THE COMPLETE IDIOT'S GUIDE® TO

A Well-Trained Dog

by Jack and Wendy Volhard

alpha books

A Division of Macmillan General Reference
A Pearson Education Macmillan Company
1633 Broadway, New York, NY 10019

Copyright © 1999 by Jack and Wendy Volhard

Cover photography by Mary Bloom

Macmillan General Reference books may be purchased for business or sales promotional use. For information please write: Special Markets Department, Macmillan Publishing USA, 1633 Broadway, New York, NY 10019.

International Standard Book Number: 1-58245-034-X
Library of Congress Catalog Card Number: 99-11570

01 00 99   8 7 6 5 4 3 2 1

Interpretation of the printing code: the rightmost number of the first series of numbers is the year of the book's printing; the rightmost number of the second series of numbers is the number of the book's printing. For example, a printing code of 99-1 shows that the first printing occurred in 1999.

Printed in the United States of America

Alpha Development Team

Publisher
Kathy Nebenhaus

Editorial Director
Gary M. Krebs

Managing Editor
Bob Shuman

Marketing Brand Manager
Felice Primeau

Acquisitions Editor
Jessica Faust

Development Editors
Phil Kitchel
Amy Zavatto

Assistant Editor
Georgette Blau

Production Team

Development Editor
Amanda Pisani

Production Editor
Michael Thomas

Copy Editor
Bryan Yates

Cover Designer
Mike Freeland

Photo Editor
Richard H. Fox

Illustrator
Kevin Spear

Book Designers
Scott Cook and Amy Adams of DesignLab

Indexer
Riofrancos & Co. Indexers

Layout/Proofreading
Troy Barnes
Marie Kristine Parial-Leonardo
Angel Perez

Contents at a Glance

Contents

14 Graduating from High School— The Canine Good Citizen   183

15 Going to College—Tricks 101   197

Foreword

New puppy and dog owners can easily be intimidated by the prospect of training their energetic charges. Once the initial excitement of getting a new dog passes and the usual problems arise, many owners panic and begin to doubt their ability to survive the experience, much less to successfully train their dog. Without clear and intelligent guidelines to follow that are based on sound principles and compassionate understanding, they may conclude too quickly that they made a mistake, and miss out on discovering the joys of living with a beautifully trained companion dog. *The Complete Idiot's Guide to a Well-Trained Dog* is just the resource needed. It addresses an impressive range of dog training challenges, from newly-acquired pup to developing an advanced utility dog. More importantly, it clearly shows that dog training is not only for specialists; it is certainly within the reach of ordinary dog owners as well. But you do need the willingness to learn and a real desire to get involved in the training, to lead your dog to success and happiness in the human/dog relationship.

Jack and Wendy Volhard have been helping people and their dogs for over thirty years through their writing, training camps and seminars, judging, and videotape series, all the while emphasizing the crucial importance of good canine nutrition and health to a quality relationship. Their publications reflect their generosity in sharing with us the wealth of their knowledge in easy-to-understand language. They always avoid the pitfall of obscuring their subject by speaking over the heads of their audience, and they go to great lengths to explain challenging concepts in concrete terms. Being involved in all facets of dog care, they show that training embraces our whole life and communication with our dogs, and their teaching helps us acquire a deeper sensitivity to the way dogs actually are. They know owners and their fears, and their style of presentation encourages students to move forward toward realizing their goals. They communicate their proven expertise and experience in a way that is engaging, sensible, never-boring, easy-to-follow, and often even humorous.

Good dog trainers and teachers are always creative and will adapt their own specific approaches to particular dogs and situations based on their experience and knowledge. Therefore, different trainers will, at times, use different techniques. Rather than one rigid method of training, then, what we need are well-defined, proven techniques based on the principles of how dogs actually learn. There is no question that Jack and Wendy Volhard successfully present just such practical guidance, and we at New Skete have learned much from them through the years. By carefully following their program, readers will be able to confidently bring out the amazing potential present in their dog or pup. At the same time, they will begin to participate in an immensely rewarding and enjoyable activity.

The Monks of New Skete

Introduction

Both of us have had a dog of one kind or another ever since we were children. Although neither one of us was the primary care giver, we did have the responsibility of walking the dog.

Children have entirely different expectations of their dogs than do adults. For one thing, they don't believe in leashes. And, because both of us were brought up in a city, that meant training our respective dogs to stay close by during our walks. Neither one of us remembers exactly how we did that. No doubt our dogs were smarter than we were and viewed their daily outings as having to keep an eye on us rather than the other way around.

It wasn't until 1968 that we got involved in training in a more structured way. We had obtained a Landseer Newfoundland and were encouraged to join the local obedience-training club. As these things go, one thing led to another, and before we knew it, a pleasant pastime turned into a hobby and then an avocation. Before long we were conducting seminars and five-day training camps, which have taken us to almost every state in this country, Canada, and England.

So here we are, some 30 years later, sharing with you what we have learned along the way. Every dog we have ever had has been more of a teacher than a pupil, and we have learned much more from our dogs than we could ever have hoped to teach them. This book is an attempt on our part to pass on to you what our dogs have taught us.

Following the Trail

Not many of us can become proficient, much less expert, in a given field without some help. We certainly had lots of that. The well-trained dog is the result of education, actually more yours than that of your dog. You need to know what makes a dog a dog, how he thinks, how he reacts, how he grows, how he expresses himself, what his needs are, and most importantly, why he does what he does. When you understand your dog, you will achieve a mutually rewarding relationship. Dogs are not a homogenous commodity. Each one is a unique individual, and in their differences lies the challenge.

In structuring this book, we used the educational format, all the way from kindergarten to college, to turning pro, and, heaven forbid your dog should wind up there, reform school. All of it can be applied to your dog.

Part 1: The Education of Your Dog. Here we cover some basic concepts of interacting with your dog, choosing the right dog for you, his growth stages, housetraining, leadership exercises, and going to kindergarten where he learns not to jump on people and to come when called.

Part 2: Understanding Your Dog. We continue with a personality profile of your dog and the various factors that affect his ability to learn, as well as choosing the right equipment for the job. This part includes a chapter on the importance of proper nutrition.

Part 3: From Grade School to College. This is where your dog begins to shine. He perfects the lessons to become a well-trained dog. He also learns how to retrieve on command and perform lots of neat tricks.

Part 4: Turning Pro. You never knew dogs could turn pro, but they do. Participating in organized dog sports is a wonderfully rewarding hobby and brings out the best in your dog.

Part 5: Reform School. We don't expect that after you have followed the program in this book that your dog will wind up here. On the off chance that he might, we offer a few tips that will rehabilitate him.

Interpreting the Scent

To help you through the text, we have included some highlights of important material, some definitions, some hints, and some whimsical facts. These are contained in little boxes.

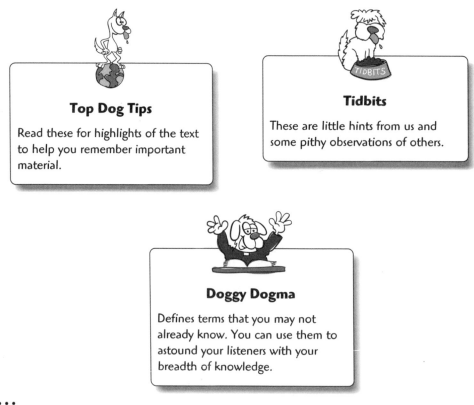

Top Dog Tips

Read these for highlights of the text to help you remember important material.

Tidbits

These are little hints from us and some pithy observations of others.

Doggy Dogma

Defines terms that you may not already know. You can use them to astound your listeners with your breadth of knowledge.

Bet You Didn't Know

Their purpose is to dispel old myths and half-truths as well as to provide the occasional interesting nugget of useless information.

Part 1
The Education of Your Dog

We know you are anxious to get started on training your dog to become the well-trained dog he deserves to be. But, before you can begin his training, there are a few details about your dog that you need to know.

Knowing the function for which your dog was bred and how he thinks will help you enormously in your efforts. Similarly, an understanding of his developmental stages will prevent misunderstandings between you and your dog, and guide you through what could be trying times.

To be successful, you also need to become your dog's pack leader and we will show you an easy way to do this. Once you are pack leader, your dog will readily participate in becoming a well-trained dog.

Having a dog that is housetrained, comes when called, and has proper table manners, are just a few of the benefits of being the proud owner of a well-trained dog.

Chapter 1

Before You Get Started

In This Chapter

➤ Guess what? Your dog is already busy training you!

➤ If he can train you, you can train him

➤ A trained dog is a lot more fun than an untrained dog

➤ Understanding how your dog thinks

➤ How to win your dog over to your way of thinking

A well-trained dog is a joy to have around. He is welcome almost anywhere because he behaves around people and dogs. He knows how to stay and he comes when called. He is a pleasure to take for a walk, and he can be let loose for a romp in the park. He can be taken on trips and family outings. He is a member of the family in every sense of the word.

The most important benefit for your dog, let's call him Rascal, is his own safety. A dog that listens and does what he is told, rarely gets into trouble. Instead of being a slave to a leash or a line, a trained dog is truly a free dog—he can be trusted to come when called, not to chase a cat across the road, or try to retrieve a car.

Tidbits

As a gift to yourself and your dog, your family, and your friends and neighbors, train your dog. It will mean sanity for you, safety for your dog, and you will reap compliments from those you meet. Make him an ambassador of good will for all dogs.

The untrained dog has few privileges. When guests come, he is locked away because he is too unruly. When the family sits down to eat, he is locked up or put outside because he begs at the table. He is never allowed off leash because he runs away and stays out for hours at a time. Nobody wants to take him for a walk because he pulls, and he never gets to go on family outings because he is such a nuisance.

Your dog has a life expectancy of 8 to 16 years. Now is the time to ensure these years are going to be mutually rewarding. Teach him to be the well-trained dog you want him to be. Believe us, it's well worth the investment.

The well-trained dog is a member of the family.

What Is a Well-Trained Dog?

For more than 25 years we have been teaching dog training classes, two-day seminars, and five-day training camps. During this time we carefully listened to what our students told us what a well-trained dog should be. First and foremost, he has to be housetrained, of course. After that, in the order of importance, he is a dog who:

➤ Doesn't jump on people.

➤ Doesn't beg at the table.

➤ Doesn't bother guests.

➤ Comes when called.

➤ Doesn't pull on the leash.

Note that these requirements, with one exception, are expressed in the negative—dog, don't do that. For purposes of training, we need to express them in the positive so we can teach the dog exactly what we expect. Here is what it looks like:

➤ Sit when I tell you.

➤ Go somewhere and chill out.

➤ Lie down when I tell you and stay there.

➤ Come when called.

➤ Walk on a loose leash.

You are beginning to get the picture—sit and down-stay are the building blocks for the well-trained dog; if Rascal knew nothing else, you could live with him. Of course, your Rascal might have some additional wrinkles that may need ironing out.

What Is Training?

We use the term training to describe two different activities:

1. To teach Rascal to do something that we want him to do, but that he would not do on his own. For example, Rascal knows how to sit and will sit on his own, but we want him to sit on command, something he will not do on his own without training.

2. To teach Rascal to stop doing something he would do on his own, but that we don't want him to do. For example, Rascal chases bicyclists, something he will do on his own that we want him to stop.

We call this *action* and *abstention* training. For action training, we mainly use positive reinforcement, such as a treat or lots of praise; for abstention training, we may have to use negative reinforcement, such as a check on the leash. More about that later.

The object of any training is to have your dog respond reliably to your command. Ideally, he responds on the first command. There is nothing more frustrating than telling your dog to do something only to be ignored. It is especially annoying when somebody is watching or you are trying to show off. Male dogs in particular have that favorite trick of absolutely having to lift a leg just one more time, and sometimes several times, before they deign to acknowledge our presence.

Think of it in terms of choices. Do you want a dog that thinks he has a choice of responding to you? We don't think so. We think you want a dog who understands, after you have trained him, that he has to do what you tell him, no ifs or buts.

Who Is Training Whom?

Training is a two-way street: Rascal is just as involved in training you as you are in trying to train him. The trouble is that Rascal is already a genius at training you, a skill with which he was born. You, on the other hand, have to learn the skills of training him, just as we had to learn it.

To succeed, you must become aware of how he is training you so he doesn't by accident become the one "in charge."

Take the following quiz: What do you do when Rascal

1. Drops his ball in your lap while you are watching television?
2. Nudges or paws your elbow when you are sitting on the couch?
3. Rattles his dish?
4. Sits at the door?

If your answers are:

1. Throw it for him,
2. Pet him,
3. Give him something to eat, and
4. Open it to let him out,

he has you well trained. There is nothing wrong with this—all five of our dogs have us perfectly trained to perform these tricks—so long as we all understand who is in charge.

Training Models

There are basically three training models, each with varying degrees of effectiveness. We are going to take a quick look at them and then decide which one we are going to use to train Rascal.

Training Model	Method	Efficiency	Stress Involved
No-No	The dog is always wrong—he is punished unless he can figure out on his own by trial and error what his trainer wants	Takes a long time and sometimes the dog doesn't get it, depending on what the dog is expected to learn	Extremely high, to the point where the dog may give up trying altogether
Yes-Yes	The dog is always right—he is rewarded for every correct response, but still has to learn on his own what is expected	Takes a considerable amount of patience and time	Can be high, depending on the dog
Yes-No	The dog knows immediately whether he is right or wrong	Very fast	Very little

Because you are a busy, result-oriented person, we are going to use the Yes-No method of training Rascal.

Taking Charge

Dogs are pack animals, and a pack consists of followers and one leader. The leader is in charge and dictates what happens when.

You and your family are now Rascal's pack and someone has to be in charge, the leader. The principles of democracy do not apply to pack animals. Your dog needs someone he can respect and look up to for direction and guidance.

Tidbits

"To his dog, every man is Napoleon; hence the constant popularity of dogs." Aldous Huxley

You may just want to be friends, partners, or peers with your dog. You can be all of those, but for the well being of your dog, you must be the one in charge. In today's complicated world you cannot rely on him to make the decisions.

Debbie did not think much about the "being in charge" theory. She wanted to be pals with Thor, her Labrador Retriever. After all, he had always listened to her before and never given her any trouble.

She changed her mind when one day Thor made the decision that "now I will chase the cat across the road" just as a car was coming. She realized that if she wanted Thor to be around for a while, he had to learn that she was in charge and that she made the decisions.

Few dogs actively seek leadership and most are perfectly content for you to assume the role, so long as you do. But you must do so, or even the meekest of dogs will take over. Remember, it's not a matter of choice. For his safety and your peace of mind, you have to be the one in charge.

How do you know which of you is in charge? Here are a few signs to watch for:

➤ Does Rascal get on the furniture and growl at you when you tell him to get off?

➤ Does Rascal demand attention from you, which you then give?

➤ Does Rascal ignore you when you want him to move out of the way, when he is in front of a door or cupboard?

➤ Does Rascal shoot out of doors ahead of you?

If the answer to two or more of these questions is "yes," you need to become pack leader, and we will show how to do that.

Top Dog Tips

Whenever your dog comes to you, be nice to him. Put another way, don't do anything he perceives as unpleasant. If you want to give him a bath or a pill, don't call him to you. Instead, go get him, or call him, but first give him a cookie before the bath or pill.

Ground Rules

In Chapter 4 you will begin Rascal's education, but before you do, you need to know the ground rules.

Building Trust

Picture Rascal chasing a cat across the road. Your heart is in your mouth because you are afraid he might get run over. When he finally returns, you are angry and soundly scold him for chasing the cat and giving you such a scare.

Here is how Rascal looks at this situation. First, he chased the cat, which was lots of fun. Then he came back to you and was reprimanded, which was no fun at all.

What you wanted to teach him was not to chase the cat. What you actually taught him was that coming to you can be unpleasant.

One of the commands you will want your dog to learn is to come when called. To be successful, remember this principle: whenever your dog comes to you, be nice to him.

No matter what he may have done, be pleasant and greet him with a kind word, a pat on the head and a smile. Teach your dog to trust you by being a safe place for him. When he is with you, follows you or comes to you, make him feel wanted.

If you call him to you and then punish him, you undermine his trust in you. When your dog comes to you on his own and you punish him, he thinks he is being punished for coming to you.

Tidbits

Consistency in training means handling your dog in a predictable and uniform manner. If there is more than one person in the household, everyone needs to handle the dog in the same way. Otherwise the dog will become confused and unreliable in his responses.

You may ask, "How can I be nice to my dog when he brings me the remains of one of my brand new shoes, or when he wants to jump on me with muddy paws, or when I just discovered an unwanted present on the carpet?"

For the answers, you will have to read this book—it will show you how to deal with all these situations without undermining his trust in you.

Consistency

If there is any magic to training, it is consistency. Your dog cannot understand sometimes, maybe, perhaps, or only on Sundays. He can and does understand yes and no. For example, it is confusing to your dog to encourage him to jump up on you when you are wearing old clothes, but then be angry with him when he joyfully plants muddy paws on your best suit.

Bill loved to wrestle with Brandy, his Golden Retriever. Then one day, when Grandma came to visit, Brandy flattened her. Bill was angry and Brandy was confused—he thought roughhousing was a wonderful way to show affection. After all, that's what Bill had taught him.

Does this mean you can never permit your puppy to jump up on you? Not at all, but you have to train him that he may only do so when you tell him it's "OK." But beware: It is more difficult to train a dog to make this distinction than to train him not to jump up at all. The more "black and white" or "yes and no" you can make it, the easier it will be for Rascal to understand what you want.

Persistence

Training your dog is a question of who is more persistent—you or your dog. Some things he will learn quickly, others will take more time. If several tries don't bring success, be patient, remain calm and try again. It may take many repetitions before a dog understands a command and responds to it each and every time.

No "No"

As of right now, eliminate the word "no" from your training vocabulary. All too often, this is the only command a dog hears and he is expected to figure out what it means. There is no exercise or command in training called "no."

Bet You Didn't Know

Avoid negative communications with your dog; they undermine the relationship you are trying to build. Eliminate "no" from your training vocabulary. Don't use your dog's name as a reprimand. Don't nag your dog by repeatedly using his name without telling what you want him to do.

Begin to focus on the way in which you communicate with Rascal. Does he perceive the interaction as positive or negative, pleasant or unpleasant, friendly or unfriendly? How many times do you use the word "no," and how many times do you say "good dog" when communicating with your dog? It has been our experience during more than 25 years of teaching that by the time we see the dogs, most have been "no'ed" to death. Everything the dog does brings forth a stern "don't do this," "don't do that," "no, bad dog."

The dogs are sick of it and have no interest or desire in learning what the owners want them to do.

In dealing with your dog, ask yourself "what exactly do I want Rascal to do or not to do?" Use a "do" command whenever possible so you can praise your dog instead of reprimanding him. You will find there is a direct relationship between your dog's willingness to cooperate and your attitude. Get out of the "blaming" habit of assuming it's the dog's fault. Your dog only does what comes naturally. More importantly, your dog's conduct is a direct reflection of your training. Show Rascal in a positive way what you expect from him, and that means training him.

Does this mean you can never use the "n" word? In an emergency you do what you have to do: But remember, only in dire need.

Does Your Dog Think?

Certainly your dog thinks. He just thinks like a dog, and to anyone who has been around dogs sometimes it's uncanny! It's almost as though they can read your mind. But is it your mind they are reading, or have they simply memorized patterns of your behavior?

Here is an example: Before leaving for work, Wendy always put Heidi in her crate. It wasn't long before Heidi went into her crate on her own when Wendy was about to leave. "What a clever puppy," thought Wendy, "she knows I am going to work."

Tidbits

"I've seen a look in dogs' eyes, a quickly vanishing look of amazed contempt, and I am convinced that basically dogs think humans are nuts." John Steinbeck

Dogs often give the appearance of being able to read our minds. What happens in actuality is that by observing us and studying our habits, they learn to anticipate our actions. Because they communicate with each other through body language, they quickly become experts at reading ours.

Dogs communicate with each other through body language and quickly become experts at reading ours.

What Heidi observed was that immediately before leaving for work, Wendy invariably put on her make-up and then crated her. Heidi's cue to go into her crate was seeing Wendy putting on her make-up.

Then one evening, before dinner guests were to arrive, Wendy started "putting her face on." When Heidi immediately went into her crate, Wendy realized the dog had not been reading her mind, but had learned the routine through observation.

"Reading" Your Dog

Just as your dog takes his cues from watching you, so can you learn to interpret what's on his mind by watching him.

You know Rascal has the propensity to jump on the counter to see whether there is any food he can steal. Since he has done this a number of times before, you begin to recognize his intentions by the look on his face—head and ears are up, whiskers pointed forward, intent stare—and the way he moves in the direction of the counter—deliberate, tail wagging.

What should you do? You interrupt Rascal's thought process by derailing the train. Say "just a minute, young man, not so fast," in a stern tone of voice. You can also whistle or clap your hands, anything to distract him.

After that, tell him to go lie down and forget about stealing food.

What if he has already started the objectionable behavior? He has his paws firmly planted on the counter and is just about to snatch the steak. Use the same words to stop the thought process, physically remove him from the counter by his collar, and take him to his corner and tell him to lie down.

Bet You Didn't Know

Punishment after the fact is useless and inhumane. Your dog cannot make the connection. "Go to bed without supper" doesn't work any better with dogs than it does with children. The ideal time to intervene is when your dog is thinking about what you don't want him to do.

Do not attempt any discipline after the offending deed has been accomplished. Your dog cannot make the connection between the discipline and his actions. Your dog may look guilty, but not because he understands what he has done; he looks guilty because he understands you are upset.

Visualize yourself preparing a piece of meat for dinner. You leave the counter to answer the phone and after you return, the meat is gone. You know Rascal ate it. Your first reaction is anger. Immediately Rascal looks guilty and you assume it is because he knows he has done wrong.

Rascal knows no such thing. He is reacting to your anger and wonders why you are mad and, perhaps based on prior experience, expects to be the target of your wrath.

Look at it from Rascal's point of view. He thoroughly enjoyed the meat. Unfortunately it's gone and you can't bring it back. Nor can you make him un-enjoy it. What's worse, if you punish Rascal now, he will not even understand why because he can't make the connection between the punishment and the meat he just ate. He can only make the connection between your anger and being punished.

He knows you are angry, but does not know it has anything to do with the meat. Punch a pillow, if you have to, but not your dog.

If you don't believe us, try this experiment. Without Rascal seeing you, drop a crumpled up piece of paper on the floor. Call Rascal to you and point accusingly at the paper and say in your most blaming voice "what have you done, bad dog!" He will reward you with his most guilty look without having a clue what it's all about.

Moral of the story: don't leave your valued belongings such as shoes, socks, or anything else near and dear to your heart lying about, where your dog can destroy them. Look at it this way—if you weren't a neat freak before you got your dog, you will be now.

If you attribute human qualities and reasoning abilities to your dog, your dealings with him are doomed to failure. He certainly does not experience guilt. Blaming the dog because "he ought to know better," or "he shouldn't have done it," or "how could he do this to me" will not improve his behavior. He also does not "understand every word you say," and is only able to interpret your tone of voice and body language.

Bet You Didn't Know

Dogs begin to learn at 3 weeks of age. At 7 weeks their brains are neurologically complete and all the circuits are wired. Their mind is a blank page, and all you have to do is fill it with the right information. What they learn in the next few weeks will never be forgotten. If you wait until your dog is older, he will probably have picked up a lot of bad habits. That means erasing the page and starting all over, a much more tedious job than starting when he is a puppy.

Your dog is already an expert at reading you. With a little time and practice you, too, will be able to tell what's on his mind and read him like a book. His behavior is just as predictable as yours.

Can Dogs "Reason"?

The answer is "no," not in the sense that we can. Dogs can, however, solve simple problems. By observing your dog, you learn his problem-solving techniques. Just watch him try to open the cupboard where the dog biscuits are kept to help himself for a between-meal snack. Or see how he works at trying to retrieve his favorite toy from under the couch.

Our favorite story involves a very smart English Springer Spaniel who had been left on our doorstep. The poor fellow had been so neglected that we did not know he was a purebred Spaniel until after he had paid a visit to the groomer. He became a delightful member of the family for many years. One day his ball had rolled under the couch. He tried everything—looking under the couch, jumping on the back rest to look behind it, and going around to both sides. Nothing seemed to work. In disgust, he lifted his leg on the couch and walked away. So much for problem solving.

The Least You Need to Know

➤ Dogs are pack animals and you need to be your dog's pack leader.

➤ Train your dog as well as he is training you.

➤ The well-trained dog does what you tell him.

➤ Yes, your dog thinks, but he thinks like a dog.

➤ Eliminate the word "no" from your training vocabulary.

Chapter 2

Choosing the Well-Trained Dog

In This Chapter

➤ Selecting the right breed to suit your life-style

➤ The ideal age at which to get a puppy

➤ Evaluating a puppy using the Volhard Puppy Aptitude Test

➤ Considering an older dog and the tests you can use

"I already have a dog and that is why I bought this book. I am past the choosing stage." Even so, this chapter will give you additional insights into what you have chosen and will definitely help you with selecting your next dog.

Getting a dog or puppy on impulse is rarely a good idea. Remember that dogs, like cars, were designed for a particular function. You need to decide what you want, a Corvette or a Suburban, a Fox Terrier or a Newfoundland.

When the various breeds were originally developed, there was a greater emphasis on the ability to do a job, such as herding, guarding, hunting, drafting, and the like, than on the dog's appearance. If a particular breed interests you, find out first what the dog was bred to do. There are so many different breeds to choose from and if there is a secret to getting that "perfect puppy," it lies in doing your homework.

Deciding What Kind of Dog to Get

The well-trained dog begins with some idea of what role the dog is expected to play in your life and then selecting a dog that is suitable for the job. Some of the reasons for selecting a dog follow:

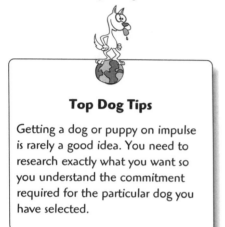

➤ Companionship

➤ Playmate for the kids

➤ Protection

➤ A special activity, such as hunting, herding, breeding, or showing

➤ Status symbol

➤ A combination of the above

> **Top Dog Tips**
>
> Getting a dog or puppy on impulse is rarely a good idea. You need to research exactly what you want so you understand the commitment required for the particular dog you have selected.

Some dogs are able to fill all of these expectations, while others have more limited talents.

Getting a dog for a status symbol usually means one of the guarding or rarer breeds, and often these represent some special challenges. If you want a rare breed, first find out why the breed is rare, and if there are any potential drawbacks to owning this type of dog.

The Labrador Retriever is a good multi-purpose dog that can serve as a wonderful companion.

Conversely, one of the most popular dogs and number 1 in American Kennel Club registrations is the Labrador Retriever. The reason is simple—the Lab is a good multi-purpose dog that can serve as a companion and playmate for the kids, is naturally protective, generally enjoys good health, makes a good guide dog, and with little time and effort can be transformed into a well-trained dog.

You also need to take into account your own life-style and circumstances. For most of us this means a dog that can satisfy our need for companionship, is easily trained and doesn't require a lot of upkeep.

Keeping Up Appearances

Everyone has his or her own preference and there is an enormous choice, from the four-pound Yorkshire Terrier to the 200-pound Mastiff. Many dogs, such as Poodles and Schnauzers, come in different sizes. Others have a smaller version that is similar in appearance, such as Collies and Shelties, or Dobermans and Miniature Pinschers, or German Shepherds and Corgis, or Greyhounds and Whippets, the "poor man's race horse."

Tidbits

Poodles and Terriers don't shed like other dogs, but have to be groomed regularly. Unless you are willing to spend the time and effort learning how to do it yourself, this means periodic visits to a professional groomer, an expensive proposition.

Bet You Didn't Know

Why do the breed standards for many dogs sound so similar when describing the dog's temperament? Because so many of them were written by the same man. In 1874, J.H. Walsh, under the pen name of Stonehenge, published *The Dog: Its Varieties and Management in Health,* the first major effort to describe the more than 60 breeds recognized at that time.

Breeds with long hair require more upkeep than those with short hair. It's pretty obvious when you think about it, but often completely overlooked when selecting a puppy or dog.

Some breeds, such as terriers and some of the herding dogs, bark a lot more than others. If you live in an apartment, such a dog would not be a good choice.

The Time Factor

In selecting a dog or puppy be aware of the time factor. How much exercise does this particular breed require and are you in a position to give it to your dog? Some breeds require less exercise than others, but all require two daily 20-minute walks, at a minimum, and some, such as the Sporting breeds, much more. Just letting the dog out in a backyard is not sufficient.

Tidbits

When choosing a dog or puppy, consider the amount of time you can (or are willing) to devote to exercising with your dog. Some breeds are more demanding in this respect than others—and if you fail to take an active role, your dog will not be a happy pet. Remember that all dogs, at a minimum, will need to take two 20-minute walks each day.

In the selection process you need to remind yourself continuously that your dog is going to be with you anywhere from 8 to 16 years. And, the older he or she gets, the more important regular exercise becomes.

How much time do you have available to devote to training that cute little bundle of fur? If you have little, or no more that 10 to 15 minutes a day, then you need to select a breed that is easily trained and doesn't require much exercise.

What Are You Looking For?

A good place to start is *The Complete Dog Book*, by the American Kennel Club, a tremendous resource. It describes in detail the 148 different breeds recognized by that organization. In addition to the breed's history and physical features, the descriptions often include a discussion of the breed's special qualities. For example, the description of the Labrador Retriever states: "Today's Labrador Retriever has several important roles in society. Its fine temperament and dependability have established its reputation as an excellent breed for guiding the blind, for search and rescue work, and, of course, for rounding out the family."

Having been the proud owners of a lovely Lab, we can attest to the accuracy of this profile.

Another wealth of information can be found at dog shows where you can see most of these dogs and talk to their owners.

To help you get the dog you want, we have devised a test that is amazingly accurate in predicting inherited behavioral tendencies and how the puppy will turn out as an adult.

What Is Puppy Testing?

Some of the tests we use were developed as long ago as the 1930s for dogs bred to become Guide Dogs. Then in the 1950s, studies were conducted on puppies to see how quickly they could learn. These studies were actually done to identify children's learning stages.

More tests were developed by Clarence Pfaffenberger and, most notably, William Campbell, to determine if pups could be tested for dominance and submission. These tests proved that it was indeed possible to predict future behavioral traits of adult dogs by testing puppies at 49 days of age. Testing before or after that age, affected the accuracy of the test, depending on the time before or after the 49th day.

Top Dog Tips

The ideal age to test the puppy is at 49 days of age when the puppy is neurologically complete and it has the brain of an adult. With each passing day after the 49th day, the responses will be tainted by prior learning.

We took these tests, added some of our own, and put together what is now known as the Volhard Puppy Aptitude Test, or PAT. PAT uses a scoring system from 1-6 and consists of ten tests. The tests are done consecutively and in the order listed. Each test is scored separately, and interpreted on its own merits. The scores are not averaged, and there are no winners or losers. The entire purpose is to select the right puppy for the right home.

The tests are as follows:

1. Social Attraction—degree of social attraction to people, confidence, or dependence.
2. Following—willingness to follow a person.
3. Restraint—degree of dominant or submissive tendency, and ease of handling in difficult situations.
4. Social Dominance—degree of acceptance of social dominance by a person.
5. Elevation Dominance—degree of accepting dominance while in a position of no control, such as at the veterinarian or groomer.
6. Retrieving—degree of willingness to do something for you. Together with Social Attraction and Following, a key indicator for ease or difficulty in training.
7. Touch Sensitivity—degree of sensitivity to touch and a key indicator to the type of training equipment required.
8. Sound Sensitivity—degree of sensitivity to sound, such as loud noises or thunderstorms.
9. Sight Sensitivity—degree of response to a moving object, such as chasing bicycles, children, or squirrels.
10. Stability—degree of startle response to a strange object.

During the testing, make a note of the heart rate of the pup, which is an indication of how it manages stress, as well as its energy level. Puppies come with high, medium, or low energy levels. You have to decide for yourself the level that suits your life-style.

Dogs with high energy levels need a great deal of exercise, and will get into mischief if this energy is not channeled in the right direction.

Bet You Didn't Know

"Don't worry, he'll grow out of it." Famous last words—and it won't happen. You see what you get and you get what you see. If the puppy has a noticeable structural flaw now, he will have that same flaw as an adult dog.

Finally, look at the overall structure of the puppy. You see what you get at 49 days of age. If the pup has strong and straight front and back legs, with all four feet pointing in the same direction, it will grow up that way, provided you give it the proper diet and environment in which to grow. If you notice something out of the ordinary at this age, it will stay with the puppy for the rest of its life; he will not grow out of it.

How to Test

Here are the ground rules for performing the test:

➤ The testing is done in a location unfamiliar to the puppies. This does not mean they have to taken away from home. A 10-foot square area is perfectly adequate, such as a room in the house where the puppies have not been.

➤ The puppies are tested one at a time.

➤ There are no other dogs or people, except the scorer and the tester, in the testing area.

➤ The puppies do not know the tester.

➤ The scorer is a disinterested third party and not the person interested in selling you a puppy.

➤ The scorer is unobtrusive and positions him or herself so he or she can observe the puppies' responses without having to move.

➤ The puppies are tested before they are fed.

➤ The puppies are tested when they are at their liveliest.

➤ Do not try to test a puppy that is not feeling well.

➤ Puppies should not be tested the day of or the day after being vaccinated.

➤ Only the first response "counts."

The tests are simple to perform, and anyone with some common sense can do them. You can, however, elicit the help of someone who has tested puppies before and knows what they are doing.

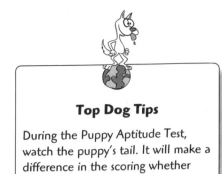

1. Social attraction—the owner or caretaker of the puppies places it in the test area about four feet from the tester and then leaves the test area. The tester kneels down and coaxes the puppy to come to him or her by encouragingly and gently clapping hands and calling. The tester must coax the puppy in the opposite direction from where it entered the test area. Hint: Lean backward, sitting on your heels instead of leaning forward toward the puppy. Keep your hands close to your body encouraging the puppy to come to you, instead of you trying to reach for the puppy.

2. Following—the tester stands up and slowly walks away encouraging the puppy to follow. Hint: Make sure the puppy sees you walk away and get the puppy to focus on you by lightly clapping your hands and using verbal encouragement to get the puppy to follow you. Do not lean over the puppy.

3. Restraint—the tester crouches down and gently rolls the puppy on its back and holds it on its back for 30 seconds. Hint: Hold the puppy down without applying too much pressure. The object is not to keep it on its back but to test its response to being placed in that position.

4. Social Dominance—let the puppy stand up or sit and gently stroke it from the head to the back while you crouch beside it. See if it will lick your face, an indication of a forgiving nature. Continue stroking until you see a behavior you can score. Hint: When you crouch next to the puppy avoid leaning or hovering over the puppy. Have the puppy at your side with both of you facing in the same direction.

5. Elevation Dominance—the tester cradles the puppy with both hands, supporting the puppy under its chest and gently lifts it two feet off the ground and holds it there for 30 seconds.

The Restraint test with an older dog.

The Elevation test with an older dog.

6. Retrieving—the tester crouches beside the puppy and attracts its attention with a crumpled up piece of paper. When the puppy shows some interest, the tester throws the paper no more than four feet in front of the puppy encouraging it to retrieve the paper.

7. Touch Sensitivity—the tester locates the webbing of one the puppy's front paws and presses it lightly between his index finger and thumb. The tester gradually increases pressure while counting to ten and stops when the puppy pulls away or shows signs of discomfort.

8. Sound Sensitivity—the puppy is placed in the center of the testing area and an assistant stationed at the perimeter makes a sharp noise, such as banging a metal spoon on the bottom of a metal pan.

9. Sight Sensitivity—the puppy is placed in the center of the testing area. The tester ties a string around a bath towel and jerks it across the floor, two feet away from the puppy.

10. Stability—an umbrella is opened about five feet from the puppy and gently placed on the ground.

Scoring the Results

The following are the responses you will see and the score assigned to each particular response. You will see some variations and will have to make a judgment on what score to give them.

Test	Response	Score
Social Attraction	Came readily, tail up, jumped, bit at hands	1
	Came readily, tail up, pawed, licked at hands	2
	Came readily, tail up	3
	Came readily, tail down	4
	Came hesitantly, tail down	5
	Didn't come at all	6
Following	Followed readily, tail up, got underfoot, bit at feet	1
	Followed readily, tail up, got underfoot	2
	Followed readily, tail up	3
	Followed readily, tail down	4
	Followed hesitantly, tail down	5
	Did not follow or went away	6

continues

continued

Test	Response	Score
Restraint	Struggled fiercely, flailed, bit	1
	Struggled fiercely, flailed	2
	Settled, struggled, settled with some eye contact	3
	Struggled, then settled	4
	No struggle, no eye contact	5
	No struggle, strained to avoid eye contact	6
Social Dominance	Jumped, pawed, bit, growled	1
	Jumped, pawed	2
	Cuddled up to tester and tried to lick face	3
	Squirmed, licked at hands	4
	Rolled over, licked at hands	5
	Went away and stayed away	6
Elevation Dominance	Struggled fiercely, tried to bite	1
	Struggled fiercely	2
	Struggled, settled, struggled, settled	3
	No struggle, relaxed	4
	No struggle, body stiff	5
	No struggle, froze	6
Retrieving	Chased object, picked it up, and ran away	1
	Chased object, stood over it, and did not return	2
	Chased object, picked it up, and returned with it to tester	3
	Chased object and returned without it to tester	4
	Started to chase object, lost interest	5
	Does not chase object	6
Touch Sensitivity	8-10 count before response	1
	6-8 count before response	2
	5-6 count before response	3
	3-5 count before response	4
	2-3 count before response	5
	1-2 count before response	6

Test	Response	Score
Sound Sensitivity	Listened, located sound, and ran toward it barking	1
	Listened, located sound, and walked slowly toward it	2
	Listened, located sound, and showed curiosity	3
	Listened and located sound	4
	Cringed, backed off, and hid behind tester	5
	Ignored sound and showed no curiosity	6
Sight Sensitivity	Looked, attacked, and bit object	1
	Looked and put feet on object and put mouth on it	2
	Looked with curiosity and attempted to investigate, tail up	3
	Looked with curiosity, tail down	4
	Ran away or hid behind tester	5
	Ignored, showed no curiosity	6
Stability	Looked and ran to the umbrella, mouthing or biting it	1
	Looked and walked to the umbrella, smelling it cautiously	2
	Looked and went to investigate	3
	Sat and looked, but did not move toward the umbrella	4
	Ran away from the umbrella	5
	Showed no interest	6

What the Scores Mean

The scores are interpreted as follows:

Mostly 1s

➤ Strong desire to be pack leader and is not shy about bucking for a promotion.

➤ Has a predisposition to be aggressive to people and other dogs and will bite.

➤ Should only be placed into a very experienced home where the dog will be trained and worked on a regular basis.

Top Dog Tips

Stay away from the puppy with a lot of 1s or 2s. It has strong leadership aspirations and may be difficult to manage. This puppy needs an experienced owner. Not good with children.

Mostly 2s

➤ Also has leadership aspirations.

➤ May be hard to manage and has the capacity to bite.

➤ Has lots of self-confidence.

➤ Should not be placed with an inexperienced owner.

➤ Too unruly to be good with children and elderly people, or with other animals.

➤ Needs strict schedule, loads of exercise and lots of training.

➤ Has the potential to be a great show dog with someone who understands dog behavior.

Mostly 3s

➤ Can be a high-energy dog and may need lots of exercise.

➤ Good with people and other animals.

➤ Can be a bit of a handful to live with.

➤ Needs training, does very well at it and learns quickly.

➤ Great dog for second-time owner.

Mostly 4s

➤ The kind of dog that makes the perfect pet.

➤ Best choice for the first-time owner.

➤ Rarely will buck for a promotion in the family.

➤ Easy to train, and rather quiet.

➤ Good with elderly people, children, although may need protection from the children.

➤ Choose this pup, take it to obedience classes, and you'll be the star, without having to do too much work!

Mostly 5s

➤ Fearful, shy, and needs special handling.

➤ Will run away at the slightest stress in its life.

➤ Strange people, strange places, different floor or ground surfaces may upset it.

➤ Often afraid of loud noises and terrified of thunder storms.

➤ When you greet it upon your return, may submissively urinate.

➤ Needs a very special home where the environment doesn't change too much and where there are no children.

➤ Best for a quiet, elderly couple.

➤ If cornered and cannot get away, has a tendency to bite.

Mostly 6s

➤ So independent that it doesn't need you or other people.

➤ Doesn't care if it is trained or not—it is its own person.

➤ Unlikely to bond to you, since it doesn't need you.

➤ A great guard dog for gas stations!

➤ Do not take this puppy and think you can change it into a lovable bundle—you can't, so leave well enough alone.

Interpreting the Scores

Few puppies will test with all 2s or all 3s—there will be a mixture of scores.

For that first time, wonderfully easy to train, potential star, look for a puppy that has quite a few 4s and 3s. Don't worry about the score on Touch Sensitivity—you can compensate for that with the right training equipment.

Avoid the puppy with a score of 1 on the Restraint and Elevation tests. This puppy will be too much for the first-time owner.

It's hard not to become emotional when picking a puppy—they are all so cute, soft, and cuddly. Remind yourself that this dog is going to be with

Tidbits

The puppy with mostly 3s and 4s can be quite a handful, but should be good with children and does well with training. Energy needs to be dispersed with plenty of exercise.

Top Dog Tips

Avoid the puppy with several 6s. It is so independent it doesn't need you or anyone. It is its own person and unlikely to bond to you.

Tidbits

Think with your head, not your heart, when selecting the puppy for you. Don't forget that you are choosing a companion that will be with you for up to 16 years. This is not a decision to make in haste. Give yourself the time you need to reflect on the puppies you are attracted to, and how you expect each of them to fit into your life-style.

you for 8 to 16 years. Don't hesitate to step back a little to contemplate your decision. Sleep on it and review it in the light of day.

It's a lot more fun to have a good dog, one that is easy to train, one you can live with, and one you can be proud of, than one that is a constant struggle.

Choosing a Breeder

Once you have done your research and you have decided the breed that is most suited to your life-style and expectations, it is time to choose a breeder. You can meet breeders at dog shows, through the local newspaper, or popular dog magazines, such as *American Kennel Club Gazette*, *Dog World* or *Dog Fancy*.

Here are some of the criteria you want to follow in selecting a breeder:

➤ Choose an experienced breeder, one who has had several litters and who knows his breed.

➤ Choose a breeder who has shown his dogs and has done some winning, which is a fairly good indication that his or her dogs conform to the standard of the breed and will grow up resembling the dogs that attracted you to the breed in the first place.

➤ Choose a breeder who is using our Puppy Aptitude Test. If he hasn't heard of it, show it to him; avoid one that says "I don't believe in that."

➤ Choose a breeder whose dogs are certified by the applicable registries against breed-related genetic disorders, such as eye problems, hip dysplasia, and the like.

➤ Choose a breeder where you can interact with adult dogs, and get some idea how long they live.

➤ Choose a breeder where the dogs are well housed and everything is clean.

Tidbits

Puppy testing is permitted by most breeders, as it gives them useful information for breeding future litters. Test results also help breeders "match" their puppies with interested buyers. A good breeder wants every dog he sells to have a happy life in a good home.

The majority of breeders today show a great willingness to have their puppies tested, and are interested in the results. It shows them the inherited behaviors of their breeding stock, valuable information for future breedings. The results make it easier for them to place the right puppy into the right home where people will be happy with it. After all, no breeder wants a puppy returned when it is 8 months old and may have been ruined by being improperly raised.

Always interact with a puppy individually, away from its littermates. Whatever you do, don't try to pick a puppy by examining the entire litter together—you will not be able to pick the right one for you.

Getting a Dog from a Shelter

Don't overlook an animal shelter as a source for a good dog. Not all dogs wind up in a shelter because they are bad. After that cute puppy stage, when the dog grows up, it may become too much for its owner. Or, there may have been a change in the owner's circumstances, forcing him or her into having to give up the dog.

Most of the dogs waiting to be adopted are housetrained and already have some training. If the dog has been properly socialized to people, he will be able to adapt to a new environment. Bonding with a new owner may take some time, but once accomplished, you will have a devoted companion.

While you can't use the entire puppy test at a shelter, there are some tests that will give you a good indication of what to look for.

1. Restraint—try putting the dog into a down position with some food, and then gently rolling him over and see what happens. If the dog jumps up and runs away or tries to bite you, this is not the dog for you. Rather, look for a dog that turns over readily, but squirms around a bit. Apply just enough pressure to keep the dog on his back; ease up if he struggles too much. Intermittent squirming is OK, constant squirming is not OK.

2. Social Dominance—directly after the Restraint Test, if the dog didn't struggle too much and if you think it's safe, try sitting the dog and just stroking him, getting your face relatively close to him while talking to him softly, to see if he licks you and forgives you for the upside down experience. A dog that wants to get away from you is not a good candidate.

3. Retrieving—crumple up a small piece of paper and show it to the dog. Have him on your left side with your arm around him and throw the paper with your right hand about six feet, encouraging the dog to get it and bring it back. You are looking for a dog that brings the paper back to you.

> **Top Dog Tips**
>
> There are lots of loving, lovable dogs waiting to be adopted at animal shelters all over the country. Some people give up their dogs when they learn that dog ownership is more demanding than they expected. Others may have to move to a place where they cannot keep a dog. Many shelter dogs are just waiting to prove their pet potential.

Guide dog trainers have the greatest faith in this test. A dog that retrieves nearly always works out to be a Guide Dog because it indicates a willingness to please the owner. Other organizations that use dogs from a shelter, such as those who use dogs to sniff out contraband or drugs, and police departments, place almost sole reliance on this test. They know that if a dog brings back the object, they can train him to do almost anything.

Bet You Didn't Know

Guide Dog trainers and organizations that use bomb-or drug-detection dogs have great faith in the Retrieve test. It indicates a dog's willingness to work for the owner.

Wherever you get your dog, use the tests that you can do and act accordingly. By the way, it's not too late to use some of the tests with the dog you already have. It just might explain some of your dog's behaviors.

The Least You Need to Know

➤ There are many breeds to choose from and if there is a secret in getting that "perfect puppy," it is doing your homework.

➤ A good place to start is *The Complete Dog Book* by the American Kennel Club, which describes in detail the 148 different breeds recognized by that registry.

➤ Carefully consider the time you have available for the necessary up-keep and exercise the dog requires.

➤ Don't get a dog on impulse.

➤ Use the Volhard Puppy Aptitude Test in selecting your dog, whether it's a puppy or an older dog.

Chapter 3

Your Dog's Growth Stages

In This Chapter

➤ The ideal time for bonding with your new puppy

➤ Predicting your dog's behavior by watching him grow

➤ Becoming a teenager with everything that entails

➤ To breed or not to breed

➤ The advantages and disadvantages of altering your dog

From birth until maturity, your dog goes through physical and mental developmental periods. What happens during these stages can, and often does have a lasting effect on your dog. Its outlook on life will be shaped during these periods, as will its behavior.

The age at which a puppy is separated from its mother and littermates will have a profound influence on its behavior as an adult. Taking a pup away from the mother too soon may have a negative effect on its ability to handle training. For example, housetraining may be more difficult under these circumstances. A pup's ability to learn is important to becoming a well-trained dog. It will also affect its dealings with people and other dogs.

So what is the ideal time for your puppy to make the transition to its new home? All the behavioral studies that have been done recommend the 49th day, give or take a day or two.

Socialization

At about the 49th day of life, when the puppy's brain is neurologically complete, that special attachment between the dog and his owner, called *bonding*, begins. It is one of the reasons why this is the ideal time for puppies to leave the nest for their new homes so that *bonding* with the new owner or family can take place.

Bonding to people becomes increasingly difficult the longer a puppy remains with its mother or littermates. With each passing day, the pup loses a little of its ability to adapt to a new environment.

In addition, there is the potential for built-in behavior problems:

➤ The pup may grow up being too dog-oriented.

➤ The pup will probably not care much about people.

➤ The pup may be difficult to teach to accept responsibility.

➤ The pup may be more difficult to train, including housetraining.

You must also be wary of taking a puppy away from the mother too soon, because it deprives the puppy of important lessons. Between three to seven weeks of age, the mother teaches her puppies basic doggy manners. She communicates to the puppies what is acceptable and what is unacceptable behavior.

For example, after the puppies' teeth have come in, nursing them will become a painful experience, so she teaches them to take it easy. She does whatever it takes from growls to snarls, and even snaps, and continues this throughout the weaning process when she wants the puppies to leave her alone. After just a few repetitions, the puppies get the message and respond to a mere look or a curled lip from mother. The puppy learns dog language, or lip reading, as we call it, and learns not to bite too hard.

Bet You Didn't Know

When the puppies are from three to seven weeks old, the mother dog teaches them basic dog manners. During play with each other, they also learn to inhibit biting too hard, an important lesson.

The mother dog teaches the puppy respect.

The puppies also learn from each other. While playing, tempers will flare because one will have bitten another one too hard. The puppies learn from these exchanges what it feels like to be bitten and, at the same time, to inhibit biting during play. Those that have not had these important lessons may find it difficult to accept discipline while growing up and may use their mouths too much.

Puppies separated from their canine family before they have had the opportunity for these experiences tend to identify more with humans than with other dogs. To put it simply, they don't know they are dogs, and tend to have their own sets of problems, such as

➤ mouthing and biting their owner,

➤ an unhealthy attachment to humans,

➤ aggression toward other dogs,

➤ nervousness,

➤ excessive barking,

➤ difficulty with housetraining, and

➤ a dislike of being left alone.

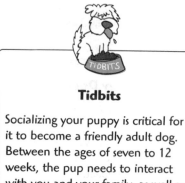

Tidbits

Socializing your puppy is critical for it to become a friendly adult dog. Between the ages of seven to 12 weeks, the pup needs to interact with you and your family, as well as other humans and dogs. When your puppy is developing, expose it to as many different people as possible, including children and older people. Let it meet new dogs too. These early experiences will pay off big time when your dog grows up.

Top Dog Tips

Puppies learn from other dogs, but can only do so if they have a chance to spend time with them. Make a point of introducing your young dog to other puppies and adults on a regular basis. In the ideal situation, the puppy will have a mentor, an older dog who can teach it the ropes.

Your dog is a social animal. To become an acceptable pet, the pup needs to interact with you and your family, as well as other humans and dogs during the seventh through the twelfth week of life. If denied these opportunities, your dog's behavior around other people or dogs may be unpredictable—your dog may be fearful or perhaps even aggressive. For example, unless regularly exposed to children during this period, a dog may not be comfortable or trustworthy around them.

Your puppy needs the chance to meet and to have positive experiences with those beings that will play a role in its life.

➤ You are a grandparent whose grandchildren occasionally visit—have your puppy meet children as often as you can.

➤ You live by yourself, but have friends visit you—make an effort to let your puppy meet other people, particularly members of the opposite sex.

➤ You plan to take your dog on family outings or vacations—introduce riding in a car.

Socialization with other dogs is equally important, and should be the norm rather than the exception. It also needs to occur on a regular basis. Ideally, the puppy has a mentor, an older dog who can teach it the ropes. We have been fortunate enough in always having had a mentor dog who supervised the upbringing of a new puppy, making our task that much easier.

If you plan on taking your puppy to obedience class or dog shows or ultimately using the dog in a breeding program, it needs to have the chance to interact with other dogs. Time spent now is well worth the effort. It will result in a well-adjusted adult companion dog.

This is also a time when your puppy will follow your every footstep. Encourage this behavior by rewarding the puppy with an occasional treat, a pat on the head or a kind word.

Suddenly He Is Afraid

Weeks eight through 12 are called the *Fear Imprint Period.* During this period any painful or particularly frightening experience will leave a more lasting impression on your pup than if it occurred at any other time in its life. If it is sufficiently traumatic it could literally ruin your pup for life.

During this time, avoid exposing the puppy to traumatic experiences. For example, elective surgery, such as ear cropping, should be done, if at all, before eight or after eleven weeks of age. When you need to take your puppy to the veterinarian, have the doctor give the puppy a treat before, during and after the examination to make the visit a pleasant experience. While you should stay away from stressful situations, do continue to train your puppy in a positive and non-punitive way.

Doggy Dogma

The *Fear Imprint Period* lasts from about eight to 12 weeks, During that time do not expose your puppy to traumatic experiences that could have a lasting impact.

During the first year's growth you may see fear reactions at other times. Do not respond by dragging your puppy up to the object that caused the fear. On the other hand, don't pet or reassure the dog—you may create the impression that you approve of this behavior. Rather, distract the puppy and go on to something that is pleasant. After a short time, the fearful behavior will disappear.

Now He Wants to Leave Home

Sometime between the fourth and eighth month, your puppy will begin to realize there is a big, wide world out there. Up to now, every time you have called, Rascal willingly came to you. But now, he may prefer to wander off and investigate. Rascal is maturing and cutting the apron strings. This is normal. He is not being spiteful or disobedient, just becoming an adolescent.

While going through this phase, it is best to keep Rascal on a leash or in a confined area until he has learned to come when called. Otherwise, not coming when called will become a pattern—annoying to you and dangerous to the dog. Once this becomes a habit, it will be difficult to break and prevention is the best cure. It is much easier to teach your dog to come when called before he has developed the habit of running away.

Do not, under any circumstances, play the game of chasing the dog. Instead, run the other way and get your dog to chase you. If that does not work, kneel on the ground and pretend you have found something extremely interesting, hoping your puppy's curiosity will bring it to you. If you do have to go to the pup, approach slowly until you can calmly take hold of the collar.

During this time your puppy also goes through teething and needs to chew—anything and everything. Dogs, like children, can't help it. Your job is to provide acceptable outlets for this need, such as chew bones and toys. If one of your favorite shoes is demolished, try to control yourself. Puppies have the irritating habit of tackling many shoes, but only one from each pair. Look at it as a lesson to keep your possessions out of reach. Scolding will not stop the need to chew, but it may cause your pet to fear you.

These Can Be Trying Times— Four Months to Two Years

The "adolescent" stage, depending on the breed, takes place anywhere from four months until two years, and culminates in sexual maturity. Generally, the smaller the dog, the sooner he will mature. Larger dogs enter (and end) adolescence later in life. It is a time when the cute little puppy can turn into a teenage monster. He starts to lose his baby teeth and his soft, fuzzy puppy coat; he goes through growth spurts and looks gangly, either up in the rear or down in front; he is entering the ugly-duckling stage.

As Rascal is beginning to mature, he starts to display some puzzling behaviors, as well as some perfectly normal, but objectionable ones.

The *Juvenile Flakies*

We use the term *juvenile flakies* because it most accurately describes what is technically known as a second fear imprint period. The timing of this event (or events) is not as clearly defined as the first *Fear Imprint Period,* and coincides with growth spurts; hence it may occur more than once as the dog matures. Even though he may have been outgoing and confident before, your puppy now may be reluctant to approach someone or something new and unfamiliar, or he may suddenly be afraid of something familiar.

Fear of the new or unfamiliar has its roots in evolution. In a wolf pack, once the pups become four months of age, they are now allowed to come on a hunt. The first lesson they have to learn is to stay with the pack; if they wander off, they might get lost or into trouble. They also have to develop some survival techniques, one of which is fear. The message to the puppy is "if you see or smell something unfamiliar, run like hell the other way."

Apprehension or fear of the familiar is also caused by growth spurts. At this point in a puppy's life, hormones start to surge. Hormones can affect the calcium uptake in the body, and coupled with growth, this can be a difficult time for the growing puppy.

For example, one day, when our Dachshund, Manfred, was six months old, he came into the kitchen after having been outside in the yard. Then he noticed on the floor, near his water bowl, a brown paper grocery bag. He flattened, looked as though he had seen a ghost and tried to run back out into the yard.

If Manfred was going through a growth spurt at this time, which would be normal at six months, he could be experiencing a temporary calcium deficiency, which in turn would produce his fear reaction.

He had seen brown paper grocery bags many times before, but this one was going to get him. We reminded ourselves that he was going through the *flakies* and ignored the behavior.

Should you observe something like this with your puppy, do not try to drag him up to the object in an effort to "teach" the puppy to accept it. If you make a big deal out of it, you create the impression that there is a good reason to be afraid of whatever triggered the reaction. Leave the puppy alone, ignore the behavior, and it will pass.

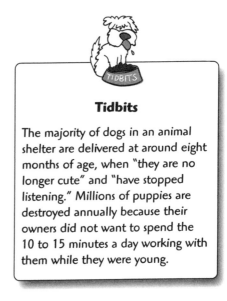

Tidbits

The majority of dogs in an animal shelter are delivered at around eight months of age, when "they are no longer cute" and "have stopped listening." Millions of puppies are destroyed annually because their owners did not want to spend the 10 to 15 minutes a day working with them while they were young.

Puppy Discovers Sex

Sometime during this four-month to two-year period, depending on the size of your dog, the puppy will discover sex, and you will be the first to know about it.

When our Landseer Newfoundland, Evo, was almost two, he fell in love. He had always enjoyed playing with other dogs. He is generally well behaved and gets along with people and all the dogs he has met. We took him to a training facility where we were to meet up with friends who had just adopted an 11-month-old female Labrador Retriever named Indy. Evo was very sweet with her and at first they played nicely together, chasing and batting at each other with their paws. All of a sudden a strange look came over Evo's face, and with his face crinkled up he jumped on Indy's back and with his front paws clasped her firmly around her chest. We realized that his puppy days were over.

Sex is sex in any language! Evo was a bit of a late developer, since he lives with spayed females and had not yet had the pleasure of being involved with an unspayed female before.

We handled Evo by going up to him, putting his lead on and taking him away from Indy. He wanted to go back to her and tried several times, but we occupied his mind with some training and he soon forgot all about her.

Bet You Didn't Know

Forty to seventy percent of adult growth, depending on the size of the dog, is achieved by seven months of age. If you have one of the larger breeds, you better start training now, before the dog gets so big that you can't manage him.

Puppy's Hormones Kick-In

During this period, the puppy's hormones surge to four times their normal level and this surge can have important effects on his behavior. Rascal may decide the time has come to buck for a promotion to pack leader. His attempted coup can take the form of an outright challenge, or it can be more subtle, as in "I'm not going to listen to you anymore."

Some puppies become aggressive in protecting their toys, their food or their owners. It's also a time when puppies are not looking their best. With puppy fur falling out and adult fur coming in, they can appear quite moth-eaten. They are getting tall and gangly. It's just as well we loved them as pups, because right now, they are not looking or behaving in a very lovable way.

Hormones drive behavior, which means that the intensity of behaviors is increased in direct proportion to the amount of hormones coursing through his system. So if you want your male puppy to become calmer, and not to assert himself quite so much, neutering him is a good idea.

Although female puppies going through puberty may show all of the above traits, they more often show greater dependency upon their owners. They will follow their owners around, looking at them constantly, as if to say, "something is happening to my body, but I don't know what. Tell me what to do." Females are just as apt to show mounting behaviors as males, and spaying has to be considered.

If you don't want to neuter your pet, the necessity for training increases. The freedom that the male puppy had before will now become limited. The better trained he is, the easier this transition will be, but it requires a real commitment on your part. The female, in turn, needs to be protected during her heat cycle, which usually occurs every six months and lasts around 21 days. Her attraction is so potent that you may discover unwanted suitors around your house, some of whom may have come from miles away.

Our first experience with a female in season involved our Landseer, Heidi. When we came home from work we found a good-sized Basset Hound on our front stoop; he was patiently waiting for Heidi. As we approached, he made it perfectly clear that he was taking a proprietary attitude toward Heidi, as well as the house.

We had to enter the house via the back door. We then managed to subdue the little fellow with a few dog biscuits just long enough to check his collar. We were surprised to learn that the horny hound had traveled close to three miles to visit.

To Spay or Neuter

Unless you intend to exhibit your dog in dog shows to get a championship, or to breed the dog, you should seriously consider neutering your dog.

You should not even contemplate breeding, if:

➤ your dog is not purebred and registered;

➤ you got your dog from an animal shelter, pet store, or found him;

➤ you don't have a three- to five-generation pedigree for your dog;

➤ your dog does not have at least four titled dogs, such as conformation or working titles, in the last three generations;

➤ your dog is not certified free of genetic disorders applicable to the breed;

➤ your dog does not fit the standard for its breed;

➤ or, your dog does not have a stable temperament.

Bet You Didn't Know

Breeding dogs for the purpose of exposing your children to the miracle of birth is *not a* good idea. Rent a video!

The advantages of neutering your pet generally outweigh the disadvantages.

For the male it will:

➤ keep him calm,

➤ reduce the tendency to roam,

➤ diminish mounting behavior,

➤ make training easier,

➤ improve overall disposition, especially toward other dogs.

In short, he will be easier to live with and easier to train. It will also curb the urge to roam or run away. So if the front door is left open by accident, he will not, like our friend the Basset, go miles to find a female in season.

Bet You Didn't Know

It is not true that dogs who have been neutered lose their protective instincts—it depends on the age when the dog was neutered. Generally, dogs neutered after one year of age retain their protective instincts.

If you spay your female, she too will stay closer to home. Perhaps even more important:

➤ you won't have to deal with the mess that goes along with having her in season,

➤ you won't have to worry about unwanted visitors camping on your property and lifting a leg against any vertical surface,

➤ you won't have to worry about accidental puppies, which are next to impossible to place in good homes.

When to Spay or Neuter

Altering your pet during the juvenile period means that his or her behavior remains more juvenile. So if you want a dog that retains puppy-like characteristics for the rest of its life, then alter your dog at around six to nine months of age. This can be advantageous if there are very young children in the family.

When you have your pet altered, make sure that the operation occurs at least one month apart from his or her rabies shot, which should not be given before six months of age. Until six months of age, the puppy is protected against rabies through the antibodies passed along in the mother's milk. Vaccines should also not be given to a dog that is undergoing surgery because this can have long-term adverse effects. So, if you decide to alter your dog, think about having the surgery after seven months of age, for both sexes.

Depending on the breed and size of the female, she will go into her first season anytime after seven months of age. For a Yorkshire Terrier it is apt to be sooner, and for one of the giant breeds, it is likely to be later, sometimes as late as 18 months of age.

If you want a dog to show more adult behaviors and take more responsibility, like being a protector or guard dog, training for competitive events, or working for a living, then you should think about altering later.

A dog that has not been neutered until after one year of age, or a female that has gone through two seasons, is generally easier to train for competitive events such as obedience or agility trials. They have become fully grown by that time, are emotionally mature, have learned more adult behaviors and can accept more responsibility.

Tidbits

Neutering your pet in the juvenile period means that his or her behavior remains more juvenile. So if you want a dog who retains puppy-like characteristics for the rest of its life, then spay or neuter around six to nine months of age. This can be advantageous if there are very young children in the family.

Disadvantages to Spaying and Neutering

Altering changes the hormones in the body. Some dogs that are altered develop hypothyroidism as they mature. Hypothyroidism can cause:

➤ increased shedding,

➤ dull, oily, smelly coats,

➤ separation anxiety,

➤ skin problems,

➤ a tendency to gain weight.

Finally He Grows Up

No matter how much you wish that cute little puppy to remain as is, your pup is going to grow up. It happens anywhere from one to four years. Over the course of those years, your dog will undergo physical and emotional changes. For you, as the owner, the most important one is your dog's sense of identity—the process of becoming an individual in his own right. By providing leadership through training, he will reward you with many years of loyal devotion.

Socialization at all ages is very important. Keep reacquainting your dog with good doggy manners his whole life. It pays off!

The Least You Need to Know

➤ The ideal time to bring your puppy home is his 49th day so the puppy can bond to his new family.

➤ Socialization with other dogs should be the norm and not the exception.

➤ When the puppy is between eight and 12 weeks of age, avoid traumatic experiences, especially elective surgery, such as ear cropping.

➤ Altering your dog after one year of age will not effect his protective instincts.

➤ Teach your dog to come when called before he has developed the habit of running away.

Housetraining and Other Basics

The well-trained dog's education begins with housetraining. As with any training, some dogs catch on more readily than others. Some of the toy breeds are notoriously dense in this regard and vigorously resist all efforts requiring their cooperation.

As a general rule, however, the majority of dogs do not present a problem, provided you do your part. To speed along the process, we strongly recommend that you use a crate or similar means of confinement.

Initially you may recoil from this concept as cruel and inhumane. Nothing could be further from the truth. You will discover that your puppy likes his crate and that you can enjoy your peace of mind.

Puppy's Own Baby-Sitter—A Crate

When Jim and Laura went to pick up their puppy, the breeder asked them what they thought was a peculiar question. "When you were raising your children, did you use a play pen?" "Of course," said Laura, "I don't know what I would have done without it." "Fine," said the breeder, "a crate for a puppy is like a play pen for a child."

Whatever your views on play pens, dogs like crates. It reminds them of a *den*, a place of comfort, safety, security and warmth. Puppies, and many adult dogs, sleep most of the day, and they prefer the comfort of their *den*. For your mental health, as well as that of your puppy, get a crate.

Here are just a few of the many advantages to crate training your dog:

➤ It's a baby sitter—when you are busy and can't keep an eye on your dog, but want to make sure he will not get into trouble, put him in his crate. You can relax and so can he.

➤ It's ideal for getting him on a schedule for housetraining.

➤ Few dogs are fortunate enough to go through life without ever having to be hospitalized. Your dog's private room at the veterinary hospital will consist of a crate. His first experience with a crate should not come at a time when he is sick—the added stress from being crated for the first time will retard his recovery. There may also be times when you have to keep your dog quiet, such as after being altered or after an injury.

➤ Driving any distance, even around the block, with your dog loose in the car is tempting fate. An emergency stop and who knows what could happen. Having the dog in a crate protects you and your dog.

➤ When we go on vacation we like to take our dog. His crate is his home away from home, and we can leave him in a hotel room knowing he won't be unhappy, stressed, or tear up the room.

➤ It is a place where he can get away from the hustle and bustle of family life and hide out when the kids become too much for him.

Your dog will like his crate because it will remind him of the security of a *den*. He will use it on his own, so he should always have access to it. Depending on where it is, your dog will spend much of his sleeping time in his crate.

Selecting a Crate

Select a crate that is large enough for your dog to turn around, stand up or lie down comfortably. If he is a puppy, get a crate for the adult size dog so he can grow into it.

Crates are available in a variety of materials including wire mesh, cloth mesh, and plastic. Some crates are more durable than others and most are easy to assemble.

We recommend a good quality crate that easily collapses and is portable so you can take it with you when traveling with your dog. If you frequently take your dog with you in the car, consider getting two crates, one for the house and one for the car. It will save you having to lug one back and forth.

Introducing Rascal to the Crate

Set up the crate and let your dog investigate it. Put a crate pad or blanket in the crate. Choose a command, such as "crate," or "go to bed." Physically place Rascal in the crate using the command you have chosen. Close the door, tell him what a great little puppy he is, and give him a bite-sized treat, then let him out.

Next, use a treat to coax him into the crate. If he does not follow the treat, physically place him into the crate and then give him the treat. Again, close the door, tell him what a great little puppy he is, and give him a bite-sized treat, then let him out.

Do this until Rascal goes into the crate with almost no help from you, each time using the command and giving him a treat after he is in the crate.

For the puppy that is afraid of the crate, use his meals to overcome his fear. First, let him eat his meal in front of the crate, then place his next meal just inside the crate. Put each successive meal a little further into the crate until he is completely inside and no longer reluctant to enter.

Tidbits

Some crates are better than others in strength and ease of assembly. You can get crates in wire mesh type material, cloth mesh, or in plastic, called airline crates. Most are designed for portability and are readily assembled.

Top Dog Tips

There's no rule against gentle persuasion to get your pup enthused about his crate. A treat placed inside can work wonders. If your puppy is not lured in, physically place him inside the crate and close the door. Next comes a little praise, a little treat, and the opportunity to exit.

Manfred looks for his treat, having gone into his crate.

Getting Rascal Used to the Crate

Tell your dog to go into the crate, give him a treat, close the door, and tell him what a good puppy he is, then let him out again. Each time you do this, leave him in the crate a little longer with the door closed, still giving him a treat and telling him how great he is.

Finally, put him in his crate, give him a treat, and then leave the room, first for

➤ 5 minutes, then

➤ 10 minutes, then

➤ 15 minutes, and so on.

Each time you return to let him out, tell him how good he was before you open the door.

How long can you ultimately leave your dog in his crate unattended? That depends on your dog and your schedule, but for an adult dog, it should not be more than 8 hours.

A word of caution: *Never* confine Rascal to his crate in order to punish him. It is not in your interest for Rascal to develop negative feelings about his crate. You want him to like his private *den*.

Bet You Didn't Know

Your dog's crate is never used as a form of punishment. If it is, he will begin to dislike the crate and it will lose its usefulness to you.

Housetraining Puppy

Keys to successful housetraining are:

➤ Crate training your puppy first.

➤ Setting a schedule for feeding and exercising your dog.

➤ Sticking to that schedule, even on weekends, at least until your dog is housetrained and mature.

➤ Vigilance, vigilance, and vigilance until your dog is trained.

Using a crate to housetrain your puppy is the most humane and effective way to get the job done. It is also the easiest way because of the dog's natural desire to keep his *den* clean.

Over the course of a 24-hour period, puppies have to eliminate two to three times more frequently than adult dogs. A puppy's ability to control elimination increases with age, from not at all up to eight hours and more. During the day, when active, the puppy can last for only short periods. Until he is six months of age, it is unrealistic to expect him to last for more than four hours during the day without having to eliminate. When sleeping, most puppies can last through the night.

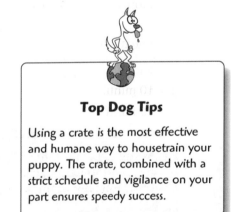

Top Dog Tips

Using a crate is the most effective and humane way to housetrain your puppy. The crate, combined with a strict schedule and vigilance on your part ensures speedy success.

Basic Principle—A Schedule

Dogs thrive on a regular routine. By feeding and exercising Rascal at about the same time every day, he will also relieve himself at about the same time every day.

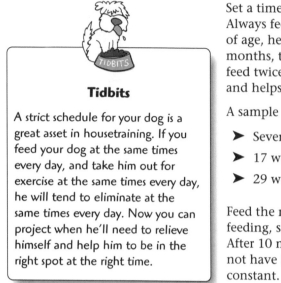

Tidbits

A strict schedule for your dog is a great asset in housetraining. If you feed your dog at the same times every day, and take him out for exercise at the same times every day, he will tend to eliminate at the same times every day. Now you can project when he'll need to relieve himself and help him to be in the right spot at the right time.

Set a time to feed the puppy that is convenient for you. Always feed at the same time. Until he is four months of age, he needs four meals a day; from four to seven months, three daily meals is appropriate. From then on feed twice a day—it is healthier than feeding only once and helps with housetraining.

A sample feeding schedule follows:

➤ Seven weeks through 16 weeks—four times a day

➤ 17 weeks through 28 weeks—three times a day

➤ 29 weeks on—two times a day.

Feed the right amount—loose stools are a sign of over-feeding, straining or dry stools a sign of underfeeding. After 10 minutes, pick up the dish and put it away. Do not have food available at other times. Keep the diet constant. Abrupt changes of food may cause digestive upsets that will not help your housetraining efforts.

Fresh water must be available to your dog at all times during the day. You can pick up his water dish after 8:00 p.m. so he can last through the night.

Establish a Toilet Area

Start by selecting a toilet area and always take Rascal to that spot when you want him to eliminate. If possible, pick a place in a straight line from the house. Carry your puppy or put him on leash. Stand still and let him concentrate on what he is doing. Teach him a command, such as "hurry up." Be patient, let him sniff around. After he is done, tell him what a clever puppy he is and take him back inside.

Sample Housetraining Schedule

First thing in the morning, Mary takes her 12-week-old poodle puppy, Colette, out of her crate and straight outside to her toilet area. Fifteen minutes after Colette's morning meal, she is let out again. Mary then crates Colette and leaves for work.

On her lunch break, Mary goes home to let Colette out to relieve herself, feeds her and then, just to make sure, takes her out once more. For the afternoon, Colette is crated again until Mary returns. Colette is then walked and fed, after which she spends the rest of the evening in the house where Mary can keep an eye on her. Before bedtime, Colette goes out to her toilet area one more time and is then crated for the night.

When Colette becomes seven months old, Mary will drop the noontime feeding and walk. From that age on, most dogs only need to go out immediately or soon after waking up in the morning, once during the late afternoon and once again before bedtime.

Vigilance

Take your puppy to his toilet area after eating or drinking, after waking up, and after he has played or chewed. A sign that he has to go out is sniffing the floor in a circling motion.

Special vigilance is required when it is raining because many dogs, particularly those with short hair, do not like to go out in the wet anymore than you do. Make sure the puppy actually eliminates before you bring him back into the house.

> **Top Dog Tips**
>
> When you see your puppy sniffing and circling, take note! He is letting you know that he is looking for a place to go. Take him out to his toilet area so he doesn't make a mistake.

Dealing with Accidents

No matter how conscientious you are and no matter how vigilant, there are going to be times when your puppy will have an accident. Housetraining accidents may be simple mistakes, or they can be indicative of a physical problem. The key to remember is that, as a general rule, dogs want to be clean.

When Rascal has had an accident in the house, do not call him to you to punish him. It is too late. If you do punish your dog under these circumstances, it will not help your housetraining efforts and you will make him wary of wanting to come to you.

There is a popular misconception that the dog knows "what he did" because he looks "guilty." *Absolutely not so!* He has that look because from prior experience he knows that when you happen to come across a mess, you get mad at him. He has learned to associate a mess with your response. He has not and cannot make the connection between having made the mess in the first place and your anger. Discipline after the fact is the quickest way to undermine the relationship you are trying to build with your dog.

> **Bet You Didn't Know**
>
> Dogs are smart, but they do not think in terms of cause and effect. When you come home from work and yell at your dog for having an accident in the living room, you are not encouraging your dog to use his toilet area. All you are doing is letting him know that sometimes you're really nice and sometimes you're really mean.

Swatting your dog with a rolled-up newspaper is cruel and only makes him afraid of you and rolled-up newspapers. Rubbing his nose in it is unsanitary and disgusting. Dogs may become housetrained in spite of such antics, but certainly not because of them.

When you come upon an accident, always keep calm. Put your dog out of sight so he cannot watch you clean up. Use white vinegar as a cleaner. Do not use any ammonia-based cleaners because the ammonia does not neutralize the odor and the puppy will be attracted to the same spot.

Regressions

Regressions in housetraining will occur, especially during teething. Regressions after six months of age may be a sign that your dog is ill. If accidents persist, take him to your veterinarian for a check up.

Catching Rascal in the Act

If you catch your dog in the act, sharply call his name and clap your hands. If he stops, take him to his toilet area. If he doesn't, let him finish and don't get mad. Do not try to drag him out because that will make your clean-up job that much more difficult. Hint: Until your puppy is reliable, it is not a good idea to let him have the run of the house unsupervised.

Alternative to Crate Training

While a puppy can last in his crate for the night when he is asleep, you cannot leave a puppy for purposes of housetraining in his crate for longer than four hours at a time during the day. Your puppy will soil in his crate, which is definitely not a habit you want to establish.

Tidbits

An X-pen is intelligent confinement and uses the same principle as a crate, except it is bigger and has no top.

If your schedule is such that you cannot keep an eye on Rascal during the day or come home to let the puppy out in time, the alternative is an exercise pen. An X-pen is intelligent confinement and uses the same principle as a crate, except it is bigger and has no top.

First, you need to acquire an X-pen commensurate to the size of your dog. For a dog the size of a Labrador, the X-pen needs to be 10 square feet. Set up the X-pen where the puppy will be confined during your absence.

To get your dog comfortable in his X-pen, follow the same procedure as you would in introducing him to his crate. When Rascal is "at home" in the X-pen and you are ready to leave him for the day, cover one-third of the area with newspapers. Rascal will quickly understand what the paper is for. Cover one-third of the remaining area with a blanket, and leave one-third uncovered.

Rascal will need to have access to water during the day, so put his water dish on the uncovered area in the corner of the X-pen (some is bound to splash out and the uncovered floor is easy to clean). Before you leave, place a couple of toys on Rascal's blanket, put him into the X-pen with a dog biscuit, and leave while he is occupied with the biscuit. Don't make a big deal out of leaving—simply leave.

Some people try to rig up confinement areas by blocking off parts of a room or basement or whatever. Theoretically this works, but it does permit Rascal to chew the baseboard, corners of cabinets, or anything else he can get his teeth on.

You will find that in the long run, your least expensive option, as is so often the case, is the right way from the start. Don't be penny-wise and pound-foolish by scrimping on the essentials at the risk of jeopardizing more expensive items.

Bet You Didn't Know

You may want to confine your dog to part of a room with baby gates. This option works well for some people and some dogs, but remember it's no holds barred for whatever items Rascal can access. Lots of chew toys are a must!

Leaving a dog on a concrete surface is also not a good idea. There is something about concrete that impedes housetraining—many dogs don't seem to understand why it can't be used as a toilet area.

Marking Behavior

Marking behavior is a way for Rascal to leave his calling card by depositing one or two or more drops of urine in a particular spot. The frequency with which dogs can accomplish this never ceases to amaze us. Male dogs invariably prefer vertical surfaces, hence the fire hydrant.

Behaviorists inform us that *marking* is a dog's way of establishing his territory and provides a means to find his way back home. They also claim that our dogs are able to tell the rank order, sex and age—puppy or adult dog—by smelling the urine of another dog.

Doggy Dogma

Marking behavior is a way for your dog to leave his calling card by depositing a small amount of urine in a particular spot, marking it as his territory. Males tend to engage in this behavior with more determination than females.

Those who take their dogs for a regular walk through the neighborhood quickly discover that *marking* is a ritual, with favorite spots that have to be watered. It is a way for the dog to maintain his rank in the order of the pack, which consists of all the other dogs in the neighborhood or territory that come across his route.

Adult male dogs lift a leg, as do some females. For the male dog, the object is to leave his calling card higher than the previous calling card. This can lead to some comical results, as when a Dachshund or a Yorkshire Terrier will try to cover the calling card of an Irish Wolfhound or Great Dane. It is a contest.

Annoying as this behavior can be, it is perfectly natural and normal. At times it can also be embarrassing, such as when Rascal lifts his leg on the leg of a person, a not uncommon occurrence. What he is trying to communicate here we will leave to others to explain.

When this behavior is expressed inside the house it becomes a problem. Fortunately, this is rare, but it does happen.

Here are the circumstances requiring special vigilance:

➤ Taking Rascal to a friend's or relative's house for a visit, especially if that individual also has a dog or a cat.

➤ When there is more than one animal in the house, another dog, or dogs, or a cat.

➤ When you have redecorated the house with new furniture and/or curtains.

➤ When you have moved to a new house.

Top Dog Tips

Distract your dog if you see that he is about to mark in an inappropriate spot. Call his name, and take him to a place where he can eliminate.

When you take Rascal to someone else's home, keep an eye on him. At the slightest sign that he is even thinking about it, interrupt his thought by clapping your hands and calling him to you. Take him outside and wait until he has had a chance to relieve himself.

Should it happen in your house, and you catch Rascal in the act, you already know what to do. If it persists, you need to go back to basic housetraining principles, such as the crate or X-pen until you can trust him again.

Being a Good Dog Neighbor

Being a good dog neighbor means not letting Rascal deface the property of others, and using only those areas specifically designed for that purpose. Even diehard dog lovers object to other dogs leaving their droppings on their lawn, the streets, and similar unsuitable areas. They also object to having their shrubbery or other vertical objects on their property doused by Rascal.

Be a responsible dog owner and clean up after your dog.

Becoming Pack Leader

Remaining in place, either in the sit or down position, is one of the most important exercises you can teach your dog. Aside from its practical value, it has important psychological implications.

One way a dog exerts his leadership over a subordinate dog is by restricting the movement of the subordinate, or keeping him in his place. We remember an amusing incident involving our Yorkshire Terrier, Angus. Friends had come to visit and brought their six-month-old Doberman, Blue. Things went fine with the two dogs until we noticed that Blue was sitting in a corner with Angus lying in front of him a few feet away. Every time Blue tried to move, Angus would lift his lip and Blue shrank back into the corner. It seems Angus had exploited the "home-field advantage" and convinced Blue that he was in charge.

Using the same principle, we have successfully taught countless dog owners to become pack leader in a non-violent and non-confrontational way. To accomplish this you need to learn to place your dog into a sit and a down.

Tidbits

Part of responsible dog ownership is curbing and cleaning up after your dog. Don't let Rascal become the curse of your neighborhood. Do unto others as you would have them...

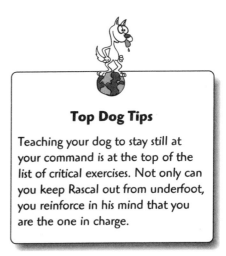

Top Dog Tips

Teaching your dog to stay still at your command is at the top of the list of critical exercises. Not only can you keep Rascal out from underfoot, you reinforce in his mind that you are the one in charge.

Placing Your Dog into a Sit and Down

For the sit, with Rascal on your left, kneel next to him, both of you facing in the same direction. If Rascal is a small dog, you can do this on a table. Place your right hand against his chest and your left hand on his withers. Say "sit" and run your left hand over his back, all the way down to his knees and with equal pressure of both hands, collapse him into a sit. Keep your hands in place to the count of five and verbally praise Rascal, saying "good dog." Then release him with "OK."

For the down, with Rascal sitting on your left, kneel next to him, both of you facing in the same direction. With your left hand, reaching over his back, place it behind his left foreleg; place the right hand behind the right foreleg. Keep your thumbs up so as not to squeeze Rascal's legs, something he may not like and may cause him to resist. Say "down" and lift Rascal into the begging position and then lower him to the ground. Keep your hands in place to the count of five and verbally praise him. Then release him with "OK."

For the down, lift your dog into the begging position...

...and lower him into the down. Note that the handler keeps her thumbs up so as not to place any pressure on the dog's legs.

> **Bet You Didn't Know**
>
> The purpose of the long sit and down exercise is to teach Rascal in a non-violent way that you are his pack leader. For this reason, it is the foundation of all further training. Training your dog is next to impossible unless he accepts you as the one in charge.

Recipe for Leadership

Week 1—Five times during the course of a week, practice the long down exercise for 30 minutes at a time as follows:

➤ sit on the floor beside your dog;

➤ place him in the down position;

➤ if he gets up, put him back;

➤ keep your hands off when he is down;

➤ stay still;

➤ after 30 minutes, release him.

As a general rule, the greater a dog's leadership aspirations, the more frequently he will try to get up and the more important this exercise becomes. Just remain calm and each time he tries to get up, replace him in the down position.

If your dog is particularly bouncy, put him on leash and sit on a chair and the leash so your hands are free to put him back.

Some dogs immediately concede that you are the pack leader, while others need some convincing. If your dog is in the latter group, your, as well as his, first experience with the long down will be the hardest. As he catches on to the idea and gradually (if not grudgingly), accepts you as pack leader, each successive repetition will be that much easier.

Practice the long down when:

➤ Your dog is tired.

➤ After he has been exercised.

➤ When interruptions are unlikely.

➤ When you are not tired.

Tidbits

Through religious use of the long down exercise, your dog will unconditionally accept you as pack leader.

If the situation allows it, you can watch television or read, so long as you don't move.

Week 2—on alternate days, practice three 30-minute downs and 10-minute sits while you sit in a chair next to your dog.

Week 3—on alternate days, practice three 30-minute downs and 10-minute sits while you sit across the room from your dog.

Week 4—on alternate days, practice three 30-minute downs and 10-minute sits while you move about the room but in sight of your dog.

After that, practice a long down and a long sit at least once a month.

We guarantee you that by following this regimen, your dog will unconditionally accept you as pack leader.

The Least You Need to Know

➤ The quickest way to housetrain your dog is by using a crate or similar means of temporary confinement.

➤ To housetrain your dog, establish a schedule for feeding and walking and stick to it.

➤ Be a good dog neighbor and pick up after your own dog.

➤ The long down and sit are designed for you to become pack leader in a non-violent and non-confrontational way.

Chapter 5

Puppy Goes to Kindergarten

In This Chapter

➤ Sit on command is lots of fun and better than jumping on people

➤ Sit and down are two different commands

➤ Table manners are taught at home

➤ Rules for teaching your dog to come to you

➤ The game of coming when called

One question almost every dog owner asks is "how do I keep my dog from jumping up on people?"

Dogs jump on people usually as a form of greeting, like saying "hello, nice to meet you!" Even the briefest of separations from the owner, as little as five minutes, can set off this behavior.

Different styles of greetings have been perfected by dogs. Bean, the Labrador, would literally launch himself at his owner from a distance of about six feet. The owner did not appreciate having to catch this missile.

As annoying as it may be at times, please remember that jumping up is a gesture of affection and good will. We certainly do not recommend any form of punishment to deal with it.

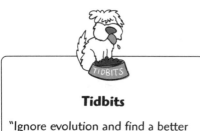

Top Dog Tips

Dogs perceive jumping up as a friendly gesture. It is a dog's way of letting the object of his affection know that he's happy to see him or her. You can train your dog to greet people in a less rambunctious fashion, but you don't want to punish your happy pet simply because he is glad to see you.

Tidbits

"Ignore evolution and find a better way to greet other dogs." *A Dog's Little Instruction Book* by David Brawn.

Tidbits

The importance of teaching a dog to sit and stay cannot be overemphasized. Not only does Rascal stop jumping up on Grandma when she walks into the room, he can't run into the street after the neighbor's cat if he knows that he must sit.

Even more annoying is the dog's habit of sniffing an area of our anatomy we would prefer he didn't. And, downright embarrassing is his apparent special fondness for engaging in this behavior with guests. While this behavior may be normal for the dog—he uses his nose to identify the rank, sex, and age of other dogs he meets—we are going to insist that he get this information in a less intrusive way.

Sit Yes, Jump No

So how do you get him to stop these behaviors without dampening his enthusiasm? By teaching him to sit and stay on command. Your dog can't jump on you when he is sitting—the two behaviors are mutually exclusive.

The sit and stay is one of the simplest and yet most useful exercises you can teach your dog. It gives you a wonderfully easy way to control him when you need to most.

Sit and stay is used when you want your dog to remain quietly in one spot for a short time. For example, Kaiser, a German Shepherd, would become so excited when Jane was about to feed him that he sent the dish flying out of her hands. Once taught the sit and stay, he sat like a perfect gentleman as she put his dish down.

Commands to Be Taught

For this exercise your dog needs to be on a leather or material buckle collar, sufficiently snug so he can't slip out of it.

You are going to teach your dog three commands:

1. Sit
2. Stay
3. OK

OK is his release command. It means he can move now and is on his own time. Make it a strict rule to give him the release command, which allows him to move again, after every time you have told him to stay. Should you get lax about it and forget, Rascal will get into the habit of releasing himself. That teaches him he can decide when to move, not a good idea and the opposite of what you want him to learn.

Unless impaired, a dog's sense of hearing is extremely acute and when giving a command there is absolutely no need to shout. In fact, the opposite is true—the quieter you give your commands, the quicker your dog learns to pay attention to you.

Commands are given in a normal tone of voice, such as "sit!" It is "sit!", the command, and not "sit?", the question. The release word "OK" is given in a more excited tone of voice, such as "that's it, you're all done."

When teaching a new command, during the initial introduction you may have to repeat it several times before your dog catches on. After the first session, teach him to respond to the first command. Give the command and if nothing happens, show your dog exactly what it is you want by physically helping him. Consistency is the key to success.

Teaching Your Dog to Sit On Command

Teaching your dog to sit on command is not usually very difficult. Try the following time-tested technique.

Begin by showing your dog a small, bite-sized treat, holding it just a little in front of his eyes, slightly over his head. Say "sit" as you bring your hand above his eyes. Looking up at the treat will cause your dog to sit.

Top Dog Tips

As quickly as you can, get into the habit of using only one command. If you do not get the desired response on the first command, reinforce the command by showing the dog what you want without repeating it. By being consistent early on, your dog learns he has to respond to the first command.

Tidbits

"The truest sign of the poorly trained dog is the repeated command or commands, quite generally given in a rising voice, and only reluctantly complied with by the dog." American Kennel Club *The Complete Dog Book*, 1964 edition.

When he does, give him the treat and tell him what a good puppy he is. Tell him without petting him. If you pet him at the same time as you praise him, he will probably get up, but what you really want him to do is sit.

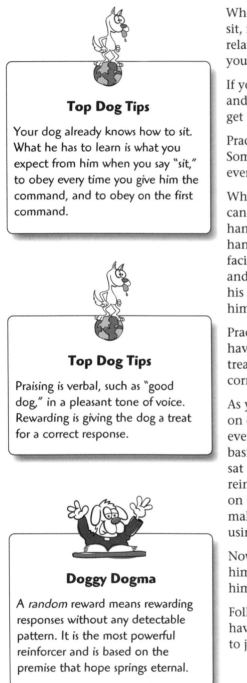

Top Dog Tips

Your dog already knows how to sit. What he has to learn is what you expect from him when you say "sit," to obey every time you give him the command, and to obey on the first command.

Top Dog Tips

Praising is verbal, such as "good dog," in a pleasant tone of voice. Rewarding is giving the dog a treat for a correct response.

Doggy Dogma

A *random* reward means rewarding responses without any detectable pattern. It is the most powerful reinforcer and is based on the premise that hope springs eternal.

When using the above method of teaching your dog to sit, it is important to properly position your hand in relation to the dog's head. If your hand is held too high, your dog will jump up; if it is too low, he will not sit.

If your dog does not respond on his own, say "sit" again and press lightly on his rump with your other hand to get him to sit and then give him the treat.

Practice making your dog sit 5 times in a row for 5 days. Some dogs catch on to this idea so quickly that whenever they want a treat they sit in front of their owner.

When he understands what the word "sit" means, you can start to teach him to obey your command. Put the hand that has the treat at your side and slide your other hand through his collar at the top of his neck, palm facing up, and tell him to sit. If he does, give him a treat and tell him how good he is; if he does not, pull up on his collar and wait until he sits, then praise and reward him with a treat.

Practice until he sits on command, that is, without having to pull up on, or touch the collar. Give him a treat and praise him with "good puppy" for every correct response.

As your dog demonstrates that he has mastered sitting on command, start to reward the desired response every other time. Finally, reward him on a *random* basis—every now and then give him a treat after he has sat on command. A *random* reward is the most powerful reinforcement of what your dog has learned. It is based on the simple premise that hope springs eternal. To make it work, all you have to do is use it and keep using it!

Now when Rascal wants to greet you by jumping up, tell him to "sit." Bend down and briefly pet him and tell him what a good puppy he is, then release him.

Following this simple method consistently, you will have changed your dog's greeting behavior from trying to jump on you to sitting to be petted.

Teaching Your Dog to Stay

An easy way to teach your dog to understand the stay command is to make him sit and stay for his supper. As you are getting ready to feed him, bowl in hand, tell him "sit," "stay" and lower the bowl to the ground. As he starts for it, pick up the bowl before he gets even a mouthful. Put him back where he was supposed to sit and stay and start all over. Repeat until you can put the bowl down and count to five before telling him "OK." Then let him eat in peace.

After several days of following this regimen, your dog will sit all on his own as soon as he sees you approaching with his supper and wait until you release him with "OK." Thus, you've created a much more pleasant way to feed your dog than having him jump up and down trying to knock his dish out of your hands.

When Rascal has proven that he can sit and stay on command, you want to begin working on being able to have him stay when the doorbell rings or someone knocks on the door. If your dog is anything like ours, the doorbell causes an immediate charge amidst paroxysms of barking. While most of us want our dogs to be alert, we then want them to stop, sit, and stay, so we can answer the door.

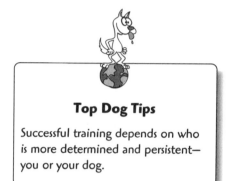

Top Dog Tips

Successful training depends on who is more determined and persistent—you or your dog.

To accomplish this goal, you will need to enlist the aid of a friend or neighbor to ring the doorbell. When the bell rings and your dog goes through his paces, take him by the collar and make him sit. Tell him "stay" and then go to open the door. When he gets up, which he surely will, put him back.

If Rascal is an excitable soul, be prepared for many repetitions of putting him back before he takes you seriously. Other dogs catch on after two or three attempts.

When he stays as you go to the door, open it to admit your accomplice. At this point, Rascal will more than likely want to say hello. Again, put him back and have your helper approach him holding out the palm of his or her hand, let Rascal sniff the palm and then have your helper ignore him. You may have to be right next to Rascal to reinforce the sit and stay.

When you work on this with your helper, instruct him or her to ring the doorbell only once and then wait until you open the door.

Tidbits

To help make your helper's arrival as traditional as possible, have him or her ring the doorbell only once. Ask him or her to wait for you to open the door.

You will need to repeat this procedure several times until Rascal is reliable and will hold the sit and stay while you open the door.

Learning Door, Stair and Car Manners

Almost as annoying as unrestrained greeting behavior, but far more dangerous, is the dog's habit of:

➤ dashing through doors just because they are open

➤ racing up and down stairs, either with, ahead or behind you

➤ jumping in and out of the car.

It is dangerous because he may find himself in the middle of the road and get run over. It is dangerous for you because you might get knocked over or down the stairs.

These potential accidents can be prevented by teaching your dog to sit and stay while you open the door and to wait until you tell him it's okay to go out.

Sit and stay also apply to going up and down stairs—we don't like the thought of having both arms full while going down a staircase with a dog dashing by, or having a dog scramble around us as we get in or out of a car.

Start by sitting your dog in front of a door closed to the outside. You know that if you open that door he will want to go through. Tell him to "stay" and start opening the door. When he starts to get up, close the door, put him back in the exact spot where you told him to stay and start all over.

You will find that after you have put him back 3 or 4 times he begins to get the message and will stay. Practice until you can open the door all the way before closing it again with your dog on a stay. From now on, each time you let him out, make him sit first, open the door, then release him with "OK."

Also, get into the habit of having him sit and stay before you open any door. Some of us prefer to go through the doorway first, while others want the dog to go through first. It makes no difference, so long as your dog stays until you release him. Practice through doors your dog uses regularly, including the car door. Every time you make him sit and stay it reinforces your position as pack leader and the one in charge.

If you have stairs, start teaching your dog to stay at the bottom while you go up. First sit him, tell him to stay. When he tries to follow, put him back and start again. Practice until you can go all the way up the stairs with him waiting at the bottom before you release him to follow.

Repeat the same procedure for going down the stairs.

Once your dog has been trained to wait at one end of the stairs, you will discover that he will anticipate the release. He will "jump the gun" and get up just as you are thinking about releasing him. Before long, he will stay only briefly and release himself when he chooses. It may happen almost as soon as he has grasped the idea, or it may take a few weeks or even months, but it will happen.

When it does, stop whatever you are doing and put him back, count to 10 and release him. Do not let him get into the habit of releasing himself. Consistency is just as important here as it is teaching any other exercise.

Learning Table Manners

Teaching Rascal table manners is your responsibility and you only have to remember one rule: Don't feed the dog from the table. This sounds a lot simpler than it is, especially in a multi-person household. Moreover, don't ever underestimate your dog's ability to train you.

Bet You Didn't Know

Every time you reward your dog's efforts with a treat from the table, you are systematically teaching him not to take "no" for an answer.

When Rascal was a puppy, nobody thought much about occasionally slipping him something from the table. But now he is six months old, almost fully grown, and has started to beg at the table. Since it is no longer cute, and embarrassing when there are guests, the family resolves to put a stop to it.

At first, Rascal does not believe you are serious; after all, you were the one who started it in the first place. He digs a little deeper into his repertoire of begging routines. He may sit up, nudge you, paw you, or whine in the most pathetic tone as though he is near death's door from starvation. Sure enough, little Sally takes pity on him and slips him something.

As this scenario repeats itself, often with longer intervals before someone gives in, Rascal is systematically being trained to persevere at all cost and never to give up. Looking at it from his point of view, you are rewarding, even encouraging, the very behavior you want to stop.

As soon as you stop giving in to Rascal, his efforts will decrease, until over time, and provided you don't have a relapse, he will stop begging altogether. In technical jargon, you have extinguished the undesired behavior by refusing to reward it.

You can also save yourself all this aggravation by teaching Rascal to lie quietly in his favorite spot while you enjoy your meals in peace.

You are going to teach your dog two new commands:

1. Go lie down
2. Down

"Go lie down" is used when you want Rascal to go to his place and remain there for an extended period until you release him. It is most commonly used when you are eating or when friends visit and you don't want him making a pest of himself. When you give him the command, he is expected to go to his favorite spot and make himself comfortable. When he can get up again, release him.

"Down" is used when you want him to lie down in place, right now and stay there until you release him.

Teaching Your Dog to Lie Down On Command

Again, your dog already knows how to lie down. What you are going to teach him is to do it when you tell him.

Start by sitting your dog at your left side. Put two fingers of your left hand, palm facing you, through his collar at the side of his neck. Have a treat in your right hand. Show him the treat and lower it straight down and in front of your dog as you apply gentle downward pressure on the collar, at the same time saying "down."

When he lies down, give him the treat and praise him by telling him what a good puppy he is. Keep your left hand in the collar and your right hand off your dog while telling him how clever he is, so that he learns he is being praised for lying down. With a small dog you may want to do this on a table.

Reverse the process by showing him a treat and bringing it up slightly above his head with upward pressure on the collar as you tell him to "sit."

Teaching your dog to lie down on command…

…using a treat and a little downward pressure on the collar.

Practice having your dog lie down at your side 5 times in a row for 5 days, or until he does it on command with minimal pressure on the collar. Praise and reward with a treat every time.

When he understands what the word means, you can move on to the next step. Sit your dog at your left side and put two fingers of your left hand, palm facing you, through his collar at the side of his neck. Keep your right hand with the treat at your right side. Say "down" and apply downward pressure on the collar. When he lies down, praise and give him a treat every other time. Practice over the course of several days until he will lie down on command without any pressure on the collar.

Top Dog Tips

Make a game out of teaching your dog to lie down on command. Get him eager about a treat and then in an excited tone of voice say "down." Then give him his treat.

After that, when he lies down on command randomly reward.

You can now start to teach your dog to lie down in one place for several minutes. Tell him to "go lie down" and take him to his favorite spot; if necessary, place him down with a little pressure on his collar and the command "down." Keep an eye on him and when he tries to get up, place him down again. Teach him to stay at that spot in the down position for five minutes, then praise and release him with "OK."

As he learns where you want him to stay, gradually and over the course of several sessions, increase the time until he will stay up to 30 minutes before you release him. If you have done the long down exercise described in Chapter 4, this will go quickly.

Remember, you must release him from the spot when he can move again. If you forget, he will get into the habit of releasing himself thereby undermining the purpose of the exercise.

From then on out, when you want him out from under foot, tell him to "go lie down." At this stage, you may still have to take Rascal to the spot, but after several repetitions he will go all by himself.

As always, the key to your success lies in how consistent you are in your dealings with Rascal.

The Game of Coming When Called

One of the greatest joys of owning a dog is going for a walk in a park or the woods and letting him run, knowing he will come when he is called. A dog that does not come when called is a prisoner of his leash and if he gets loose, is a danger to himself and others.

Rules of the Game

Rule #1: Exercise, exercise, exercise.

Many dogs do not come when called because they do not get enough exercise. At every chance, they run off and make the most of it by staying out for hours at a time.

Tidbits

"If your dog does not come when called, you don't have a dog!" Jack Volhard

Consider what your dog was bred to do and that will tell you how much exercise he needs. Just putting him out in the backyard will not do. You will have to participate. Think of it this way, exercise is as good for you as it is for your dog.

Rule #2: Whenever your dog comes to you, be nice to him.

One of the quickest ways to teach your dog not to come to you is to call him to punish him or do something the dog perceives as unpleasant. Most dogs consider being given a bath or a pill unpleasant. When Rascal needs either, go and get him instead of calling him to you.

Bet You Didn't Know

You can effectively teach your dog not to come when called by rewarding his response with something he doesn't like. When you have to give Rascal a pill, go get him. Don't call him to you. He'll remember the next time.

Another example of teaching your dog not to come is to take him for a run in the park and call him to you when it's time to go home. Repeating this sequence several times, teaches the dog "the party is over!" Soon, though, he may become reluctant to return to you when called because he is not ready to end the fun.

You can prevent this kind of unintentional training by calling him to you several times during his outing, sometimes giving him a treat, sometimes just a pat on the head. Then let him romp again.

Rule #3: Teach him to come when called as soon as you get him, no matter how young he is.

Ideally, you acquired your dog as a puppy and that is the best time to teach him to come when called. Start right away. But remember, sometime between four and eight months of age, your puppy will begin to realize there is a big, wide world out there.

While he is going through this stage, it is best to keep him on leash so that he does not learn he can ignore you when you call him.

Rule #4: When in doubt, keep him on leash.

Learn to anticipate when your dog is likely not to come. You may be tempting fate trying to call him once he has spotted a cat, another dog, or a jogger. Of course, there will be times when you goof and let him go just as another dog appears out of nowhere.

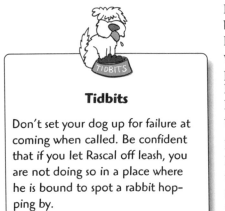

Tidbits

Don't set your dog up for failure at coming when called. Be confident that if you let Rascal off leash, you are not doing so in a place where he is bound to spot a rabbit hopping by.

Resist the urge to make a complete fool of yourself by bellowing "come" a million times. The more often you holler "come," the quicker he learns he can ignore you when he is off leash. Instead, patiently go to him and put him on leash. Do not get angry with him once you have caught him or you will make him afraid of you and he will run away from you when you try to catch him the next time.

Rule #5: Make sure your dog always comes to you and lets you touch his collar before you reward him with a treat or praise. Touching his collar prevents the dog from developing the annoying habit of playing "catch"—coming towards you and then dancing around you, just out of reach.

The Game

Needed: Two people, one hungry dog, one six-foot leash, plenty of small treats and two whistles (optional). Some people prefer to train their dog to come to a whistle instead of the verbal command "come." Some people train their dog to do both.

What works best will depend on the dog and you may want to experiment. Considering trying the verbal command first, because there may be times when you need to call your dog but don't have your whistle.

You can then do it over with a whistle, which will go very quickly since Rascal already has some understanding of what he is supposed to do.

Step 1: Inside the house, with your dog on a six-foot leash, you and your partner sit on the floor, six feet apart, facing each other. Your partner gently restrains the dog, you hold the end of the leash. Call your dog by saying "Rascal, come," and use the leash to guide him to you. Put your hand through his collar, give him a treat, pet and praise him enthusiastically.

Now you hold the dog and pass the leash to your partner who says "Rascal, come," guides the dog in, puts his hand through the collar, gives him a treat, and praises the dog.

Repeat the exercise until your dog responds on his own to being called and no longer needs to be guided in with the leash.

Step 2: Repeat Step 1 with your dog off leash.

Gradually increase the distance between you and your partner to 12 feet.

Step 3: Have your partner hold your dog by the collar while you hide from him in another room. Then call your dog. When he finds you, put your hand through the collar, give him a treat, and praise him. If he can't find you, go to him, take him by the collar and bring him to the spot where you called. Reward and praise. Now have your partner hide and then call your dog.

Repeat the exercise until the dog doesn't hesitate in finding you or your partner in any room of the house.

Top Dog Tips

Some dogs find it entertaining to come when you call, only to prance around you when they arrive. Prevent this habit by training your dog to allow you to touch his collar prior to a treat or praise.

Going Outside

Take your dog outside to a confined area, such as a fenced yard, tennis court, park or school yard and repeat Steps 1, 2 and 3.

You are now ready to practice by yourself. Let your dog loose in a confined area and ignore him. When he is not paying any attention to you, call him. When he gets to you, give him a treat and make a big fuss over him. If he does not come, go to him, take him by his collar and bring him to the spot where you called him, then reward and praise him.

Repeat until he comes to you every time you call him.

Once your dog is trained, you don't have to reward him with a treat every time, but do so frequently.

The Least You Need to Know

➤ When your puppy sits on command he cannot jump up on people—the two behaviors are mutually exclusive.

➤ Every time you give your puppy a tidbit from the table, you are rewarding the unacceptable behavior of begging.

➤ Teaching your puppy to "go lie down" establishes good table manners.

➤ The down on command is used when you want your puppy to lie down in place.

➤ When your dog comes to you, always be nice to him.

➤ If in doubt about your dog's response, keep him on leash.

Part 2
Understanding Your Dog

Your dog comes with instincts and behaviors that can help or hinder in his training. The most important of these are the three major "drives." We have developed a Personality Profile for your dog that helps you in understanding what makes him the way he is.

Environmental factors, such as your attitude, as well as what you feed your dog, play an important role in how he responds to training and how well he remembers his lessons. Just like you, your dog is subject to stress, which can interfere with learning.

The right tools for the job are also important. What you need to succeed is determined by a combination of factors, including your aptitude, and size and weight in relation to that of your dog.

Influences on Learning

Several factors influence how successful you will be in turning your pet into a well-trained dog. Some of these are under your direct control, and some of them come with your dog.

The factors that are under your direct control are:

➤ Your Expectations

➤ Your Attitude

➤ Your Dog's Environment

➤ Your Dog's Social Needs

➤ Your Dog's Emotional Needs

➤ Your Dog's Physical Needs

➤ Your Dog's Nutritional Needs

There is a direct relationship between your awareness and understanding of these factors and your success as a trainer.

Your Expectations

All of us have varying ideas of what we expect from our companions. Some of these expectations are realistic, others are not. You have heard people say "my dog understands every word I say," and perhaps you think that your dog does. If it were as easy as that, there would be no need for books like this one.

Bet You Didn't Know

Sometimes our dogs seem to really understand what we say. If a dog understands every word his owner says, how come the dog doesn't do what he is told?

Still, there is enough truth here to perpetuate the myth. Although dogs don't understand the words we use, they do understand tone of voice, and sometimes even our intent.

Do you believe your dog obeys commands because he:

1. loves you

2. wants to please you

3. is grateful

4. has a sense of duty

5. feels a moral obligation?

We suspect that you answered "yes" to the first and second question, became unsure at the third question, and then realized that we were leading you down a primrose path.

No doubt your dog loves you, but he will not obey commands for that reason. Does he want to please you? Not exactly, but it sometimes seems like he does. What he is really doing is pleasing himself. Unfortunately, Rascal also does not have the least bit of gratitude for anything you do for him and will not obey commands for that reason either. He is interested in only one thing—what are you doing for me right now?

Rascal certainly has no sense of duty or feelings of moral obligation. The sooner you discard beliefs like that, the quicker you will come to terms with how to approach his training.

Do you believe your dog does not obey commands because he:

1. is stubborn

2. is hardheaded

3. is stupid

4. is ungrateful

5. lies awake at night thinking of ways to aggravate you?

Top Dog Tips

If your approach to training is based on moral ideas regarding punishment, reward, obedience, duty, and the like, you are bound to handle the dog in the wrong way.

If you answered yes to any of the questions, you are guilty of *anthropomorphizing,* that is, attributing human characteristics and attributes to an animal. It's an easy habit to fall into, but will not help in your training.

Dogs are not stubborn or hardheaded. To the contrary, they are quite smart when it comes to figuring out how to get their way. And, they do not lie awake at night thinking of ways to aggravate you—they sleep, just like everybody else.

So why does your dog obey your command? Usually, for one of three reasons:

1. he wants something,

2. he thinks its fun, like retrieving a ball, or

3. he has been trained to obey.

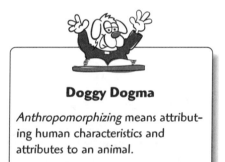

Doggy Dogma

Anthropomorphizing means attributing human characteristics and attributes to an animal.

When he obeys for either the first or the second reason, he does it for himself; when he obeys for the third reason he does it for you. This is an important distinction because it deals with reliability and safety.

Ask yourself this question: If Rascal only obeys because he wants something or because it's fun, will he obey when he does not want something or when it is no longer fun? The answer is obvious.

The well-trained dog obeys because he has been trained. This does not mean you and he can't have fun in the process, so long as the end result is clearly understood. When you say "come," there are no options, even though he may want to play a little longer, and even though you don't have a cookie.

Your Attitude

One of the most important aspects of training is your attitude toward your dog. During training, you want to maintain a friendly and positive attitude.

For many of us this can be enormously difficult because frequently we don't start to think about training until Rascal has become an uncontrollable nuisance. He is no longer cute, he has become incredibly rambunctious, everything he does is wrong and he certainly doesn't listen.

Your communications by this time consist of "no," "bad dog," "how could you do this," and "get out and stay out." You are unhappy and Rascal is unhappy.

A better approach is to train him with firm kindness, so both of you can be happy. An unfriendly or hostile approach will not gain you your dog's cooperation and will needlessly prolong the training process. When we become frustrated or angry, the dog becomes anxious and nervous, and is unable to learn.

When you feel that you are becoming a little irritable, it is best to stop training and come back to it in a better frame of mind. You want training to be a positive experience for Rascal.

Top Dog Tips

Don't train your dog when you are irritable or tired. You want training to be a positive experience for your dog. Should you get frustrated during training, stop and come back to it at another time.

Your Dog's Environment

Your dog has a keen perception of his environment. Continuous or frequent strife or friction in the household will have a negative impact on the dog's ability to learn. Many dogs are also adversely affected by excessive noise and activity, and may develop behavior problems.

Signs that the dog has a negative perception of his environment are:

➤ lethargy

➤ hyperactivity

➤ irritability

➤ aloofness

➤ aggression

Under these circumstances, learning will be retarded—if it takes place at all—or the lesson will not be retained.

Impact of the First Impression

You have heard the saying "you don't get a second chance to make a first impression." You also know that the first impression leaves the most lasting impact. The stronger that impression, the longer it lasts.

For example, Rascal's first visit to the veterinarian should be a pleasant experience or he will have an unpleasant association with going to the veterinarian. Have the doctor give him a dog biscuit first and then do the examination, and give another treat at the end.

A particularly traumatic or unpleasant first experience can literally ruin a dog for life. The object is to make your dog's first impression of training as pleasant as you can. Any introduction to a new activity should be a pleasant experience.

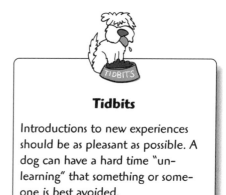

Tidbits

Introductions to new experiences should be as pleasant as possible. A dog can have a hard time "unlearning" that something or someone is best avoided.

Your Dog's Social Needs

Dogs are social animals that do not do well being isolated. Those of us who work have to leave our dogs alone at home. Then when we get back, the dog is terribly excited and wants to play and be with us. Then, we might go out in the evening, leaving the dog alone again.

Sometimes the dog retaliates. In our younger (and more socially active) days we had a lovely, well-trained Collie named Duke. Both of us worked and frequently went out in the evening. If this happened three days in a row Duke would urinate on the bed. It took us a while before we had this pattern figured out and solved the problem by not going out three days in a row, or by taking Duke with us.

Bet You Didn't Know

Day-care centers for dogs are being established in many communities. You can leave your dog for the day without having to feel guilty while he spends much of his time socializing.

If you simply do not have the time to give your dog the attention he craves, consider finding a day-care center for dogs. Their popularity is proof of the need for these services. You can leave your dog for the day without having to feel guilty. He will spend much of his time socializing with other dogs and having a good time.

In addition to keeping Rascal entertained and amused, many dog day-care facilities provide other services such as bathing and grooming, and training. Perhaps the best feature, depending on your perspective, is that when you pick up Rascal on your way home, he will be too tired to make many demands on you.

Do Dogs Have Emotional Needs?

Whether dogs have emotional needs depends on whether you accept that dogs have emotions. We certainly do, and here are some of them:

➤ joy

➤ happiness

➤ sadness

➤ depression

➤ anger

➤ apprehension

➤ fear

You can see your dog exhibit some of these emotions, such as joy and happiness, on a daily basis, but what about sadness and depression? Dogs react with the same emotions we do to the loss of a loved one, be it a member of the family or another dog.

For the last 30 years we have always had more than one dog, at times as many as ten. When one of them passed on, there is no question that those closest to him or her experienced grief. We had a brother and sister pair of Landseers named Cato and Cassandra. When Cassandra died, Cato showed all the signs of clinical depression.

This happened when Cato was seven years old and had been retired from a very successful dog show career. Since he really enjoyed pre-show training and going to dog shows, we started him all over in Canada to get him out of his depression. And it worked. He competed for another three years and was finally retired at the age of ten.

Your Dog's Physical Needs

Every dog, whether shorthaired or longhaired, needs to be groomed on a regular basis. They also need to be bathed regularly. Dogs love to be clean and groomed, evidenced by how playful they become after their grooming sessions. They enjoy being told how beautiful they look.

Bathing

The rule of thumb about bathing is when the dog smells like a dog, bathe him. Some dogs' coats repel dirt and pollution more effectively than others. Dogs live in a variety of environments and depending on how much your dog is exposed to dirt, or how dirty your dog becomes just eating his food, will dictate how often to bathe.

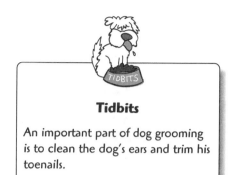

Tidbits

An important part of dog grooming is to clean the dog's ears and trim his toenails.

We have a Briard, a French sheep-herding dog. We look at him as a giant Yorkshire Terrier. He has huge mustaches, and a long coat. He must be brushed at least three times a week and bathed once a week, otherwise he begins to smell and his hair mats. He is a high-maintenance dog.

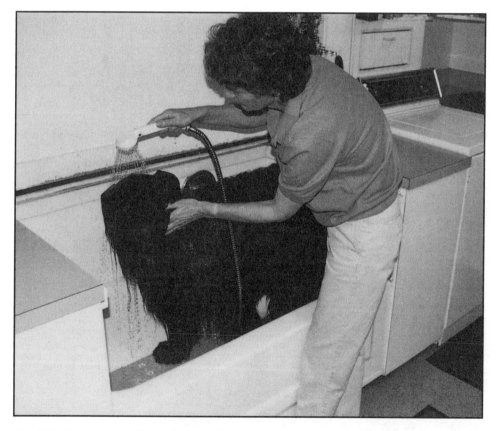

Our Briard needs a weekly bath, but other breeds need less frequent bathing.

Top Dog Tips

How often your dog should be bathed is relatively simple to assess. Let your nose be your guide.

Our Standard Wirehaired Dachshunds require little grooming. Their hair, which does not shed, is taken out three times a year. Apart from a comb through whiskers, eyebrows, and legs, there is practically no maintenance at all. Still, our little female Diggy, loves to roll in anything she can find in the woods, so she frequently finds herself in the bath tub. The difference between the two dogs is that Diggy takes only 5 minutes to shampoo and towel dry, whereas the Briard takes half an hour in the tub, and several hours to dry.

For bathing Rascal, choose a mild herbal shampoo, something you would use yourself. Rinsing your dog in a solution of apple cider vinegar and water—half vinegar and half water—will help to repel fleas and other skin parasites. It also balances out the pH levels of the skin and is excellent for minor skin irritations. Your dog will have a wonderfully shiny coat after this treatment.

Toenails

A dog's toenails need to be trimmed once a week. If the nails are not cut, the dog is unable to use the pads of his feet. Ultimately, the nails will grow and turn backwards into the feet, causing a great deal of pain and discomfort to the dog. In breeds that have long backs, such as Corgis, Dachshunds, Bassets, and the like, it is critical to keep their nails short. Left unattended, the nails force the dog to walk on the back pad on his feet, which in turn pushes the shoulders back and ultimately causes horrible back problems.

Cut on the dotted line.

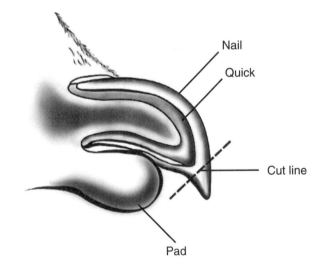

How can you tell when Rascal's nails need to be trimmed? If you can hear his toenails when he walks across the floor, they are too long.

Here is how you can train your dog to accept nail cutting. Of course, you can also take him to a groomer or the veterinarian.

Tidbits

A grinder makes nail trimming very easy. Your dog may object to the sound of the grinder at first, but many dogs adjust comfortably. Remember, when you hear Rascal clicking across the kitchen floor, it's time for a trim!

1. Sit with your dog on the floor or the couch. Take his paw, one at a time, and gently get him used to having them touched and looked at. Give him a treat when he allows you to hold his paw without jerking it away.

2. Once Rascal is comfortable with this, hold his paw in your hand, and with your index finger gently apply pressure to a nail. Pat it a couple of times, praise your dog and give him a treat. Do this until your dog is comfortable with having his nails touched.

3. Show your dog the nail clipper and let him smell it. Take his foot and hold it firmly, but not hard, and clip off the end of one nail. You need usually remove about one-eighth of an inch. Praise your dog and reward with a treat. Finish up one foot per session.

4. Trim the nails at the rate of one foot per day until all four feet are done.

5. After that, you can move to trimming once a week and do all four feet at the same session. Always remember to reward your dog.

If you have let your dog's nails go, take him to your veterinarian or a groomer. Nail cutting can be painful to your dog if you don't do it on a regular basis. Dogs that have had bad experiences are fretful when it comes to nail cutting time. With these dogs, training them to accept a grinder is often the best route to take. We also use the grinder to round off the rough edges left after cutting the nails with a clipper.

Ears

Ears need to be cleaned out once a week as part of your grooming sessions.

Take a piece of cotton and wet it with a solution of apple cider vinegar (ACV) and warm water (50 percent of each). The solution is a good maintenance cleaner, because the acidity of the vinegar prevents the growth of all sorts of bacteria and fungi. Wipe out ears, paying attention to the little folds that collect earwax. Do not go down too deep inside the ear.

Anal Glands

Anal glands are small sacks inside the rectum. In earlier times, dogs used to express these glands to mark their territory. Little use is found for these holdover glands today.

All dogs have them, and they can become a nuisance. If you see your dog scooting along the ground, chances are he is trying to express them himself. If this behavior continues, take him to your veterinarian and have him show you how to express these glands; it is childishly simple. Left unattended, they can block the end of the rectum, become infected and painful, and your dog will not be able to eliminate. In severe cases, surgery is required.

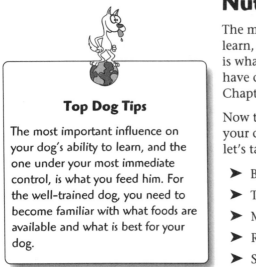

Top Dog Tips

The most important influence on your dog's ability to learn, and the one under your most immediate control, is what you feed him. For the well-trained dog, you need to become familiar with what foods are available and what is best for your dog.

Nutritional Needs

The most important influence on your dog's ability to learn, and the one under your most immediate control, is what you feed him. Because it is so important, we have devoted a separate chapter to this topic. (See Chapter 9.)

Now that we have covered the principal influences on your dog's ability to learn that are under your control, let's take a look at those that come with your dog:

➤ Breed-Specific Behaviors

➤ Temperament

➤ Mental Sensitivity

➤ Responses to Visual Stimuli

➤ Sound Sensitivity

➤ Touch Sensitivity

Breed-Specific Behaviors

Whether you have a designer dog—a dog of mixed origin—or a purebred, he will come with breed-specific behaviors, such as hunting or herding, among others. These, in turn, have been further refined. Some dogs hunt large game, some small, others birds, some close by, others far away, and so on. Some herd and guard, others just herd, some were developed to herd cows, others sheep. You get the picture.

The American Kennel Club, the main governing body of dogdom, recognizes 148 different breeds. These are divided into seven groups, largely based on behavioral similarities. Some of these breeds are fairly close cousins, whereas others are as different as night and day. (There is also a Miscellaneous Class for newly accepted breeds.)

Bet You Didn't Know

There are many different breeds of dogs. The American Kennel Club recognizes 148 different breeds, but there are many others that are not recognized.

For example, Group VII, the Herding Breeds, includes the Belgian Malinois, the Belgian Sheepdog, and the Belgian Tervuren, which are closely related. It also includes the two Welsh Corgis, the Cardigan and the Pembroke, which have no resemblance to any of the other dogs in that group, but in turn are related to one another. The most obvious difference between the two is that the Cardigan has a tail and the Pembroke's tail is docked. Appearance aside, what all the dogs in that group share in common is the instinct to herd. In addition, many of them share the instinct to guard. The German Shepherd , for example, is a member of that group.

The breeds in the various groups are:

Group I	The Sporting Dogs—Pointers, Retrievers, Setters, and Spaniels
Group II	The Hounds
Group III	The Working Dogs—includes sled and draft dogs, water dogs, and guard dogs
Group IV	The Terriers
Group V	The Toys—from Affenpinscher to Yorkshire Terrier
Group VI	The Non-Sporting Dogs—sort of a catch-all category for those that don't fit into any of the other groups
Group VII	The Herding Dogs—those that herd, some of which also guard

Tidbits

The very traits for which dogs were bred in the first place are the ones that sometimes interfere with being a good pet, such as the instinct to hunt or herd.

83

Because the dogs in a given group, with the exception of Group VI, are there because of behavioral traits, you can get a pretty good idea of what is going to be easy for your dog and what is going to be hard.

Terriers, for example, like to dig because they were bred to go after little furry things that live in holes in the ground. Shetland Sheepdogs like to roundup kids, because they were bred to herd. The Pointer is bred to finger the game, retrievers to bring it back, Spaniels to flush it, and so on, each one with its own special talents.

Because dogs were bred to work with or under the direction of man, these talents help with our training efforts. But sometimes the dog's instinct to do what it was bred for is what gets him into trouble today. Put another way, we may not want him hunting, or herding, or whatever. Thus, some of our training efforts are spent in redirecting these energies. Whenever you run into a roadblock in your training, ask yourself "is that what this dog was bred to do?" If not, it will take him more time to learn that particular exercise, and you have to be patient.

What Is *Temperament?*

Most of us will readily agree that good *temperament* is the most important quality for our pets. Unfortunately, the explanation of exactly what that means is often vague and elusive, and sometimes contradictory. The official breed standard of most breeds will make a statement to the effect that the dog you are considering is loyal, loving, intelligent, good with children and easy to train.

If it were only true!

Doggy Dogma

Temperament is having the personality traits suitable for the job you want the dog to do.

Simply defined, *temperament* is having the personality traits suitable for the job you want the dog to do. If you want your dog to be good with children and your dog has that personality trait, then he has good temperament. He may not do so well on other things, such as guarding or herding, but then that may not have been what you were looking for.

Similarly vague and elusive have been attempts to define the dog's *intelligence*. Again, it goes back to function. We define a dog's *intelligence* as the ease with which he or she can be trained for the function for which the dog was bred. For example, as a general rule it is childishly simple to teach a Labrador Retriever to retrieve. After all, that is what he was bred to do.

On the other hand, you would be dead wrong to refer to an Afghan Hound as stupid just because he may have difficulty in learning to retrieve. That's not what he was bred to do; it's not his job.

And that is the whole point. You need to recognize and be aware of your dog's strengths and limitations. They have a profound influence on the ease or difficulty of teaching your dog a particular task.

Circus trainers have an old saying: "Get the dog for the trick, and not the trick for the dog." Exploit your dog's strengths.

Doggy Dogma

Intelligence in a dog is defined as the ease with which a dog can be trained for the function for which it was bred.

Mental Sensitivity

Dogs, like people, vary in their ability to deal with negative emotions. Most dogs, however, are keenly aware of our emotions. Moreover, the more you work with Rascal, the greater the bond that develops. It seems as though he can read your mind.

He may not be able to read your mind, but he certainly senses your emotions. If you are feeling frustration, disappointment or anger, Rascal will sense it.

Because dogs are ill equipped to deal with these emotions, they tend to become anxious and confused. That slows down or even prevents the learning process. Your job in training Rascal is to maintain an up-beat attitude.

Blaming Rascal for what you perceive to be a shortcoming on his part does not help and undermines the very relationship you are trying to build. Remember, Rascal only does what comes naturally and it is your responsibility to teach him what is acceptable and what is not.

You are the trainer and Rascal is the student. He only responds to the commands you have taught him.

Top Dog Tips

It is your job, as your dog's trainer, to teach him what you want him to do and what you do not want him to do. Without your guidance, your dog will simply do what comes naturally to him—he's a dog!

Responses to Visual Stimuli

Responses to visual stimuli is a fancy way of saying how a dog responds to moving objects. For purposes of training it relates to the dog's distractibility when faced with something that moves.

This, too, varies from breed to breed, as well as the nature of the moving object. Terriers are notoriously distractible. Our Yorkshire Terrier, although technically a member of the Toy Group, was convinced that every moving leaf or blade of grass had to be investigated. While this made perfect sense to him, it made training him to pay attention a real challenge.

In the Hound Group, some breeds, such as Afghan Hounds, Borzois, or Salukis, called sight hounds, are not much interested in objects close by and instead focus on those far away. Others, such as the Basset Hound, Beagle, or Bloodhound, are more stimulated by scents on the ground or in the air than by moving objects. Training a Beagle to heel, that is, walking on a loose leash while paying attention to you and without sniffing the ground, becomes a herculean task.

The guarding breeds, such as the German Shepherd Dog, Doberman Pinscher or Rottweiler, were bred to survey their surroundings, to keep everything in sight, as it were. They, too, find it difficult to focus exclusively on you in the presence of distractions. Remember, it is their job to be alert to what is going on around them.

The Bernese Mountain Dog was used as a draft dog by the weavers of the Canton of Berne, drawing small wagons loaded with baskets to the marketplace. As a breed, these dogs are usually not excited by moving objects. After all, it would hardly do for the little fellow to chase a cat with the little wagon bouncing behind him.

The Newfoundland, an ordinarily sedate companion, becomes a raving maniac near water with his instinctive desire to rescue any and all swimmers, totally disregarding that they may not want to be rescued.

Sound Sensitivity

Some dogs have a keener sense of hearing than others, to the point where loud noises literally hurt their ears. One of our Landseers would leave the room anytime the TV was turned on. Fear of thunder can be the result of sound sensitivity.

Under ordinary circumstances, this is not a problem, but it can affect the dog's ability to concentrate in the presence of moderate to loud noises. A car backfiring will cause this dog to jump out of its hide, whereas it will only elicit a curious expression from another dog.

Touch Sensitivity

A dog's threshold of discomfort depends on two things:

➤ his touch sensitivity, and

➤ what he is doing at the particular time.

For purposes of training, and knowing what equipment to use, you need to have some idea of Rascal's touch sensitivity. When a dog doesn't readily respond to the training collar, he is all too quickly labeled as stubborn or stupid.

Nothing could be further from the truth. It is the trainer's responsibility to select the right training equipment so that the dog does respond.

Shetland Sheepdogs, for example, tend to be quite touch sensitive and respond promptly to the training collar. What one dog hardly notices, makes another one sit up and take notice. And therein lies the secret of which piece of training equipment to use.

Touch sensitivity is not size-related. Our Yorkshire Terrier had a very high discomfort threshold. That, plus his sight sensitivity, made training him a real challenge.

Neither is it age-related. A puppy will not start out as touch sensitive and, as it grows older, become insensitive. There may be some increase in insensitivity, but it will be insignificant.

Finally, a dog's touch sensitivity is affected by what he is doing. In hot pursuit of a rabbit, his discomfort threshold goes up, as it would during a fight.

Tidbits

Discomfort thresholds tend to be breed specific. We would expect that a Labrador Retriever, which is supposed to be able to cover all manner of terrain, as well as retrieve in ice-cold water, would have a high discomfort threshold.

Once you have an idea of Rascal's discomfort threshold you will know how you have to handle him and the type of training equipment you need.

The Least You Need to Know

➤ The function for which your dog was bred determines the ease or difficulty in training him.

➤ The tasks that are in harmony with his instincts are quickly learned.

➤ Among the most important influences on your dog's ability to learn is his environment.

➤ Dogs have physical and emotional needs.

➤ Dogs vary in sensitivity to sight, sound, and touch.

Chapter 7

Your Dog's Personality

In This Chapter

➤ Complete Volhards' Canine Personality Profile to find out what makes your dog tick

➤ There are three sets of behaviors that are used in training your dog

➤ Successful training often requires neutralizing chase behaviors

➤ Keep your dog's focus on the job at hand

To give you a better understanding of your dog, we have grouped instinctive behaviors into three *drives*.

 prey

➤ pack

➤ defense

These *drives* reflect instinctive behaviors your dog has inherited from his ancestors and that are useful to you in teaching him what you want him to learn. Each one of these *drives* is governed by a basic trait.

Your dog and every other dog is an individual who comes into the world with a specific grouping of genetically inherited, predetermined behaviors. How those behaviors are arranged, their intensity, and how many component parts of each *drive* the dog has will determine temperament, personality, and suitability for the task required. It also determines how the dog perceives the world.

Doggy Dogma

Drives are instinctive behaviors our dogs have inherited from their ancestors that are useful in teaching our dogs to learn what we want them to know.

Doggy Dogma

Prey drive includes those inherited behaviors associated with hunting, killing prey and eating.

Doggy Dogma

Pack drive consists of behaviors associated with reproduction, being part of a group or pack, and being able to live by the rules.

The Three Major "*Drives*"

Prey drive includes those inherited behaviors associated with hunting, killing prey and eating.

It is activated by motion, sound and smell. Behaviors associated with *prey drive* are:

- ➤ seeing and hearing
- ➤ scenting and tracking
- ➤ stalking and chasing
- ➤ pouncing
- ➤ high-pitched barking
- ➤ jumping up and pulling down
- ➤ shaking
- ➤ tearing and ripping apart
- ➤ biting and killing
- ➤ carrying
- ➤ eating
- ➤ digging and burying

You see some of these behaviors when Rascal is chasing the cat or gets excited and barks in a high-pitched tone of voice as the cat runs up a tree. Rascal may also shake and rip soft toys, or bury dog biscuits in the couch.

Pack drive consists of behaviors associated with reproduction and being part of a group or pack. Our dogs are social animals that evolved from the wolf. To hunt prey that is mostly larger than themselves, wolves have to live in a pack. To assure order, they have to adhere to a social hierarchy governed by strict rules of behavior. An ability to be part of a group and to fit in is important, and, in the dog, is translated into a willingness to work with us as part of a team.

It is stimulated by rank order in the social hierarchy. Behaviors associated with *pack drive* are:

- ➤ physical contact with people and/or other dogs
- ➤ playing with people and/or other dogs
- ➤ behaviors associated with social interaction with another dog, such as reading body language

➤ reproductive behaviors, such as licking, mounting, washing ears, and all courting gestures

➤ the ability to breed and to be a good parent

A dog with many of these behaviors is the one that follows you around the house, is happiest when with you, loves to be petted and groomed, and likes to work with you. The dog may be unhappy when left alone too long, which can express itself in separation anxiety.

Defense drive is governed by survival and self preservation, and consists of both fight and flight behaviors. It is complex, because the same stimulus that can make a dog aggressive (fight), can also elicit avoidance (flight) behaviors, especially in the young dog.

Fight behaviors are not fully developed until the dog is about two years of age, and sometimes later, although tendencies toward these behaviors will be seen at an earlier age. Behaviors associated with fight are:

➤ hackles up from the shoulder forward

➤ standing tall and staring at other dogs

➤ standing ground or going to unfamiliar objects

➤ guarding food, toys, or territory against other people and dogs

➤ dislike of being petted or groomed

➤ lying in front of doorways or cupboards and refusing to move

➤ growling at people or dogs

➤ putting the head over the shoulder of another dog

➤ biting people or other dogs

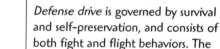

Doggy Dogma

Defense drive is governed by survival and self-preservation, and consists of both fight and flight behaviors. The same stimulus can cause a dog to fight, as well as elicit flight behaviors, especially in the young dog.

Flight behaviors demonstrate that the dog is unsure and young dogs tend to exhibit more flight behaviors than older dogs. Behaviors associated with flight are:

➤ hackles that go up the full length of the body, not just at the neck

➤ hiding or running away from a new situation

➤ a dislike of being touched by strangers

➤ general lack of confidence

➤ urinating when being greeted by a stranger or the owner

➤ flattening of the body when greeted by people or other dogs

Freezing—not going forward or backward—is interpreted as inhibited flight behavior.

Doggy Dogma

Volhards' Canine Personality Profile catalogs ten behaviors in each drive that influence the dog's responses and that are useful to us in training.

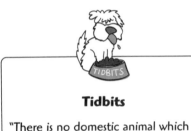

Tidbits

"There is no domestic animal which has so radically altered its whole way of living, indeed its whole sphere of interests, that has become domestic in so true a sense as the dog."
Konrad Lorenz

Your Dog's Personality Profile

To help you understand how to approach your dog's training, we created *Volhards' Canine Personality Profile*. The Profile catalogs ten behaviors in each drive that influence the dog's responses and that are useful to us in training. The ten behaviors chosen are those that most closely represent the strengths of the dog in each of the drives. The Profile does not pretend to include all behaviors seen in a dog, nor the complexity of their interaction. Although it is an admittedly crude index of Rascal's behavior, you will find it surprisingly accurate.

The results of the Profile will give you a better understanding of why Rascal is the way he is and the most successful way to train him. You can then make use of his strengths, avoid needless confusion, and greatly reduce training time.

Evaluating the Profile

When completing the Profile, keep in mind that it was devised for a house dog or pet with an enriched environment, perhaps even a little training, and not a dog tied out in the yard or kept solely in a kennel—such dogs have fewer opportunities to express as many behaviors as a house dog. Answers should indicate those behaviors Rascal would exhibit if he had not already been trained to do otherwise. For example, did he jump on people to greet them, or jump on the counter to steal food, before he was trained not to do so?

Volhards' Canine Personality Profile

The questionnaire for the profile suggests three possible answers to each question with a corresponding point value. The possible answers and their corresponding values are:

➤ Almost always—10

➤ Sometimes—5

➤ Hardly ever—0

For example, if Rascal is a Beagle, the answer to the question "when presented with the opportunity, does your dog sniff the ground or air?" is probably "almost always," giving him a score of 10.

You are now ready to find out who Rascal really is.

You may not have had the chance to observe all of these behaviors, in which case you leave the answer blank.

When presented with the opportunity, does your dog

1. Sniff the ground or air _____
2. Get along with other dogs _____
3. Stand his ground or investigate strange objects or sounds _____
4. Run away from new situations _____
5. Get excited by moving objects, such as bikes or squirrels _____
6. Get along with people _____
7. Like to play tug-of-war games to win _____
8. Hide behind you when he feels he can't cope _____
9. Stalk cats, other dogs, or things in the grass _____
10. Bark when left alone _____
11. Bark or growl in a deep tone of voice _____
12. Act fearfully in unfamiliar situations _____
13. When excited, bark in a high-pitched voice _____
14. Solicit petting, or like to snuggle with you _____
15. Guard his territory _____
16. Tremble or whine when unsure _____
17. Pounce on his toys _____
18. Like to be groomed _____
19. Guard his food or toys _____
20. Cower or turn upside down when reprimanded _____
21. Shake and "kill" his toys _____
22. Seek eye contact with you _____
23. Dislike being petted _____
24. Show reluctance to come close to you when called _____
25. Steal food or garbage _____
26. Follow you around like a shadow _____

27. Guard his owner(s) _____

28. Have difficulty standing still when groomed _____

29. Like to carry things _____

30. Play a lot with other dogs _____

31. Dislike being groomed or petted _____

32. Cower or cringe when a stranger bends over him _____

33. Wolf down his food _____

34. Jump up to greet people _____

35. Like to fight other dogs _____

36. Urinate during greeting behavior _____

37. Like to dig and/or bury things _____

38. Show reproductive behaviors, such as mounting other dogs _____

39. Get picked on by older dogs when young _____

40. Tend to bite when cornered _____

Scoring the Profile

Prey	Pack	Fight	Flight
1._____	2._____	3._____	4._____
5._____	6._____	7._____	8._____
9._____	10._____	11._____	12._____
13._____	14._____	15._____	16._____
17._____	18._____	19._____	20._____
21._____	22._____	23._____	24._____
25._____	26._____	27._____	28._____
29._____	30._____	31._____	32._____
33._____	34._____	35._____	36._____
37._____	38._____	39._____	40._____
Total Prey	Total Pack	Total Fight	Total Flight

After you have obtained the totals, enter them into the appropriate column of the Profile at a Glance at the end of the chapter.

What Do You Want Rascal to Do?

Before you can use the results of the Profile, you need to look at what you want Rascal to do or, and this is often more important, stop doing. For example, when you walk Rascal on leash and want him to pay attention to you, he has to be in pack drive. Rascal, on the other hand, wants to sniff, maybe follow a trail or chase the neighbor's cat; he is in prey drive.

For most of what you want Rascal to do, such as:

> ➤ come
> ➤ walk on a loose leash
> ➤ sit
> ➤ down
> ➤ stay

he needs to be in pack drive.

For most of what Rascal wants to do, such as:

> ➤ chase the cat
> ➤ follow the trail of a rabbit
> ➤ retrieve a ball or stick
> ➤ sniffing the grass
> ➤ digging

he is going to be in prey drive.

You can readily see that those times when you want him to behave, you have to convince Rascal to forget about being in prey drive. Most often it is prey drive that gets dogs into trouble. The dog with high pack and low prey drive rarely needs extensive training.

Such a dog doesn't:

> ➤ chase bicycles, cars, children or joggers
> ➤ chase cats or other animals
> ➤ roam from home
> ➤ steal food
> ➤ chew your possessions
> ➤ pull on the leash

> ## Top Dog Tips
>
> To use the concept of drives, you need to know what you want Rascal to do or stop doing. Usually, you want him to be in pack drive and he wants to be in prey. Once you have mastered how to get him out of prey and into pack, you have a well-trained dog.

In other words, he is a perfect pet.

Theoretically, Rascal does not need defense drive (fight) behaviors for what you want him to learn, but the absence of these behaviors has important ramifications. A very low defense drive will determine how Rascal has to be trained.

The beauty of the drives theory is that, if used correctly, it gives you a tool to overcome areas where your dog may be weak.

Bringing Out Drives

The basic rules for bringing out drives are as follows:

1. Prey drive is elicited by the use of motion—hand signals (except stay)—a high-pitched tone of voice, or an object of attraction (stick, ball, or food), chasing or being chased, and leaning backward with your body as the dog comes to you.

2. Pack drive is elicited by touching, praising and smiling at the dog, grooming, and playing and training with your body erect.

3. Defense drive behavior is elicited by leaning or hovering over the dog, either from the front or the side, checking (a sharp tug on the leash), a harsh tone of voice, and exaggerated use of the stay hand signal.

Switching Drives

Rascal can instantaneously switch himself from one drive to another. Picture this scene—Rascal is lying in front of the fireplace:

➤ playing with his favorite toy

➤ when the doorbell rings he drops the toy, starts to bark and goes to the door

➤ you open the door, it is a neighbor and Rascal goes to greet him and then

➤ returns to play with his toy

Rascal has switched himself from:

➤ prey into

➤ defense into

➤ pack and back into

➤ prey

JJ is in pack drive—his attention is focused on Jeannette.

Here, JJ is in prey drive—his attention is focused on the bumper.

During training, your task is to keep Rascal in the right drive, and if necessary, switch him from one drive into another. For example, you are teaching Rascal to walk on a loose leash in the yard when a rabbit pops out of the hedge. He immediately spots it, runs to the end of the leash, straining and barking excitedly in a high-pitched voice. He is clearly in full-blown prey drive.

Now you have to get him back into pack where he needs to be to walk at your side. The only way you can do that is by going through defense. You cannot, for example, show him a cookie in an effort to divert his attention from the rabbit. The rabbit is going to win out.

The precise manner in which you get Rascal back into pack drive—remember, you must go through defense—depends on the strength of his defense drive. If he has a large number of defense (fight) behaviors, you can give him a firm tug on the leash (check), which switches him out of prey into defense. To get him into pack, touch him gently on the top of his head, smile at him and tell him how clever he is. Then continue to work on your walking on a loose leash.

If he is low in defense (fight) behaviors, a check may overpower him, and a voice communication, such as "Ah, ah" will be sufficient to get him out of prey into defense, after which you put him back into pack drive.

For the dog that has few fight behaviors and a large number of flight behaviors, a check on the leash is often counter-productive. Body postures, such as bending over the dog, or even using a deep tone of voice, are usually enough to elicit defense drive. Your dog, by his response to your training—cowering, rolling upside down, not wanting to come to you for the training session—will show you when you overpower him, thereby making learning difficult, if not impossible.

The basic rules for switching from one drive to another are:

1. From prey into pack, you must go through defense. How you put your dog into defense will depend on the number of defense (fight) behaviors he has. As a general rule, the more defense (fight) behaviors the dog has, the firmer the check needs to be. As the dog learns, a barely audible voice communication or a slight change in body posture will suffice to encourage your dog to go from prey through defense into pack drive.

2. From defense into pack by touching or smiling; and

3. From pack into prey with an object (food) or motion.

Applying the concept of drives, learning which drive Rascal has to be in and how to get him there, will speed up your training process enormously. As you become aware of the impact your body stance and motions have on the drive he is in, your messages will be perfectly clear to your dog. Your body language is congruent with what you are trying to teach. Since Rascal is an astute observer of body motions, which is how dogs communicate with each other, he will understand exactly what you want.

Top Dog Tips

Your dog can switch himself from one drive into another. To switch your dog from prey into pack you must go through defense.

Practical Application

By looking at your dog's profile, you will know the training techniques that work best and are in harmony with your dog's drives. You now have the tools to tailor your training program to your dog.

➤ Defense (fight)—more than 60.

Your dog will not be bothered too much by a firm hand. Correct body posture is not critical, although incongruent postures on your part will slow down the training. Tone of voice should be firm, but pleasant and non-threatening.

➤ Defense (flight)—more than 60.

Your dog will not respond to force training and you will have to rely mainly on the other drives. Correct body posture and a quiet, pleasant tone of voice are critical. Avoid using a harsh tone of voice and any hovering, either leaning over or toward your dog. There is a premium on congruent body postures and gentle handling.

➤ Prey—more than 60.

Your dog will respond well to a treat or a toy during the teaching phase. A firm hand may be necessary, depending on strength of defense drive (fight), to suppress prey drive when in high gear, such as when chasing a cat or spotting a squirrel. This dog is easily motivated, but also easily distracted by motion or moving objects. Signals will mean more to this dog than commands. There is a premium on using body, hands, and leash correctly so as not to confuse the dog.

➤ Prey—less than 60.

Your dog is probably not easily motivated by food or other objects, but is also not easily distracted by or interested in chasing moving objects.

➤ Pack—more than 60.

This dog responds readily to praise and touch. The dog likes to be with you and will respond with little guidance.

➤ Pack—less than 60.

Start praying. Rascal probably does not care whether he is with you or not. He likes to do his own thing and is not easily motivated. Your only hope is to rely on prey drive in training. Limited pack drive is usually breed-specific for dogs bred to work independently of man.

Dogs that exhibit an overabundance in prey or pack are also easily trained, but you will have to pay more attention to the strengths of their drives and exploit those behaviors most useful to you in training. You now have the tools to do it!

Important hints:

1. If your dog is high in defense (fight), you need to work especially diligently on your leadership exercises and review them frequently.

2. If your dog is high in prey, you also need to work on these exercises, not necessarily because your dog wants to become pack leader, but to control him around doorways and moving objects.

3. If your dog is high in both, you may need professional help.

> **Top Dog Tips**
>
> If your dog is high in both prey and defense (fight), you may need professional help. This is by no means a bad dog, but you may become exasperated with your lack of success. The dog may simply be too much for you.

Here are the nicknames for some of the profiles. See if you can recognize your dog.

➤ The Couch Potato—low prey, low pack, low defense. Difficult to motivate and probably does not need extensive training. Needs extra patience if training is attempted since there are few behaviors with which to work. On the plus side, this dog is unlikely to get into trouble, will not disturb anyone, will make a good family pet and does not mind being left alone for considerable periods of time.

➤ The Hunter—high prey, low pack, low defense. This dog will give the appearance of having an extremely short attention span, but is perfectly able to concentrate on what he finds interesting. Training will require the channeling of his energy to get him to do what you want. Patience will be required because the dog will have to be taught through prey drive.

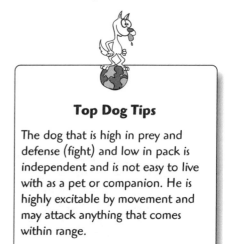

> **Top Dog Tips**
>
> The dog that is high in prey and defense (fight) and low in pack is independent and is not easy to live with as a pet or companion. He is highly excitable by movement and may attack anything that comes within range.

➤ The Gas Station Dog—high prey, low pack, high defense (fight). This dog is independent and not easy to live with as a pet. Highly excitable by movement, he may attack anything that comes within range. He doesn't care much about people or dogs and will do well as a guard dog. Pack exercises such as walking on a leash without pulling need to be built up through his prey drive. This dog is a real challenge.

➤ The Runner—high prey, low pack, high defense (flight). Easily startled and/or frightened. Needs quiet and reassuring handling. A dog with this profile is not a good choice for children.

➤ The Shadow—low prey, high pack, and low defense. This dog will follow you around all day and it is doubtful that he will get into trouble. He likes to be with you and is not interested in chasing much of anything.

➤ Teacher's Pet—medium (50–75) prey, pack, and defense (fight). Easy to train and motivate, and mistakes on your part are not critical. At our training camps and seminars we have the owners put the profile of their dogs in graph form for easy "reading." The graph for Teacher's Pet looks like this:

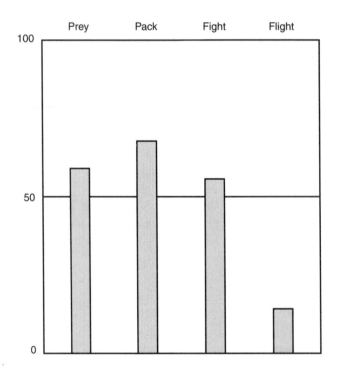

By now you have gathered that the easiest dogs are those that are balanced among all drives. No matter what you do, the dog seems to be able to figure out what you want. If you are lucky enough to have a dog like that, take good care of him. By applying the principles of drives, he will be easy to turn into a well-trained dog.

For your dog's Profile at a Glance, use the following graph.

Profile at a Glance

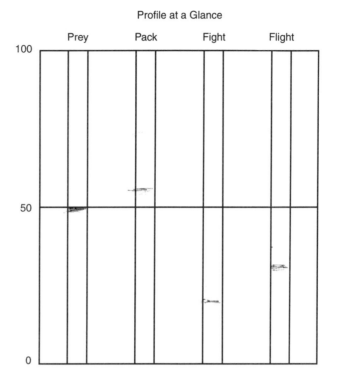

Enhancing Drives

One question we are frequently asked is "can I increase my dog's score in a particular drive?" The answer is "yes," but only to a limited extent.

When we got our first Wirehaired Dachshund, Demi, she was quite low in prey. Her numbers increased after she had been taught to retrieve and been shown in obedience competition. She then started playing with sticks and toys, and carrying things around, something she had not done before.

The other drives can also be somewhat increased through training, as well as the life experiences of the dog.

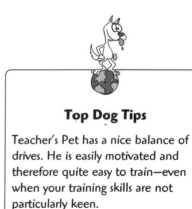

Top Dog Tips

Teacher's Pet has a nice balance of drives. He is easily motivated and therefore quite easy to train—even when your training skills are not particularly keen.

The Least You Need to Know

➤ Drives reflect the instinctive behaviors your dog has inherited from his ancestors.

➤ Prey drive includes those behaviors associated with hunting, killing, and eating prey, and is stimulated by motion, sounds, and odors.

➤ Pack drive consists of behaviors associated with being part of a pack, including reproduction, and is stimulated by an inviting body posture, touching, and a friendly voice.

➤ Defense drive consists of behaviors associated with survival and self preservation, and includes both fight and flight behaviors. Defense drive is stimulated by a threatening body posture, hitting, and an unfriendly voice—this is how people get bitten.

➤ The dog can switch at will from one drive to another.

➤ To switch the dog from prey drive into pack drive, your dog must go through defense drive.

➤ Your dog's personality profile tells you the correct way to train.

Good Grief, My Nerves

In This Chapter

➤ Stress also affects your dog

➤ Recognizing the signs of stress

➤ Stress can interfere with learning

➤ Stress can be managed

Stress, the buzzword of the '90s. If it isn't one thing, it's another—our health, our family, our job, the state of the economy, the state of the country, the state of the world. Even pleasurable experiences, such as taking a vacation, are a source of *stress*.

In order to deal with all these stresses, we get ourselves a (check appropriate response)

➤ boat

➤ motor home

➤ cabin in the woods

➤ dog

➤ _____ (fill in blank)

and now *it* is a source of *stress,* and so it goes.

Stress is a natural part of our daily lives and it affects each of us in different ways. Dogs are no different. Just like us, they experience stress. As your dog's teacher it becomes your job to recognize the circumstances that produce stress, its manifestations, and how to manage it.

Doggy Dogma

Stress is defined as the body's response to any physical or mental demand. It is a physiological, genetically predetermined reaction over which the individual, be it a dog or person, has no control.

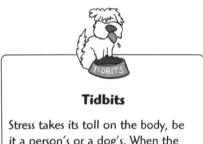

Tidbits

Stress takes its toll on the body, be it a person's or a dog's. When the body's ability to counteract stress has maxed-out, the stress is expressed behaviorally. This is as true for your dog as it is for you.

Your personal experiences with stress will help you be able to relate to what your dog is experiencing. Learning the signs and symptoms is not difficult once you know what you are looking for.

What Is *Stress?*

Stress is defined as the body's response to any physical or mental demand. The response prepares the body either to fight or flee. It increases blood pressure, heart rate, breathing, metabolism and there is a marked increase in the blood supply to the arms and legs. It is a physiological, genetically predetermined reaction over which the individual, be it a dog or person, has no control.

When stressed, the body becomes chemically unbalanced. To address the imbalance, the body releases chemicals into the bloodstream in an attempt to re-balance itself. The reserve of these chemicals is limited. You can dip into it only so many times before it runs dry and the body loses its ability to re-balance. Prolonged periods of imbalance result in neurotic behavior and the inability to function.

Mental or physical stress ranges from tolerable all the way to intolerable—that is, the inability to function. Our interest here lies with the stress experienced during training, whether we are teaching a new exercise or practicing a familiar one, or during a test, as for example, the Canine Good Citizen test (see Chapter 14, Graduating From High School—The Canine Good Citizen). You need to be able to recognize the signs of stress and what you can do to manage the stress your dog may experience.

Positive and Negative Stress—Manifestations

Stress is characterized as "positive"—manifesting itself in increased activity, and "negative"—manifesting itself in decreased activity.

Picture yourself returning home after a hard day at work. You are welcomed by a mess on the brand-new white living room carpet. What is your response? Do you explode, scream at poor Rascal, your spouse, the children, and then storm through the house slamming doors? Or, do you look at the mess in horror, shake your head in resignation, feel drained of energy, ignore the dog, the spouse and the children, and retire to your room?

In the first sample response, your body was energized by the chemicals released into the bloodstream. In the second sample response, your body was debilitated. Dogs react in a similar manner.

Help, I'm Hyperactive

So-called positive *stress* manifests itself in hyperactivity, such as running around, bouncing up and down or jumping on you, whining, barking, mouthing, getting in front of you, or anticipating commands. You may think your dog is just being silly and tiresome, but for the dog those are coping behaviors.

Why Am I So Depressed?

So-called negative *stress* manifests itself by lethargy, such as freezing, slinking behind you, running away, or a slow response to a command. In new situations, Rascal seems tired and wants to lie down, or he seems sluggish and disinterested. These are not signs of relaxation, but are the coping behaviors for negative *stress*.

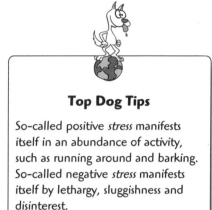

Top Dog Tips

So-called positive *stress* manifests itself in an abundance of activity, such as running around and barking. So-called negative *stress* manifests itself by lethargy, sluggishness and disinterest.

Recognizing the Symptoms

In dogs, signs of either form of *stress* are muscle tremors, excessive panting or drooling, sweaty feet that leave tracks on dry, hard surfaces, dilated pupils, and in extreme cases urination or defecation—usually in the form of diarrhea—or self-mutilation.

Stress is a normal part of our lives and it is the little stresses that go on every day that add to the wear and tear of the body, the mess on the rug being the last straw. It becomes the threshold beyond which you can no longer concentrate or function normally and thereby become anxious.

Anxiety is a state of apprehension, uneasiness. When it is prolonged, two things happen.

1. The ability to learn and to think clearly is diminished and ultimately stops. It can also cause a panic attack.

2. Anxiety depresses the immune system thereby increasing our chances of becoming physically ill. It affects our dogs in the same way. The weakest link in the chain is attacked first. If the dog has structural flaws, such as weak pasterns (the region of foreleg between the wrist and digits), it may begin to limp or show signs of pain. Digestive upsets are another common reaction to *stress*.

Stress, in and of itself, is not anything bad or undesirable. A certain level of stress is vital for the development and healthy functioning of the body and its immune system. It is only when there is no behavioral outlet for *stress*—when the dog is put in a no-win situation—that the burden of coping is born by the body and the immune system starts to break down.

Origins of *Stress*—Intrinsic and Extrinsic

Intrinsic sources of *stress* are all the things that come with the dog, including structure and health. They are inherited and come from within the dog. Dogs vary in coping abilities and *stress* thresholds. Realistically, there is not much you can do to change your dog, such as training a dog to deal better with *stress*. You can use *stress*-management techniques to mitigate its impact.

Extrinsic sources of *stress* range from the diet you feed to the relationship you have with your dog. They come from outside the dog and are introduced externally. Extrinsic sources include:

➤ lack of adequate socialization.

➤ appropriateness of the training method being used.

➤ the location where the training takes place.

➤ frustration and indecision on your part.

➤ how the dog perceives his environment.

Fortunately, all these are under your control.

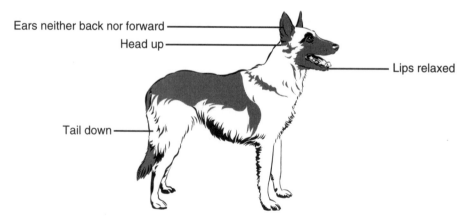

Ears neither back nor forward

Head up

Lips relaxed

Tail down

A dog's posture will convey when he feels relaxed.

Body low

Pupils dilated

Panting

Lips pulled way back

Sweating feet

A dog's posture also will convey when he is stressed.

Stress and Learning

All learning is stressful. For many people, ourselves included, one of the most recent learning experiences was brought on by the computer revolution. In our case, there were plenty of times during the learning process when we were tempted to throw the agonizing contraption out the window. At that moment, learning, and the ability to think rationally had stopped. There was no point in trying to go on until the body had the chance to re-balance itself.

When you train Rascal, you cannot prevent him from experiencing some *stress*, but you can keep it at a level where he can still learn. Recognize the signs of *stress* and when you should stop. When Rascal reaches the point where he can no longer learn, whatever he does will not be committed to memory.

Top Dog Tips

If you find that your dog is over-stressed during a training session, it is time to stop the session. At that point, your dog's ability to learn is critically diminished and neither of you will benefit from continuing.

There are going to be times when Rascal just doesn't get the message. It can happen at any time, especially when you are working with distractions (see Chapter 12, Going to High School). Nothing you do works and you feel that you are not making any progress.

"What can I do?" we are often asked. "If I stop, Rascal will think he has won and he will never do it for me." This argument is completely without merit because it presumes that you and Rascal are adversaries, in some kind of a contest, such as, "you will do it no matter what." If you approach training with this attitude, you are doomed to failure; at best, you will have an unrewarding relationship with your dog.

Training Rascal has nothing to do with winning, but with teaching. You can walk away from a training session at anytime, whether or not you think you have been successful. When you see that no further learning is taking place, stop! If you don't and insist on forcing the issue, you will undermine both your dog's trust in you and the relationship you are trying to build.

Tidbits

"Good training needs a kind heart as well as a cool and well-informed head ..." *Training Dogs—A Manual*, by Konrad Most, the "father" of training as we know it today, originally published in 1910.

Tidbits

Prepare to be patient when you first introduce your dog to training with distractions. Naturally, Rascal is going to be distracted (that is the point!), but over time, he will learn to respond in the way that you want. If you feel yourself becoming distraught, it is time to take five.

Let Rascal rest for four hours and try again. You will find that all of a sudden the light bulb seems to have gone on. By having taken a break at that point, you give latent learning—the process of getting the point through time—a chance to work. Our advice is to quit training when you find yourself becoming irritable or when Rascal starts to show signs of severe stress.

Konrad Most, considered to be the "father" of modern dog training, recognized the importance of maintaining the dog's equilibrium. In his 1910 training manual he wrote, "Good training needs a kind heart as well as a cool and well-informed head ..." Anyone can dominate a dog by physical or mental pressure, but only through the building of confidence by positive reinforcement can reliability and enjoyment of performance be achieved. Rascal must perceive you as trustworthy or he will begin to exhibit neurotic behaviors.

Stress and Distraction Training

When distractions are introduced in training, your dog may not respond as you expected. As a result, you may become a little frustrated, taking the attitude "How could you do this to me?" Rascal senses your feelings and becomes apprehensive and anxious. He only understands that you are upset, but does not understand why. Unless you now calm yourself and him, and reassure him that he is a good boy and should keep trying, your training session will deteriorate to the point where all learning stops.

When you take your Canine Good Citizen test (see Chapter 14, Graduating From High School—The Canine Good Citizen), it is especially important for you to remain calm and control any nervousness you may experience. Your dog is acutely aware of your emotions, which are likely to interfere with his performance. Remember, the object of training and the test is to make both a positive experience for you and your dog.

Most of the tests for the Canine Good Citizen involve some form of distraction or another. You will need to monitor your dog's reaction to these distractions so you can help him cope. One test requires you be out of your dog's sight for three minutes, which can be a source of significant *stress* to your dog. You will need to introduce him to and condition him for this exercise in such a way that any *stress* he may experience is minimized.

The first impression leaves the most lasting impact. Whenever you introduce your dog to a new exercise or distraction, make it as pleasant and as *stress*-free as possible so that it leaves a neutral, if not favorable impression.

A classic example of the impact of the first impression is the following incident: Pinny had entered her one-year old Landseer Newfoundland, Immy, in a Newfoundland Club of America Water Test. These events test the dogs' rescue abilities and when found satisfactory, result in a Water Dog title, attesting the fact the dog is a water rescue dog.

Top Dog Tips

Try to make every new exercise or distraction a positive experience for your dog. A favorable introduction will have a positive long-term impact.

The first part of this test is on land, where the dogs are expected to demonstrate a passing familiarity with basic obedience commands, such as heel, come and stay. Immy was very well trained to do all this.

Bet You Didn't Know

The Newfoundland Club of America conducts Water Tests where the dogs can demonstrate their water rescue abilities. There are two levels, Water Dog and Water Rescue Dog. The Club also conducts Draft Dog tests.

When Pinny and Immy approached the area in which they were to be tested, which had been roped off into a large square with yellow tape, she noticed that Immy was becoming extremely agitated. He outright refused to get close to, much less into, the roped off enclosure. His eyes rolled back in his head, he wanted to bolt, and became almost uncontrollable.

Pinny walked away from the area, calmed him down and tried again. No way was Immy going close to the yellow tape that was flapping in the wind. Pinny didn't push the issue, but Immy went on and did the water part of the trial with great success.

Driving home, she was trying to think why Immy should have been so frightened of the yellow tape. And then she remembered. When Immy first came to her, he was already 6 months old. He was a tall and gangly puppy with lots of energy and a propensity for jumping straight up in the air. It wasn't long before he took this great talent and experimented with jumping the fence in the back garden. He took himself for a nice walk around the neighborhood and found visiting other dogs lots of fun.

Living on a rather busy street, Pinny was worried that he would get run over. So she came to the conclusion that an electric fence was the best solution to her problem.

When the salesperson installed the fence, he asked Pinny if she had ever trained a dog to the fence before. She answered that she had not. Don't worry, I'll show you how to do it," said the salesman. He took Immy on a leash, went up to the fence which had yellow flags on it, and as Immy approached curiously, he yanked him back as hard as he could, and screamed "no." Immy fell to the ground in shock and Pinny was horrified.

Looking back, Immy clearly associated this most unpleasant experience with the yellow tape and when he encountered it again at the Water Test, he wanted nothing to do with it.

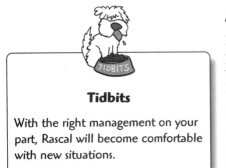

Tidbits

With the right management on your part, Rascal will become comfortable with new situations.

Stress Management

Become aware of how Rascal reacts to *stress*, that is positively or negatively, and the circumstances under which he stresses. Something you are doing, or even a location, may cause him stress.

Let's say Rascal stresses in a "positive" way, which means he gets overexcited and bouncy. In the case of a person we would say he or she is hysterical. In the old movies, when someone started screaming uncontrollably, this was handled by slapping the person on the cheek. (For Rascal, a check on the collar to settle him down would be the same thing.) However, we advise that you keep your hands still and off your dog, and keep your voice quiet or you will excite him even more. Give him the down command and enforce it. Every behavior has a time frame and experience will tell you how long it takes Rascal to calm down under different circumstances. During times of severe stress, Rascal is unable to learn or respond to commands, even those he knows well, until his body re-balances itself. Your goal is to restore your dog's breathing pattern and body posture to normal.

If Rascal stresses in a "negative" way, take him for a walk to get the circulation going and redistribute the chemicals that have been released, so his breathing can return to normal. Massage the top of his shoulders to relax him—just because he is quiet does not mean he is calm. Try to get him excited with an object or food. Do not, under any circumstances, use a check to get him "out of it." This will just produce even greater lethargy.

Understand that Rascal has no control over his response to *stress*—he inherited this behavior—and that it is your job to manage it as best as you can. Through proper management, Rascal will become accustomed, with every successful repetition, to coping with new situations and handle them like an old trooper.

Stress Management Examples

Some dogs get unduly stressed during thunderstorms. Others, perhaps because of lack of socialization, get stressed when they are away from home, left in a kennel, taken to a class for the first time, riding in the car, and the like.

There are products on the market now that make dealing with stress so much easier. Homeopathic remedies and Bach Flower Remedies are excellent to use for this purpose. For fear of thunderstorms, use Aconite 30c. This comes in liquid or pellet form. Usually one dose will give the dog a feeling of being able to cope with the storm.

When taking a dog to a place where he experiences fear, such as the animal hospital, we use a product called Calm Stress. It is a liquid homeopathic; you can put it into your dog's mouth just before you enter. It lasts about 20 minutes. Once your dog understands that he need not be afraid, and that he has coped well with the environment, further dosing will be unnecessary.

We use the Calm Stress remedy to rehabilitate rescue dogs with great success, as well as another one called Rescue Remedy. A Bach Flower Remedy is used when the dog gets so stressed there is danger of shock. It can be dropped directly into the dog's mouth, about 4 drops, or put into his water bowl.

Bet You Didn't Know

A simple remedy for carsick dogs is a ginger cookie. Ginger has a wonderful way of settling the stomach, and if you give your dog a ginger cookie just as he gets into the car, the car becomes a good place to be in.

Rescue Remedy, together with Calm Stress, works well to combat carsickness. Another simple trick is to give your dog a ginger cookie, which helps to calm the stomach. If the trip is a long one, you can give a ginger cookie periodically. Dogs can get quite stressed in a car, not only by the movement, but also by things flashing by the windows. Using a crate for such a dog is a good idea, because you can cover the crate so the dog is not constantly exposed to visual stimuli.

Stress manifests itself in so many ways, and it is up to you, the owner, to know your dog. Remember, it is a response over which the dog has no control. It is also up to you to play detective to find out what triggers the stress behavior.

Perhaps the strangest case we have had to deal with was that of one of our own dogs. D.J. is an extremely handsome black Briard. When D.J. was a young dog, he got stressed by almost everything. If we put him in the car, he would throw up and turn in circles. When he got out he would be wet from drooling, and would want to pace and pace. Around other dogs he was anxious and wanted nothing to do with them. If they came too close, he would lunge out at the end of the leash, teeth flashing—a frightening sight for any dog or person that happened to be close.

Knowing that D.J. was on the very best diet he could be on, we ruled out food-related problems. He had every medical test in the book to find out the cause of his stressful behavior. Nothing was found, and so we lived with him, always seeking some kind of answer. It came when he was nearly three years old.

We were told of a veterinarian who was also a Certified Animal Chiropractor and who was giving a clinic for dogs and horses. Since we had tried everything else, this was the last ditch attempt to help D.J. The journey to the clinic was memorable in itself. The car was a mess from the vomit, drool, and diarrhea. Every toll booth collector had to be attacked through the window.

The chiropractor was in a horse barn, working on some dogs when we arrived. Leaving D.J. in the car, we went in and introduced ourselves. The doctor was the model of patience with D.J. She told us to bring in D.J. and just let him sit and watch what was going on for a while, so he could get the feeling of his surroundings. She went on adjusting other dogs.

In the barn were horses, goats, and chickens. D.J. was fascinated by the smells and was fine so long as nothing or no one came close to him. We carefully inched him closer and closer to the doctor who was sitting on a small stool. He stood with his back to her, and all of a sudden, decided to back into her. She talked to him for a while, without touching his body. She asked him if he minded if she petted him. He sat still. She touched him and he jumped, and we all jumped.

We started again. She felt up and down his back while his attention was glued on a chicken. As she felt his back and then his tail, she told us that many vertebrae were out of alignment, and there had been some kind of break in his tail. We surmised that this must have happened during the birthing process, which apparently is not uncommon. She very gently manipulated him back into position. But she really felt the problem was his neck.

Slowly, slowly, she moved up his body and he was motionless. Thank goodness the chicken was obliging and stayed within a nose length of D.J. who was still staring at it. The doctor finally was able to feel his neck and with two rather quick movements, adjusted the vertebrae. He stood up and shook himself, sat down suddenly, and then just lay down.

She told me that his neck was such a mess that the nerves connected to his eyes were severely displaced. She felt that he had never been able to see properly, either his vision was so distorted he couldn't make out shapes, or that he was seeing upside down. My light bulb went on.

114

This of course explained all of his behavior and the severe *stress* that he felt. If his vision was poor, naturally he always felt threatened when away from home. Since he was never off leash when we took him out, and couldn't run away as he wanted to do, he would then be forced into a defensive posture, hence the teeth and the growling. We felt both relieved and saddened.

The journey home was amazing. After cleaning out the car, we put D.J. into the back of the station wagon on a nice clean blanket. He slept the whole way home, without even acknowledging the toll booth attendant. We took him out in the car every day after that, to training classes, everywhere we could think of. He was totally at ease and at almost nine years of age, has become a very cuddly and sweet dog. Most visitors to our house pick out D.J. as our most friendly dog.

So the moral of this story is that when your dog is stressing, there is a reason for it. You just have to work at it until you find the answers.

The Least You Need to Know

➤ Stress can manifest itself in hyperactivity or lethargy.

➤ Extrinsic sources of stress are under your control.

➤ When your dog stresses you need to re-balance the chemicals in his body.

➤ All learning is stressful, and it is your job to manage that stress.

Chapter 9

Feeding the Well-Trained Dog

In This Chapter

➤ The connection between nutrition and health

➤ An almost short course in canine nutrition

➤ Your dog's staff of life is meat

➤ Yes, you need to supplement processed food

➤ Making your own dog food is an option

Your dog's behavior, happiness, health, longevity, and over all well being are inextricably intertwined with what you feed him. Dogs, just like everyone else, have specific nutritional requirements that need to be met. And, not to complicate matters, the needs of dogs vary. For example, even though your first dog may have done wonderfully well on Barfo Special Blend, it may be completely wrong for Rascal.

We are not trying to turn you into an expert on canine nutrition, but you should know some basic concepts. If you do want to become an expert, see *The Holistic Guide For a Healthy Dog* by Wendy Volhard and Kerry Brown, DVM (Howell Book House, 1995).

You should also know the most common and most visible symptoms of nutritional deficiencies. Recognizing these will save you a great deal of money in veterinary bills because you can make the necessary adjustments to your dog's diet.

Choosing the Right Food

Not all dog foods are alike and there are enormous quality differences. The cliché "garbage in, garbage out" applies with terrifying validity. There are so many choices available today that trying to make an informed decision can become an overwhelming task. We are going to tackle the job by the process of elimination. Two commonly used criteria immediately come to mind: advertising and price.

1. Forget about what the ad says about how good this food is for your dog. It may be OK for Rascal, but perhaps it is not. You have to look at what's in it.

2. Forget about price. This works both ways. Just because it costs more doesn't necessarily mean it's better than a less expensive variety.

Following is a quick checklist to determine if Rascal is getting what he needs:

➤ he doesn't want to eat the food,

➤ he has large, voluminous stools that smell awful,

➤ he has gas,

➤ his teeth get dirty and brown,

➤ his breath smells,

➤ he burps a lot,

➤ he constantly sheds,

➤ he has a very dull coat,

➤ he smells like a dog,

➤ he is prone to ear and skin infections,

➤ he has no energy or is hyperactive,

➤ he easily picks up fleas,

➤ he easily picks up worms and has to be wormed frequently, or

➤ his immune system is impaired.

All of the above will happen occasionally with any dog, but only occasionally. When several of the items on the list occur frequently, or continuously, it's time to find out why.

A Carnivore Needs Meat

Your dog is a carnivore and not a vegetarian. He needs meat. His teeth are quite different from ours—they are made for ripping and tearing meat. They do not have flat surfaces for grinding up grains. His digestion starts in his stomach and not in his mouth. All the enzymes in his system are geared toward breaking down meat and raw foods. There is no doubt about it, Rascal is a carnivore.

Your dog's body, as well as yours, is made up of cells, a lot of them. Each cell needs 45 nutrients to function properly. The cells need:

1. protein, consisting of 9 to 12 essential amino acids

2. carbohydrates

3. fat

4. vitamins

5. minerals

6. water

Tidbits

A dog's body, from the shape of his teeth to his digestive system, is designed to accommodate the ingestion of meat. Dogs are carnivores and need to eat meat to stay healthy.

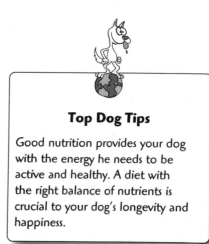

Top Dog Tips

Good nutrition provides your dog with the energy he needs to be active and healthy. A diet with the right balance of nutrients is crucial to your dog's longevity and happiness.

All these nutrients need to be in the correct proportion for the necessary chemical reactions of digestion, absorption, transportation, and elimination to occur. If the cells are going to be able to continue to live, the exact composition of the body fluids that bathe the outside of the cells needs to be controlled from moment to moment, day by day, with no more than a few percentage points variation.

These nutrients are the fuel, which is converted into energy. Energy produces heat and how much heat is produced determines the ability of your dog to control his body temperature, critical to a healthy life. Everything your dog does, from running and playing, to working and living a long and healthy life, is determined by the fuel you provide and the energy it produces.

The term "calorie" is used to measure energy in food. Optimally, every dog will eat the quantity of food he needs to meet his caloric needs. The food you feed must provide sufficient calories so your dog's body can

➤ produce energy to grow correctly,

➤ maintain health during adulthood,

➤ reproduce, and

➤ grow into a quality old age.

Tidbits

The source of protein in dog food is very important to your dog's well being. Look for foods in which the protein comes from animal and not plant sources.

The Dog's Staff of Life— Protein

On the back of dog food packages you will be told how much protein is in the food. How much protein is in it is important, but even more important is the source.

The manufacturer has choices as to what kind of protein to put into the food. The percentage of protein on the package generally is a combination of proteins found in plants or grains, such as corn, wheat, soy, rice, and the like, plus an animal protein, such as chicken, beef, or lamb.

By law, the heaviest and largest amount of whatever ingredient contained in the food has to be listed first. By looking at the list of ingredients, it is easy to see the origin of the protein. For example, if the first five ingredients listed are four grains, it tells you that the majority of the protein in that food comes from grains. The more grains in a dog food, the cheaper it is to produce. We wonder what Rascal thinks of such a food. The front of the package says:

With *Lamb & Rice*

High Quality Ingredients. Made With Real Lamb.

KEY INGREDIENTS
Ground yellow corn
Poultry by-product meal
Beef tallow
Lamb
Brewers rice, wheat
Fortified vitamins

The back of the package lists the actual ingredients.

So where's the meat? Take the time to learn how to decipher dog food labels.

Animal Protein Deficiencies

When Rascal does not get enough animal protein as part of his diet, or there is an imbalance of his nutrients, one or more of the following may occur:

- ➤ chronic skin and/or ear infections;
- ➤ reproductive system, heart, kidney, liver, bladder, thyroid and adrenal glands may be compromised;
- ➤ some kinds of epilepsy or cancers;
- ➤ spinning or tail chasing;
- ➤ aggression;
- ➤ timidity;
- ➤ lack of pigmentation;
- ➤ excessive shedding;
- ➤ gastrointestinal upsets, vomiting or diarrhea;
- ➤ poor appetite;
- ➤ impaired ability to heal from wounds or surgery, such as spaying and neutering;
- ➤ weakened immune system that cannot properly tolerate vaccines.

> **Top Dog Tips**
>
> The activity level of your dog is likely to correspond with the amount of animal protein he needs in his diet. The busy little Jack Russell is apt to need more animal protein than a pooch that spends his time lying around the house.

This is only a short list of the more common symptoms associated with an animal-protein deficiency.

It has also been our experience that the majority of the Working breeds, Sporting breeds, Toys and Terriers need extra animal protein in their diets. Dogs that lead a couch potato existence can survive on food with more plant than animal protein.

A dog that works off calories will need more animal protein in his diet than one that lies around the house.

One more thing you need to know about protein. Amino acids are the name given to the building blocks of protein, and when they are heated, they are partially destroyed. All dry and canned commercial dog food is heated in the manufacturing process. So commercial food contains protein that is somewhat deficient or destroyed through heating. We will show you how to compensate for that at the end of the chapter.

The Critical Time of Growth

During the first seven months of Rascal's life, he will increase his birth weight anywhere from 15 to 40 times, depending upon his breed. By one year of age, his birth weight will have increased 60 times and his skeletal development will be almost complete. For strength and proper growth to occur, he needs the right food. He also needs twice the amount of food of an adult while he is growing, especially during growth spurts. Nutritional deficiencies at an early age, even for short periods, can cause problems later on.

Bet You Didn't Know

In contrast to humans, dogs grow *fast.* By the time a dog is one year of age, his weight will be 60 times that of when he was born and his skeletal development will be nearly complete.

The most critical period for a puppy is between four to seven months, the time of maximum growth. His little body is being severely stressed as his baby teeth drop out and his adult teeth come in. He is growing like a weed, and at the same time his body is being assaulted with a huge number of vaccines. The right food is critical so that his immune system can cope with all these demands and onslaughts.

To find out how we can protect him as best as possible, we need to take a look at different dog foods to see the ones that best meet the criteria for young Rascal's growth.

Puppy Foods and Their Labels

Puppy foods do contain more protein than adult or maintenance foods. Manufacturers know that puppies need more protein for growth. Nonetheless, we still need to know the source of the protein, that is, animal or plant.

What we are looking for is a puppy food that has two animal proteins in the first three ingredients, or better yet, one that lists animal protein as its first two ingredients. Avoid foods that do not meet these criteria. Rascal is not a ruminant.

Once you have selected a food for young Rascal on the basis of its protein percentage, your job isn't quite done yet. You have to check a few other items.

Tidbits

Commercial dog food manufacturers address a puppy's need for significant amounts of protein by including it in puppy foods. The key to the value of the protein is whether it is derived from animal sources or plant sources.

Carbohydrates—Sparingly, Please!

Your dog also needs carbohydrates or grains, and some vegetables for proper digestion. Through the digestive process, grains are broken down first into starch, then into simple sugars and into glucose, necessary for energy and proper functioning of the brain. Grains are also needed for stool formation and correct functioning of the thyroid gland. Dogs do not need many carbohydrates to be healthy, so a diet low in carbohydrates and high in protein is an ideal diet. Diets high in carbohydrates take a long time to digest, produce voluminous and smelly stools, and gas. They also build up tartar on your dog's teeth, making his gums sore and his breath smell.

Oats, barley, and brown rice are whole grains that contain a lot of vitamins and minerals. They also contain protein and fat. Corn is a popular grain because of its low price. Soy is another carbohydrate that is found in some foods. Soy admittedly is high in protein, but binds up other nutrients and makes them unavailable for absorption. We recommended that you stay away from dog foods that contain soy. It is best fed to those species of animals with gizzards, such as birds, that can break it down.

Bet You Didn't Know

The soyburger might be a healthy food choice for us, but not for Rascal. Soy is high in protein, but it prevents dogs from absorbing other nutrients. Just say "no" to soy.

Carbohydrates have to be broken down for the dog to be able to digest them. Dog food companies use a heat process to do this and therein lies the problem. Many of the vitamins and minerals contained in grains are destroyed by the heat process. The question that comes immediately to mind is "where do dogs in the wild get the grains and vegetables they need?" The answer is from the intestines of their prey, all neatly predigested so the dog can digest them.

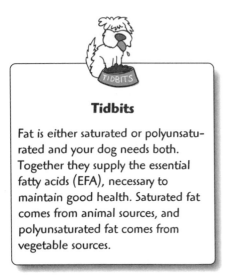

Tidbits

Fat is either saturated or polyunsaturated and your dog needs both. Together they supply the essential fatty acids (EFA), necessary to maintain good health. Saturated fat comes from animal sources, and polyunsaturated fat comes from vegetable sources.

Not All Fats Are Created Equal

Fat is either saturated or polyunsaturated and your dog needs both. Together they supply the essential fatty acids (EFA), necessary to maintain good health.

In the manufacturing of the majority of dog foods, fat is sprayed on as the last ingredient. Fat makes the dog food palatable, like potato chips and French fries.

Saturated fat comes from animal sources and is used for energy. For dogs that get a great deal of exercise or participate in competitive events, the food has to be high in animal fat. Not enough animal fat in the diet can create:

➤ lack of energy

➤ heart problems

➤ growth deficits

➤ dry skin

➤ cell damage

Too much animal fat in the diet creates:

➤ obesity

➤ mammary gland tumors

➤ cancer of the colon and rectum

Polyunsaturated fat is found in vegetable sources, such as flax seed oil, safflower oil, wheat germ oil, olive and corn oil. Polyunsaturated fat is needed by your dog for healthy skin and coat. Too little of this fat can produce skin lesions on the belly, thighs, and between the shoulder blades. If your dog has a dry coat you may need to add some oil to his food.

Linoleic acid is one of the three essential fatty acids that have to be provided daily in your dog's food. Safflower and flax seed oil provide the best source of linoleic acid and are the least allergenic. They are better than corn oil which contains only a tiny amount of linoleic acid.

Lack of polyunsaturated fat can cause:

➤ coarse, dry hair coat

➤ improper growth

➤ skin lesions on belly, inside the back legs, and between the shoulder blades

➤ thickened areas of skin

➤ horny skin growths

➤ skin ulcerations and infections

➤ poor blood clotting

➤ extreme itching and scratching

Look for food that has both animal and vegetable oils in it.

What Else Is in Here?

The manufacturer has choices on how to preserve the fat in food to prevent it from becoming rancid, such as using the chemicals BHA, BHT, ethoxyquin, or propyl gallate. If a fat is preserved with these chemicals, it will have a long shelf life and be little affected by heat and light. Even so, many of us would prefer not to feed these to our dogs, especially ethoxyquin.

A manufacturer can also use natural preservatives, such as vitamins C and E. Vitamin E will be listed as tocopherol. The down side is a shorter shelf life, no more than six months.

What Is Missing?

Vitamins are needed in your dog's food to release the nutrients and enzymes from the ingested food so the body can absorb and use it. Without vitamins, your dog cannot break down food and use it. In researching *The Holistic Guide for a Healthy Dog*, we called manufacturers to ask them their source of vitamins and how they protected them against destruction from the heat process. Their responses were astonishing. They acknowledged awareness of the problem and to overcome it, added more to the food to make up the difference. Of course, this is nonsense. If vitamins are destroyed by heat, it doesn't make any difference how much you put in the food. It will still be destroyed.

Top Dog Tips

Food preserved with chemicals, such as BHA, BHT, ethoxyquin, or propyl gallate, has a long shelf life. Even so, many of us would prefer not to feed these to our dogs, especially ethoxyquin. Food can also be preserved with vitamins C and E, but will have a shorter shelf life, no more than six months.

We also learned that most of the finished products were not tested. In other words, vitamins and minerals go into the food, but what actually reaches your dog seems as much a mystery to some of the manufacturers as it is to us.

There are two types of vitamins—water soluble and fat soluble. Water soluble vitamins are B and C. Any excess is filtered through the kidneys and urinated out between four

Tidbits

Because vitamins begin to break down when you open your dog food bag and expose the food to the elements, close the food up tight and keep it away from light. Doing so will help to retain the quality of the contents.

to eight hours after ingestion. For this reason they have to be present in each meal. Vitamins, A, D, E, and K are fat soluble and stored in the fatty tissues of the body and the liver. Both types are needed by your dog.

Vitamins are not only lost in the manufacturing process, but begin to deteriorate as soon as you open up your dog food bag and expose the food to light and air. Vitamins B and C are particularly sensitive to exposure. Vitamin C is needed for healthy teeth and gums. In the old days, sailors often suffered from vitamin C deficiency due to the lack of fresh fruits and vegetables while at sea. This malady is called scurvy and results in weakness, anemia, spongy and inflamed gums, and dirty teeth. The same thing happens to the vitamin C deficient dog.

A fairly common misconception is that dogs don't need extra vitamin C because they produce their own. While it is true that they produce their own vitamin C, it is not enough, especially in our polluted environment.

Bet You Didn't Know

Although dogs produce vitamin C in their bodies, they still need this vitamin in their diet. Vitamin C generates a wealth of benefits, including strengthening the immune system and keeping the urinary tract healthy.

Vitamin C strengthens the immune system, speeds wound healing, helps the function of the musculoskeletal system and is needed whenever the dog gets wormed, is given drugs of any kind, or put under any kind of stress. A lack of vitamin C in the diet commonly results in urinary tract infections, cystitis, and limps. Vitamin C is needed to break down the animal protein in the diet and helps to keep the immune system healthy.

The same holds true with Vitamin B, which is made up of a number of individual parts and is called vitamin B-complex. Also a water soluble vitamin and fragile, vitamin B is needed for energy and to promote biochemical reactions in the body that work with enzymes to change the carbohydrates into glucose, as well as to break down protein. Because not enough of either is contained in any processed dog food to meet our criteria for raising Rascal, you have to add these to his diet.

Minerals—A Little Goes a Long Way

Minerals make up less than two percent of any formulated diet, and yet they are the most critical of nutrients. Although the dog can manufacture some vitamins on its own, he is not able to make minerals. They are needed:

➤ so the body fluids are composed correctly,

➤ for formation of blood and bones,

➤ to promote a healthy nervous system, and

➤ to function as co-enzymes together with vitamins.

Since between 50 to 80 percent of minerals are lost in the manufacturing process, we recommend that you add extra minerals to your dog's food.

Stay with us—we're almost through the things you need to know to make intelligent decisions on feeding Rascal. We will give you some ideas of which foods to choose and what to add to them to make up for the deficiencies caused in processing. But first, one more piece of information, so everything falls into place for you.

Water

Your dog should have access to fresh water in a clean stainless steel bowl at all times. The exception would be when the puppy is being housetrained. Then you limit access to water after 8:00 p.m. so the puppy will last through the night.

Digestion Time

According to a Swedish study, raw foods pass through a dog's stomach and into the intestinal tract in 4 1/2 hours. So after that time span, the dogs were already receiving the energy from that food. Raw foods are the most easily digested by the dog.

Bet You Didn't Know

Raw foods pass through a dog's stomach and into the intestinal tract in 4 1/2 hours, and they are the most easily digested by the dog. Semi-moist food takes almost 9 hours to pass through the stomach. Dry food takes between 15 and 16 hours.

Semi-moist food, the kind that is found in boxes on the shelves in the supermarket and shaped like hamburgers, or found in rolls like sausages, takes almost 9 hours to pass through the stomach. Dry food takes between 15 and 16 hours. So if you choose to feed Rascal any kind of dry processed dog food, it will be in his stomach from morning, noon till night.

So what's the point? Well, let's take a closer look.

Enzymes and Enzyme Robbing

Enzymes make a body tick. They are already contained in the body, and made through what we feed our dogs.

When that semi-moist food or dry food sits in the stomach of the dog, it does so because there are not enough enzymes in the stomach to break it down. Remember, a dog's stomach is designed to deal with raw foods.

So the stomach sends a message to the brain. "Hey, brain, we need some more enzymes down here." And the brain responds "OK, OK, but I need some time." It then gathers enzymes from the heart, the liver, the kidneys, and other parts of the body to be transported to the stomach. In the meantime, the food sits there until enough enzymes are collected for digestion. This process is called enzyme robbing.

> **Tidbits**
>
> A dog's vital internal organs—his heart, liver, and kidneys—need the enzymes that they contain to function at their best. When a dog consumes semi-moist and dry foods, some of these enzymes must be diverted to the stomach to aid in digestion. Ultimately, it is the dog's vital organs that lose out.

Robbing various organs in the body of the enzymes that they themselves need to function correctly can have a detrimental effect on those organs. If a dog has a predisposition for problems in his heart, kidneys or liver disease, such enzyme loss can hasten that disease and reduce the life span of the dog.

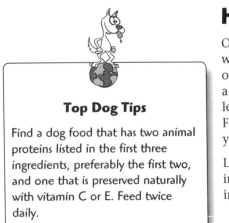

How to Feed Rascal

Over 30 years of breeding, raising, working and living with dogs of several breeds, have had a profound effect on our way of thinking. Even so, we are realists. You are a busy person and may not even cook for yourself, much less be concerned about what goes into your dog. Fortunately, you can take some shortcuts to safeguard your dog's health.

Look for a dog food that has two animal proteins listed in the first three ingredients. It is best if the first two ingredients are animal proteins. Buy a food that is

> **Top Dog Tips**
>
> Find a dog food that has two animal proteins listed in the first three ingredients, preferably the first two, and one that is preserved naturally with vitamin C or E. Feed twice daily.

preserved naturally with vitamin C or E. Feed your dog twice a day. Follow the directions for the weight of your dog. Then add:

➤ 500 mg of vitamin C in the form of calcium ascorbate two times a day

➤ Vitamin B-complex, twice a day

➤ Amino Acid complex tablet, once a day

➤ $1/8$ teaspoon digestive enzymes

➤ $1/8$ teaspoon vitamin/mineral mix, which contains probiotics, bacteria friendly to the intestines. Feed two times a day until Rascal is through teething and all his vaccinations, then stop. After that, use only when Rascal is going through a growth spurt, or during times of stress.

These supplements replace those destroyed in the manufacturing process.

Bet You Didn't Know

It is not true that raw meat makes dogs vicious. There is no sound evidence for this proposition and we have no idea who came up with this nonsense. Yet it is a widely held belief.

Rascal also needs some fresh foods that contain their own enzymes. Rotate over one week in each meal:

➤ $1/2$ cup of raw meat, or $1/2$ cup containing two-thirds raw meat and one-third raw liver. Beef or chicken are both fine. When using chicken, pour some boiling water over it to kill any bacteria before using; or

➤ Fresh yogurt with live cultures; or

➤ Cottage cheese (use only once a week); or

➤ White fish—pour boiling water over it before feeding; or

➤ Heart, kidney or tongue;

➤ 1 large egg cooked for 5 minutes, plus the shell four times per week.

Vegetables can also be added—$1/2$ cup a day is all Rascal needs. You can give them raw, such as a carrot or stalk of broccoli, or put them through a food processor and mix with the food, or slightly steam them. Do whatever it takes for your dog to enjoy them.

Vegetables to use include: carrots, broccoli, parsnips, squash, leeks, kale, collard and turnip greens, brussels sprouts, and cauliflower. Our dogs love salad vegetables, and so they always get some lettuce, cucumbers, green beans, or whatever variety we choose when making a salad for ourselves.

Because vegetables contain cellulose from the stalks of the plants and dogs can't break down cellulose, putting them through a food processor or parboiling makes them easier for your dog to digest.

Fruit should and can be fed frequently. Fruits to use are bananas, plums, prunes, raisins, apricots, apples, or anything your dog tells you he needs. Dried fruits make wonderful treats.

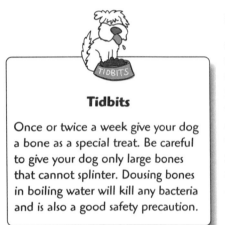

Tidbits

Once or twice a week give your dog a bone as a special treat. Be careful to give your dog only large bones that cannot splinter. Dousing bones in boiling water will kill any bacteria and is also a good safety precaution.

Give Your Dog a Bone

Once or twice a week give your dog a bone as a special treat. They love large beef bones, raw chicken necks and the tips off chicken wings. If you are not sure about how long these have been out in the supermarket case, douse with boiling water to kill any bacteria. The side product of feeding bones is that your dog has beautiful, pearly white teeth that don't need to be cleaned. Feeding too many bones will give him constipation and hard, chalky stools.

When you give your dog a bone, leave him alone. Dogs get possessive about their bones. Bones are one of the few items that may cause him to growl at you, if you try to take it away from him. It is a very special treat, and he wants to be in a place to relax and enjoy it. So if you have followed the advice in this book to date, you will have a crate for Rascal, which is the perfect place for him to enjoy his bone in peace. It will get him away from other dogs or cats in the family, the children, and you. Give him a few hours just to indulge himself. Let him be a dog. After a few days of chewing a fresh bone, it loses its magic and most dogs will allow the kids, other dogs, or you to pick them up or handle them.

Making Your Own Dog Food

Instead of leaving it to someone else, you can make your own dog food. Many people, ourselves included, do it, and there are many recipes available.

Whatever recipe you are going to use, you absolutely must follow two rules.

1. For a benchmark, you must have a blood test performed on your dog, which includes a complete blood count (CBC) and a chem screen. Your veterinarian will do the test. After you have been feeding the diet for two months, you need to get another blood test and compare it to the first one. It will immediately tell you

whether you are on the right track. This is a cardinal rule, and if you are not prepared to have the testing performed, you should not even think about a homemade diet. Not having blood tests done is like driving a car with a blindfold on—you are bound to run off the road. We have annual blood tests done on all our dogs, so that we can make dietary adjustments, if necessary.

2. The diet must contain all known required nutrients in the right proportions, that is, it must be complete and balanced. If it is not, you can cause all sorts of problems, and your dog would be better off with a good commercial food and some supplements. The diet in the *Holistic Guide* meets those requirements.

Top Dog Tips

Anyone interested in making his own dog food must start with a benchmark blood test, and test again after two months. The diet must also be complete and balanced, that is, contain all known required nutrients in the right proportion.

The Least You Need to Know

➤ Your dog's behavior, health and well being depends on what you feed him.

➤ Your dog *is* a carnivore and needs meat.

➤ Select a dog food that lists two animal proteins in the first two ingredients, or two animal proteins as the first three ingredients.

➤ Your dog needs some carbohydrates in the form of grains and vegetables.

➤ You need to supplement with vitamins and fresh foods because important nutrients are destroyed in the manufacturing process.

➤ If you make your own dog food, it must contain all known required nutrients in the right proportions, and you must get a benchmark blood test.

Training Equipment

Dog training is no different than any other activity—you need the right equipment for the job. There are many choices available to you and we will address the factors that determine what training equipment to use and under what circumstances.

Many dog collars and leashes serve purely ornamental purposes. They are perfectly fine once your dog has been trained to your level of satisfaction.

How Do You Choose?

The type of training collar and leash you need depends on:

➤ The particular training method you are using

➤ The strength or weakness of your dog's drives

➤ Your dog's touch sensitivity

➤ Your dog's size and weight in relation to your size and weight

Top Dog Tips

A combination of factors determines the correct choice of training equipment, including the method you are using, the effectiveness of the equipment, your dog's size and weight in relation to your size and weight, and your dog's safety.

Tidbits

The best training leash is a six-foot canvas leash—it is easy on the hands, easily manipulated, and just the right length. It is also the most economical.

➤ The equipment's effectiveness

➤ Your dog's safety

➤ Your aptitude for training

The combination of these factors determines the collar and leash you need to succeed. Keep in mind that training is not a matter of strength but finesse. For the trainer, it should not have to be a heavy aerobic workout.

Leashes

Leashes come in an assortment of styles, materials, widths, and lengths. The most common materials are:

➤ chain

➤ leather

➤ canvas

➤ nylon

We have never quite understood the purpose of chain leashes or why anyone would want to use them, but they exist.

For a leash, our materials of choice are canvas or nylon. Both can be readily manipulated, an important factor for the method we are using, and they are economical. Canvas, especially with larger dogs, is easier on the hands than nylon.

We use a six-foot long leash. For the average-size or larger dog, such as a Labrador, we use a canvas leash that is 1/2 inch wide. For toy dogs, such as a Yorkshire Terrier, we use a leash that is 1/4 inch wide.

These leashes are readily available in pet stores, and come in a variety of colors, although olive green seems to be the most common.

If you are like most of us, you are going to experiment with different lengths and materials, and will have a nice leather leash for Rascal's Sunday walk. Before you know it, you will have an entire assortment. Still, for training Rascal, you need that six-foot canvas leash.

Collars

Collars also come in a dazzling assortment of styles, colors, and materials. We distinguish between two types:

➤ collars for the trained dog, and

➤ training collars

Collars for the trained dog are the buckle type of either leather, nylon, or canvas. For the untrained dog, these are virtually useless. Picture yourself trying to hang on as a fully grown Rottweiler decides to take off after a cat. With a buckle collar that would definitely be a heavy aerobic workout.

For small dogs, harnesses are also quite popular.

You can find any number of training collars. The advantages and disadvantages of each are described below.

Chain or Nylon Slip-on Collars

A slip-on collar is one that slips over the dog's head. As a result, it is generally much too big to be an effective training tool.

Advantages:	Disadvantages:
1. Readily available in pet stores and through catalogs	1. Not very effective
2. Inexpensive	2. Great potential for damaging the dog's trachea and neck
3. Easy to put on	

Studies of dogs wearing this type of collar have shown a high incident of significant tracheal and spinal injuries. Animal chiropractors have made similar observations of spinal misalignment caused by this collar.

Bet You Didn't Know

Not only are chain training collars ineffective, they pose a danger to the trachea and spine of your dog: Avoid them!

Because slip-on collars aren't very effective to begin with and have a poor safety record, we recommend that you save your money and get something that works.

Nylon Snap-around Collars

The principle difference between a slip-on and a snap-around collar is that the latter has a clasp that enables you to fasten the collar around the dog's neck instead of having to slip it over his head.

Advantages:	Disadvantages:
1. Nylon collars are readily available in pet shops and through catalogs	1. Nylon will stretch and fray
2. Fairly inexpensive	2. You have to order one made from the right material
3. Can be fitted exactly to your dog's neck	3. Not as easy to put on as a slip-on collar
4. Very effective	4. A puppy will grow out of it and you may have to buy two to three before the dog is mature
5. Quite safe	
6. Can be used as a training collar or a buckle collar	

The snap-around collar is our collar of first choice because of its effectiveness and versatility. The ones we use are actually made of a material other than nylon and don't stretch or fray. (See Appendix A for sources of training equipment.)

The German, Pinch or Prong Collar

For old-time trainers, this was the only collar to use.

A prong collar certainly is effective and efficient, and the dog understands immediately where his advantage lies. Those who use one for the first time refer to it as power steering. We call it the "religious collar" because it makes an instant believer out of the dog.

Advantages:	Disadvantages:
1. Readily available in pet stores and and through catalogs	1. Looks like a medieval instrument of torture
2. Very effective	2. Twice as expensive as a snap-on collar
3. Can be fit to the exact size of the dog's neck	3. Not as easy to put on as a slip-on collar

Advantages:	Disadvantages:
4. Very safe—it is self-limiting in that it can only constrict very little and not to the point where the dog's air is cut off	

According to our veterinarian and animal chiropractor, the prong collar is the safest training collar. From our perspective, it is also the most effective.

Prong collars come in four sizes—large, medium, small and micro. We have never used or recommended the large size, as it appears to have been made for elephants. For a large, strong and rambunctious dog, the medium size is more than adequate. For a Golden Retriever–size or smaller dogs, the small size is sufficient. For the toy dogs, there is the micro version. It is handmade and must be ordered (see Appendix A).

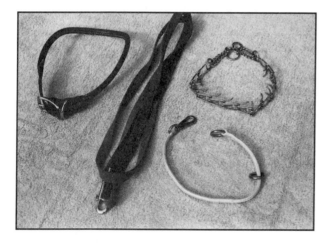

Recommended equipment: Far left— leather buckle collar. Center— six-foot canvas training leash. Upper right—prong collar. Lower right— snap-on collar (notice the stationary ring and the floating ring).

Electronic Collars

We do not recommend that you try using an electronic collar to train your dog. To use such a collar requires a great deal of skill and experience. Moreover, they are quite expensive.

(There is also an electronic bark collar, which requires virtually no skill. It is an effective tool for the chronic barker and is a lot cheaper than being evicted.)

The Head Halter

The head halter is a hybrid piece of equipment. It works on the premise that where the dog's head goes, sooner or later the rest of the body has to follow. It is an adaptation from head halters used for horses.

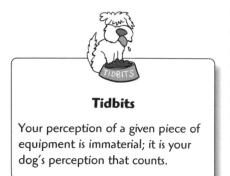

Whereas the prong collar looks downright menacing, the head halter looks quite inviting, almost user friendly. Interestingly, the dog's reaction, and he is the one that counts, is quite the opposite. He will readily accept a prong collar, but vigorously and vociferously object to the halter, at least initially.

The principal advantage of the halter, once the dog has learned to accept it, is that it has a

➤ calming and tranquilizing effect, helpful with nervous, timid, shy, or hyperactive dogs

➤ equalizing effect, whereby small handlers with large dogs, senior citizens and handicapped handlers can control their dogs

➤ muzzling effect, which helps with inappropriate sniffing behavior, whining or barking, some forms of aggression, and play biting or nibbling the owner.

Advantages:	Disadvantages:
1. Readily available in pet stores and through catalogs	1. Greatest potential for serious damage to your dog's neck
2. Not very expensive	2. Transition tool only
3. Minimum strength required to use it	3. The dog does not learn to accept responsibility for his behavior

The great potential for damage is due to the nature of the halter. Because it controls the head, a strong pull by the dog or the handler can do serious damage to the dog's neck. It is not quite the same principle as the head halter for horses. Because most people are smaller than horses, the halter is used to control the horse's head from below.

In contrast, most people are taller than dogs, and any pull or tug is going to be upward, and at times, simultaneously to the side. Tugging the dog's neck in this way creates great potential for injury. We also feel that the halter can and often does have a depressing effect on the dog. It is ironic that this highly marketable tool has such a great potential for damage, while the torturous-looking prong collar is the safest.

Finally, the halter is a transition tool, at best, because it does not teach the dog to assume the responsibility for his behavior.

Getting and Putting On a Snap-around Collar

The principal advantage of the snap-around collar is that it does not have to slip over your dog's head; it can be snapped directly around Rascal's neck, ensuring a snug fit. It should fit high on his neck, just below his ears, as snug as a turtleneck sweater.

Measure your dog's neck and get the appropriate size collar.

The snap-around collar consists of

> ➤ a clasp on one side,
>
> ➤ a ring on the other side, and
>
> ➤ a loose or floating ring.

Start with you and your dog facing each other. Then

1. take the clasp in your left hand and the two rings in your right hand;

2. place the collar under your dog's neck and bring the ends up to the top of his neck, directly behind the ears;

3. attach the clasp to the floating ring. The smooth side of the clasp should be next to the dog's skin.

When you begin to put on the collar, the dog flexes his neck muscles, expanding the circumference of the neck by as much as 1/2 inch. This creates the impression that the collar is much tighter than it actually is, and is similar to the effect produced by a horse taking in air as it is being saddled. Once the collar is on and the dog relaxes, you should be able to slip two fingers through the collar.

Tidbits

The snap-around collar is guaranteed to fit your dog properly. The collar should sit just below your dog's ears.

Tidbits

Remember that as you put on Rascal's collar, his natural response is to flex his neck muscles, making his neck wider than normal. Wait a few minutes for Rascal to calm down before checking the fit of the collar.

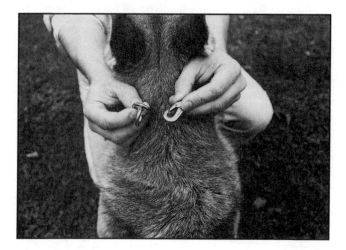

To put on the snap-around collar, take the clasp into your left hand and the two rings in your right hand. Face your dog and place the collar under his neck and bring the ends up to the top of his neck, directly behind the ears. Attach the clasp to the floating ring.

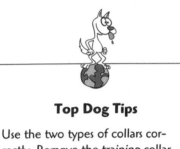

You will get the impression that the collar is much too tight and that you can barely get it around Rascal's neck. We suggest that after the first time you put the collar on you wait for five minutes. After the dog has relaxed, you then can test for correct snugness. You should be able to slip two fingers between the collar and your dog's neck (one finger if you have a toy dog). If you can't, the collar is too tight; if you can get three or more fingers through, the collar it is too loose. One way to make the collar smaller is to tie a knot in it.

Once you have the collar on, you can use it as a training collar by attaching the leash to the *live ring* of the collar, or as a buckle collar by attaching it to the *dead ring* of the collar.

The *live ring* is the stationary ring and the *dead ring* is the floating ring.

Should you have to use a prong collar, it is put on the same way. Simply expand or contract it by adding or removing links, respectively.

Take the training collar off your dog when he is not being trained and whenever he is not under your direct supervision. Do not attach any tags to the training collar.

When you are not training your dog, use a buckle collar to which you have attached his tags.

The Use of Treats

Other than your ingenuity and intellect, treats are the most powerful positive training tool you can use. Treats are used in one of two ways.

1. As a reward for a desired response. For example, the handler says "down," and the dog lies down. When used as a reward, the treat is hidden from the dog, who does not know whether he is going to get it. To be effective, the treat has to follow the desired response within a sufficient time span so the dog understands he is being rewarded for that particular response. If you want to reward your dog for having correctly responded to the down command, you can't give him a treat just as he is getting up. That would be rewarding getting up, not what you wanted at all.

2. As a lure or inducement to obtain a desired response. Now the treat is in the open and is used to entice the dog to lie down, and when he does, he gets the treat. When used as an inducement, it is within the dog's control whether he gets the treat.

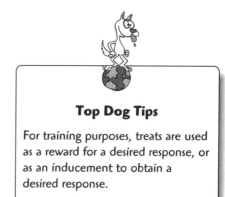

Top Dog Tips

For training purposes, treats are used as a reward for a desired response, or as an inducement to obtain a desired response.

Because you are going to use treats both as a reward and an inducement, you need to decide where to carry them. Some people use fanny packs, which may be OK, depending on your dog. Some dogs begin to focus in on the fanny pack because they know that's where the treats are kept. If that happens, you need to find another way to carry your treats.

We use our pockets and wear trousers that are loose enough so we can quickly get a treat. If your dog has to wait who knows how long while you struggle to get a treat out of your pocket, the treat may no longer mean anything. Worse yet, he may have done something else during the wait, something you don't want to reward.

Type of Treats

We like to use dry treats rather than something soggy, and there are many dry and semi-dry treats available. You do, however, need to be careful of both salt and sugar content, so that treats don't ruin your dog's diet. Experiment to see what your dog likes and to what he responds. It's of no use trying to train a dog with treats he doesn't like. Treats are also not going to be very effective after Rascal has just been fed.

Tidbits

Whatever you use for treats, be sure to keep them handy and accessible. If you can't get at the treat quickly, there's a good chance that Rascal will do something that you don't want to reward—and you'll have lost the power to reinforce the right behavior.

Our dogs' favorites are homemade liver treats. They are simple to make, and contain no salt or sugar.

➤ Parboil some beef liver;

➤ Cut into 1/4 inch cubes;

➤ Place on a baking sheet and liberally sprinkle with garlic powder;

➤ Bake in a 350-degree oven until dry;

➤ Store in refrigerator.

Our dogs also like raisins and carrots, but obviously not as much as they like liver.

Alternatives to Treats

Some dogs do not respond as well to treats as they do to other objects, such as a ball, Frisbee or stick. In that case, you use whatever turns your dog on, so long as it does not become a hindrance in your training.

Our German Shepherd, Katharina, would not take treats in training—must be that German work ethic. She would, however, respond to a stick, so that is what we used.

The Least You Need to Know

➤ Use equipment that is safe, yet effective.

➤ The dog will tell you whether you are using the right equipment.

➤ Treats are the most powerful training tool.

➤ You can use treats to reward a desired response or to obtain a desired response.

➤ Some dogs prefer a toy or a stick as a reward.

Part 3
From Grade School to College

Your dog's entire education is laid out for you in logical sequences, from basic commands to fancy tricks. He will learn not to pull on the leash when you take him for a walk, and to walk at heel, when necessary. He will learn to listen to you away from home and around distractions, such as other dogs and people.

Knowing how to retrieve on command is part of the well-trained dog's repertoire of tricks. It's easy to teach and lots of fun for you and the dog.

To show off your well-trained dog, you can take the Canine Good Citizen test, an American Kennel Club test for all dogs, regardless of parentage.

Tricks like "high five," "roll over," or "play dead" are easily mastered by most dogs and will impress your friends and neighbors.

Chapter 11

Going to Grade School

In This Chapter

➤ The joy of walking a dog that doesn't pull

➤ An introduction to heeling

➤ Teaching the sit and stay

➤ Making a game of the down command

➤ Rascal's first real trick—down with signal

In grade school we learn the fundamentals. Tedious as the process may be, it is here that we acquire the skills we need to go through life. The lessons we learn now are never forgotten.

How important are they? How often do you hear coaches or mentors talk about execution of fundamentals? Master the basics and the rest will follow.

The same rules apply to the education of your dog. For the well-trained dog the fundamentals are

➤ walking on a loose leash

➤ knowing how to heel with changes of direction and speed

➤ the sit-stay

➤ down on command and stay

You have already worked on some of these basics in kindergarten and some of them are going to be new.

Walking the Dog

Taking your dog for a nice, long walk is balm for the soul and good exercise for both of you, provided he does not drag you down the street.

Even if you don't ordinarily take him for walks, the well-trained dog knows how to walk on a leash without pulling your arms out. For example, at least once a year you will have to take him to the veterinarian. If he has been trained to walk on leash, the visit will go much more smoothly than if he bounces off the end of the leash like a kangaroo.

Most of us want to be able to take our dog for a walk on leash and have him remain within the length of his leash without pulling. A leisurely stroll is an important daily routine, and for many dogs, the only opportunity to get some fresh air.

Although for most of us, the dog's pulling on the leash is our main concern, many dogs have to have a chance to become accustomed to the leash.

Leash Training Your Dog

The majority of dogs readily accept the leash. Some, especially puppies, need a little time to get used to it.

Use his buckle collar and make sure it fits snugly so he can't slip out of it. Attach his six-foot leash to the collar and let him drag it around. You will need to supervise him so that he does not get tangled up. Once he ignores the leash, pick up the other end and follow him around. He will happily wander off wherever his fancy takes him.

You are now ready to show him where you want him to go. First use a treat to make him follow you and then gently guide him with the leash telling him what a good puppy he is. If you are teaching him outside, use the treat to coax him away from the house and the leash to guide him back towards the house. Before you know it, he will not only walk on the leash in your direction, but actually pull you along.

Teaching Your Dog Not to Pull

To teach Rascal not to pull, you need his training collar, his leash, and a few treats. Attach the leash to the live ring of the training collar.

Take him to an area without too many distractions, (you don't need other people and dogs, especially loose dogs, in the vicinity right now), and where you can walk in a straight line or a circle (about 30 feet in diameter).

Hold the leash in both hands and firmly plant them against your belt buckle, say "let's go," and start walking. Just before he gets to the end of the leash, say "easy," make an about-turn to your right and walk in the other direction. Be sure you keep your hands firmly planted.

This maneuver will produce a tug on his collar and turn him in the new direction. As he scampers to catch up with you, tell him what a clever boy he is and give him a treat.

Top Dog Tips

Make your turn deliberately and with determination. Be sure you keep your hands firmly planted against your belt buckle. When Rascal catches up—which he will—praise and reward him.

Before you know it, he will be ahead of you again, and you will have to repeat the procedure. When you make your turn, do it with determination. Make your turn, and keep walking in the new direction. Don't look back and don't worry about Rascal; he will quickly catch up. Remember to praise and reward him when he does.

The first few times you try this, you will be a little late—Rascal is already leaning into his collar. Try it again. Concentrate on Rascal and learn to anticipate when you have to make the turn.

You will need to repeat this sequence several times over the course of a few training sessions until he understands that you don't want him to pull. Your goal is to teach him to walk within the perimeter of his leash without pulling.

Most dogs quickly learn to respect the leash, and, with an occasional reminder, they become a pleasure to take for a walk. Some, on the other hand, don't seem to get it. If your Rascal seems particularly dense about this simple concept, you may need a prong collar.

Remember, how readily your dog responds to his collar depends on:

➤ how distracted he is by what is going on around him, including scents on the ground;

➤ his size and weight in relation to your size and weight; and

➤ his touch sensitivity.

The prong collar is an equalizer for these factors. It lets you enjoy training your dog without becoming frustrated or angry. Your dog, in turn, will thank you for maintaining a positive attitude and for praising him when he responds correctly.

Doggy Dogma

Heeling means walking close to the left side of the handler without swinging wide, lagging, forging or crowding, either on a loose leash or off leash.

Heeling On Leash

Heeling and walking on a loose leash are two different exercises. When Rascal is being walked for a bit of exercise, usually in order to do his business, he is on his own time. He can sniff, he can look around, or just aimlessly wander about, so long as he doesn't pull.

Heeling means he has to walk at your left side, the traditional position, and pay strict attention to you. When your dog is heeling, he is now on your time. It is his responsibility to focus on you, and you have to teach him to accept that responsibility.

Heeling is used for walking your dog in traffic—when you need absolute control—and for competitive obedience events. The American Kennel Club definition of *heeling* is walking "close to the left side of the handler without swinging wide, lagging, forging or crowding," either on a loose leash or off leash.

Here is what the above listed "don'ts" mean:

- swinging wide—leaving your left side
- lagging—falling behind, not staying up with you
- forging—getting ahead of you, not staying in *heel* position
- crowding—so close to you as to interfere with your freedom of motion, bumping into you

Rascal has to learn to *heel* whether you

- make a right turn,
- make a left turn,
- make an about-turn,
- run, or
- walk slowly.

The key to teaching *heeling* is to get Rascal to pay attention to you.

Teaching the Sit at *Heel*

Before teaching Rascal to *heel* with both of you walking, you are going to teach him what to do when you stop. This is called the automatic sit at *heel*.

Attach your leash to the live ring of your dog's training collar. Have him sit at your left side, both of you facing in the same direction, and put the leash over your left shoulder.

Say "Rascal, heel." Take a step forward on your right foot, then a step with the left past the right, drop down your right knee, put your right hand against your dog's chest and fold him into a sit at heel position. Avoid the temptation to push down on his rear end. Keep your hands in place as you tell him how clever he is.

Rascal already knows the sit command, but you are now showing him exactly where you want him to sit. Practice the sit at heel about 5 times or more until both of you feel comfortable with this maneuver.

Teaching *Heeling*

Choose a location relatively free of distractions, preferably a confined area, such as your back yard.

Attach your leash to the live ring of your dog's training collar. Have him sit at your left side, both of you facing in the same direction, and put the leash over your left shoulder. You need to allow about four inches of slack, so there is no tension on the leash when you start.

Make a funnel with both hands around the leash. Keep both hands, about waist high, in front of your body. The object is not to touch the leash until necessary.

In a pleasant, upbeat tone of voice, say "Rascal, heel" and start to walk. Move out briskly, as though you are late for an appointment. Walk in a large clockwise circle, or in a straight line.

To teach your dog to heel, put the leash over your left shoulder and make a funnel with your hands around the leash. When your dog leaves your left side, close your hands around the leash and bring him back to heel position.

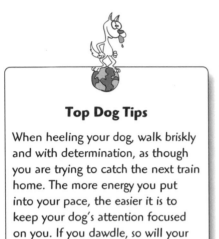

Top Dog Tips

When heeling your dog, walk briskly and with determination, as though you are trying to catch the next train home. The more energy you put into your pace, the easier it is to keep your dog's attention focused on you. If you dawdle, so will your dog.

As soon as both of you are in motion, you will notice that Rascal is forging, that is, he is getting ahead of you. Close your hands on the leash and firmly bring him back to your left side. Work on keeping his shoulder in line with your left hip. Anytime he gets out of position, bring him back and then tell him how clever he is.

After about 10 steps, stop and place him into a sit at heel, and verbally praise him. It will take you a few tries to get the hang of it. At first, you will be a little slow on the uptake. Rascal will have joyfully bounded ahead of you, the leash has fallen off your shoulder, and you are scrambling to get it back. Just start over and work on anticipating what your dog is going to do.

By paying attention to Rascal, you will learn when you need to bring him back to heel. If you can see his tail, you have waited too long.

Your initial goal is to be able to heel Rascal for 10 paces without having to touch the leash. How long it will take you depends on

➤ your dog

➤ what your dog was bred to do

➤ his response to the training collar

➤ your attitude

Generally, if you have a Shetland Sheepdog, you will reach that goal in maybe five minutes; if you have a Wirehaired Fox Terrier, you will be out there considerably longer.

When Rascal will heel without you having to touch the leash for 10 paces, gradually increase the number of steps before a halt. Bring him back to heel whenever necessary, then praise him. After about five training sessions, he should be getting the idea, at least in an area relatively free from distractions.

Changing Direction

You are now ready to introduce your dog to changes of direction while heeling. For our purposes, there are three turns—a right turn, an about-turn to the right, and a left turn.

Right Turn

In order to stay with you when you are making a right turn, Rascal needs to speed up. And, at this stage in your training, Rascal is not yet giving you 100% of his attention and you are going to antici-pate that he needs help with the right turn.

Just before you make the turn, enthusiastically say his name, make the turn and keep moving. Using his name will cause him to look up at you and he will notice that you are changing direction, which will cause him to stay with you. Without giving him that cue, chances are that as you make the turn and go one way, he will keep going the other way.

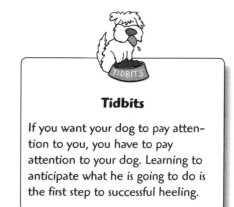

Tidbits

If you want your dog to pay atten-tion to you, you have to pay attention to your dog. Learning to anticipate what he is going to do is the first step to successful heeling.

About-Turn

An about-turn is a right turn times two. When you make your turn, keep your feet together so Rascal can keep up. As you did for the right turn, use his name just before you make the turn to encourage him to stay with you.

In the event Rascal has a particularly difficult time remaining at your side for the right or about-turn, you can use a treat or other object of interest to him to help guide him around. The treat is held in your right hand as you are heeling. Before you make the turn, show it to your dog by bringing the treat directly in front of his nose and using it to guide him around the turn, then give him the treat.

There is a potential drawback to this approach. Some dogs become overly stimulated when they know you have a treat in your hand. Make no mistake about it, Rascal knows. If you see that your dog becomes difficult to control under such circumstances, you may want to eliminate use of the treat. The hassle is not worth the potential benefit.

Left Turn

In order to make the left turn without crowding, Rascal needs to slow down as you make the turn and then resume normal speed after you made the turn. Just before you make the turn, slow down and with your left hand draw back on the leash, make the turn, and resume your normal brisk pace.

Practice heeling and the turns for a few minutes at a time as a regular part of your daily outings.

Changing Pace

Next you are going to teach your dog to change pace with you while heeling. He has to learn that whether you walk slowly or quickly, he has to stay in heel position.

For the slow pace, cut the speed of your pace in half but maintain the same length of stride. As you go into the slow pace, draw back on the leash to keep your dog in heel position.

For the fast pace, double the speed of your pace, again keeping the length of your stride the same. Just before you go into a fast pace, use your dog's name in an excited tone of voice to encourage him to stay with you.

You are still working with the leash over your shoulder. By now you should also be able to tell whether Rascal is actually *heeling*. *Heeling* means that your dog stays with you as you change direction or pace. If *heeling* properly, Rascal does not swing wide on right and about-turns, crowd you on the left turn, lag behind you as you go into a fast pace, or forge ahead of you as you go into a slow pace.

Sit-Stay

As a part of his grade school education, your dog is going to have to learn the sit-stay in a more formal manner, not just at home, but anywhere. Because he already has some idea what the concept means, reinforcing the sit-stay will go relatively quickly and the next three maneuvers can be accomplished in a few minutes in one training session.

1. With your dog sitting at your left side, put the rings of his training collar between his ears and attach the leash to the dead ring of the collar. Fold the leash neatly accordion-style into your left hand with the part going to the dog coming out at the bottom of your hand. Apply a little upward tension on the collar—just enough to let him know it's there, but not enough to make him uncomfortable.

   Say "stay" and with your right hand give the stay signal—a pendulum motion with the right hand, palm facing the dog, stopping in front of the dog's nose, and then returning to your right side. Before you step away from your dog make sure your right hand is at your side again.

   Take a step to the right, count to 10, return to your dog's side, release tension, and tell him how good he is.

2. Repeat, only this time step directly in front of your dog, count to 10, step back, release tension, and tell him what a good boy he is.

3. With your dog sitting at your left side, put the rings of the training collar under your dog's chin and attach the leash to the live ring of the collar. Neatly fold your leash accordion-style into your left hand, and place it against your belt buckle, allowing 1 foot of slack. Say and signal "stay" and place yourself 1 foot in front of your dog. Turn and face your dog, keeping your left hand at your belt buckle, and your right hand at your side, palm open, facing your dog. There is no tension on the leash.

Tidbits

When you see that your dog's attention is drifting, there's a good chance that he is about to move. When you see this happening, reinforce the stay command.

Doggy Dogma

The *review progression* is one of the sequences that is used to teach the dog a particular exercise. It refreshes the dog's recollection of what is expected from him. It is most helpful when the dog is still learning and when we think he needs to be reminded of his responsibilities.

If your dog is thinking about moving, or should actually try to move, take a step toward your dog with your right foot, and with your right hand firmly slap the leash straight up to a point directly above his head. Bring back your right foot and right hand to their original position. There is no need to repeat the command.

Count to 30, pivot back to your dog's right side. Verbally praise him and release him with "OK."

Repeat over the course of several training sessions until your dog is steady on this exercise.

You can tell your dog is thinking about moving when he starts to look around and begins to focus on something other than you. Anytime you see that, reinforce the stay command by slapping the leash straight up.

The next series of training sequences will also go quickly. They involve testing your dog's understanding of "stay," while extending the time and distance.

1. For this sequence, the leash is on the dead ring of the collar. Start in heel position, again with the left hand holding the leash, placed against your belt buckle. Say and signal "stay" and step 3 feet in front of your dog, leaving no tension on the leash.

   Slightly rotate your left hand to apply tension on the leash. This is called the sit-stay test. If your dog moves to come to you, reinforce the "stay." Test 3 times, increasing the tension until you get physical resistance on the part of your dog. Your tension should be commensurate to the size and weight of your dog.

For the sit-stay test, use a downward rotation of the left wrist. Maintain tension for a few seconds and then release tension. You are looking for physical resistance on the part of your dog.

From now on, practice a quick test before you do a sit-stay with your dog. The test is the *review progression* for the sit-stay. Every exercise has a *review progression,* which is one of the sequences used to teach the dog that particular exercise. It refreshes the dog's recollection of what is expected from him. It is most helpful when the dog is still learning, and whenever we think he needs to be reminded of his responsibilities.

2. Start at heel position. Put the leash on the live ring, and go 3 feet in front of your dog. The goal is to have him stay for one minute. If he moves, reinforce the stay.

3. Move 6 feet in front, to the end of the leash. You need to practice the sit-stay on a fairly regular basis, but you don't want to bore yourself or the dog. Once Rascal understands what you want, once or twice a week is perfectly adequate.

More on the Down Command

While the sit-stay is used for relatively short periods, the down-stay is used for correspondingly longer periods. Traditionally, it is also taught as a safety exercise—to get Rascal to stop wherever he is and stay there. For example, Rascal finds himself on the other side of the road. He sees you and is just about to cross the road when a car comes. You need a way to get him to stay on the other side until the car has passed by.

This is where the down and stay come in—the theory being that the dog is least likely to move in the down position. Be that as it may, it is not that hard to teach, and you do want to be able stop your dog in his tracks.

Down at Heel

The object of this exercise is to have Rascal lie down at heel on command. Command here means voice command, and pointing at the ground does not count. There are several sequences for accomplishing this goal, and you will be able to run through the first three quite quickly.

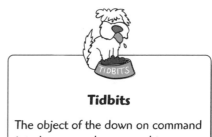

Tidbits

The object of the down on command is to have your dog respond to your command whether he is up close or at a distance. Pointing to the ground will not work from a distance, so you need to train your dog to respond to an oral command.

1. Down with pressure on the collar.

    With Rascal sitting at heel position, attach the leash to the dead ring of the collar. Neatly fold the major portion of the leash into your left hand. Put two fingers of your left hand, palm facing you, through the collar, back to front. Say "down," and with a little downward pressure guide your dog into the down position. Verbally praise him, count to 10, and release with "OK." As he already knows the word, he should readily respond. Keep your elbow stiff and apply pressure straight down so that your dog lies down facing straight ahead, not curled in front of you.

    Practice several times, each time with a little pressure.

2. Down with signal.

    The down signal is given by bringing your right arm straight up, palm facing the dog. It is the same signal students use to get a teacher's attention.

    With Rascal sitting at heel position, attach the leash to the dead ring of the collar. Neatly fold the major portion of the leash into your left hand. Say and signal "stay," and step directly in front of your dog. Kneel down on your left knee or both knees, if your prefer. Put two fingers of the left hand, palm facing down, through your dog's collar, under his chin.

    Say and signal "down" and at the same time push against his chest with your left hand and then apply downward pressure on the collar. Keep the signal up until he lies down. Then praise, count to 10 and release him.

    Practice this three times in succession and over the period of several training sessions. Your goal is to have your dog respond to the command/signal without having to apply any downward pressure on the collar.

3. With Rascal sitting at heel position, attach the leash to the live ring of the collar. Neatly fold the leash into your right hand, the part that goes to the dog coming out at the bottom of your hand, and take the end closest to your dog in your left hand, palm facing you.

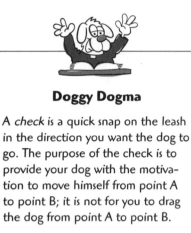

Doggy Dogma

A *check* is a quick snap on the leash in the direction you want the dog to go. The purpose of the check is to provide your dog with the motivation to move himself from point A to point B; it is not for you to drag the dog from point A to point B.

Top Dog Tips

Making a game of the down on command is a good way to maintain your dog's enthusiasm and motivation. If he is not terribly interested, use his favorite toy or a stick. Keep it fun and interesting by doing only two or three repetitions in a row.

Say "down." If Rascal responds, praise, count to 10, and release. If he does not, slowly slide your left hand down the leash, all the way to the snap, and *check* straight down. Praise, wait, and release. Keep you body upright and resist the urge to point—remember, it is the down on command and not the down on point. This is the *review progression* for this exercise.

A *check* is a quick snap on the leash in the direction you want the dog to go. It is not a pull, so there is no tension on the leash after the snap. The purpose of the check is to provide your dog with the motivation to move himself from point A to point B; it is not for you to drag the dog from point A to point B.

Repeat until your dog lies down on command without you having to *check*. Once you have reached that point, you are ready to combine the command and signal as the dog is coming toward you.

4. With Rascal sitting at heel position, attach the leash to the live ring of the collar. Say and signal "stay" and go to the end of the leash, turn and face your dog. Call with "Rascal, come" and just as he starts in motion, say "down," at the time you are giving the signal and stepping toward your dog on the right leg, keeping the left leg in place.

As soon as he responds, lower your right arm and bring back the right leg. Praise, count to 10, go to your dog's right side, and release him straight-forward. If he does not respond, review the down at heel with *check*.

The purpose of the step toward your dog is to get him to stop his forward momentum so he can lie down.

5. When your dog responds to the down command reliably from 6 feet in front on leash, you can take the leash off. Start making a game of this exercise. Have a treat in your signal hand, show it to him and say/signal "down." Keep your hand up. You may have to wait a second or two before he responds. As soon as he does, give him the treat and then release him. Two or three repetitions of this exercise is enough for one training session.

Be sure he is in the down position when you give him the treat—you want to reward the lying down. Do not give him a treat if he gets up before that—you don't want to reward the getting up.

Your dog is still within 6 feet of you, and you are still using the step toward your dog together with the signal. Once he has made the association between the signal and the down, begin to reward him on a random basis.

You can also start to increase the distance between you and your dog, but keep using the step and the signal. Make sure he lies down in place, without coming toward you. If you see this happening, decrease the distance between you.

Rascal now has a grade school education and is ready to go to high school.

The Least You Need to Know

➤ If necessary, use a treat to leash train your dog.

➤ Use the right about-turn maneuver to teach your dog not to pull.

➤ Heeling is designed for maximum control, such as in traffic.

➤ Use the leash over the shoulder technique to teach your dog to heel.

➤ A check is a quick snap on the leash in the direction you want your dog to go.

➤ The well-trained dog has to know the sit-stay and down-stay, not just at home, but anywhere.

Chapter 12

Going to High School

It is during high school when we seem to be the most distractible. Perhaps our increasing awareness of members of the opposite sex contributes to our difficulties in focusing. Although a time of conflict and confusion, in later life we fondly look back at this period as our golden years.

Distractibility is also Rascal's shortcoming. One of the cries of woe we frequently hear from our students is that Rascal does everything at home but as soon as he is away from home or there are distractions, he no longer listens.

To prevent these temporary memory lapses and intervals of selective deafness, we need to teach him how to concentrate and focus on what he is supposed to do. We do this by systematically exposing Rascal to various distractions so we can show him that he can respond even in spite of them.

Distraction Training—Teaching Rascal How to Concentrate

Distractions are introduced in a structured and orderly fashion, ranging from visual—the most innocuous—to auditory, and finally to food or a toy—the most difficult.

1. A visual distraction can be a person in a location where that person would normally not be encountered by the dog.

2. An auditory distraction would be someone else talking to the dog while it is supposed to pay attention to the handler. The dog's name is not used.

3. A favorite object distraction would be offering the dog a treat or his favorite toy while he is supposed to pay attention to his handler. The dog has to learn that when he is heeling, for example, that he has to ignore a liver treat like the one you just used to reward him, his favorite toy, and even the Frisbee or a ball.

You may ask "is all this really necessary?"

Only if you want your well-trained dog to respond under a variety of circumstances, either at home or away from home. It is easy to get Rascal to respond to a command when you are the center of his attention. It is not so easy when there are distractions.

Sit-Stay with Distractions

We use the sit-stay to start the distraction training because it is a stationary exercise. It is the easiest exercise for Rascal to understand, and the easiest for you to show him what you want.

Self-generated Distractions

As an introduction to distractions we use those that are self-generated. Start with your dog sitting at heel and attach the leash to the live ring of the training collar. Say and signal "stay," and move 3 feet in front of your dog.

Facing your dog, take a step to your right. If he moves or thinks about moving, reinforce the stay by slapping the leash with your right hand as you say "stay." Step back to the middle, then to the left, back to the middle, backward and forward. The idea is to teach Rascal not to move even when tempted and to hold his position in the face of distractions. Anytime you think Rascal may move, reinforce the stay.

After one complete set of stepping to the right, middle, etc., return to your dog's side, pause, praise, and release. Repeat the procedure except jump to the right, middle, etc. Practice this over the course of several sessions until your dog ignores your antics.

Training with a Helper

You do need a helper to be the distracter, which can be a member of the family. If your distracter is a member of the family, he or she cannot use any commands or the dog's name while distracting the dog. Rascal is supposed to obey all family members, so you don't want to confuse him with conflicting commands.

Top Dog Tips

Anytime you approach your dog to show him what you want him to do, move slowly. Charging toward your dog will just cause him anxiety, which is counterproductive to the trusting relationship that you are building.

1. With your dog sitting at heel, attach the leash to the dead ring of his training collar. Say and signal "stay," and move 3 feet in front. Have your helper approach Rascal at a 45-degree angle until he or she is 1 foot from the dog. Your helper says nothing and just smiles at the dog.

When Rascal starts to get up to go to your helper, bring your right hand up under the leash to put him back in place exactly where you left him. If you are too late and Rascal has actually reached your helper, put two fingers of each hand through the collar at the side of his neck and, and without saying anything, re-place him, from in front, exactly where you left him. From in front means you are facing each other, and in order to put him back exactly where you left him, you will have to guide your dog in a semicircle back to that spot.

Anytime you approach your dog to show him what you want him to do, do it slowly, almost in slow motion. If you dart or flail at him, he will become apprehensive and worried. Your dog should never feel anxious about you approaching him. So do it slowly and with a smile on your face.

You don't want to repeat the command because that would be giving a second command. You also don't want to start over by leaving Rascal from the heel position because he won't know anything went wrong. So you put him back from in front, and then leave him again without saying anything.

Put Rascal back as many times as it takes until he ignores your helper. When he does, tell him how clever he is, go back to him, pause to the count of five and release him. Stop working on that exercise for that training session and go to something else.

Tidbits

How many repetitions it takes for Rascal to catch on depends on his learning style. Some dogs catch on after being shown only once; others may take five or more repetitions. Once you know your dog's learning style, you can predict the number of repetitions he needs.

2. Start all over. Your helper again approaches from a 45-degree angle to within 1 foot of your dog, but this time he crouches down and starts talking to your dog in an enticing tone of voice: "What a pretty dog you are. Would you like to visit for some petting?" or whatever.

Rascal can't resist and wants to visit. You put him back as before. When he stays in place, remember to praise him, then go back to him and release him. When he ignores your helper, stop with that exercise and go to something else.

3. Start all over. This time your helper approaches to within 1 foot of your dog and offers him a treat. When Rascal goes for the treat, put him back. Under no circumstances does the helper let the dog have the treat.

Your helper can also use the treat to entice the dog to lie down by lowering it onto the ground in front of the dog. When the dog lies down—most of them will—you simply show the dog what you want by gently propping him back up without saying anything.

When he ignores the treat and stays in place, remember to praise him for being such a smart dog.

Depending on the number of prey drive behaviors your dog has, this may take a few repetitions. The number of repetitions that are required also depends on the learning style of the particular dog. For example, our German Shepherd, Katharina, would require one repetition, whereas our Labrador, Bean, required five. Once you become aware of your dog's learning style, you know how many repetitions it will take before the dog understands. Without knowing this, some handlers become frustrated and upset with the dog when he doesn't catch on after one or two repetitions.

The reason for using distraction training is threefold:

➤ It teaches the dog to pay attention, or conversely, not to allow himself to be distracted. Either way, the result is the same—a dog that is attentive to the handler in a very short period of time and a minimum amount of stress.

➤ It builds the dog's confidence. To accomplish this goal, distractions have to be introduced in a structured format, with the degree of difficulty increasing sequentially. It is especially important for the shy dog. As the dog's confidence grows so does the intensity and speed of his response. He learns to focus and concentrate on the task, critical for successful performances at any level.

➤ It builds your confidence, as well as that of your dog, one of the most important ingredients for success.

162

The key to the entire concept is to introduce the dog to distractions in a gradual and progressive way so that he can cope and is not overwhelmed. It is interesting to observe how dogs who have been introduced to distraction training on the sit-stay fairly early in their training, quickly transfer the principle to other and more complex exercises later on.

4. Start from the beginning with your dog off leash. Because you no longer have the leash to help you, use two fingers of both hands at the side of his neck, through the collar, to prop up or re-situate your dog.

> **Top Dog Tips**
>
> The purpose of *distraction* training is to teach your dog to pay attention, to concentrate and focus on what he *is* doing. It also builds your confidence, as well as that of your dog, one of the most important ingredients for success.

One of the most exciting aspects about distraction training is observing Rascal using his head. You can literally see the wheels turning as he is trying to figure out what he should do.

Here are some of Rascal's responses.

➤ He goes to your helper

➤ He tentatively goes to your helper

➤ He looks confused

➤ He understands

Distractions and Heeling

Up to now, most of your heeling has been done in areas relatively free of distractions, and probably in the same location. The time has come to expand your and Rascal's horizons. You need to get him out to new places.

For Rascal, every new location is a form of distraction training. Brand new sights and, more important, brand new smells. When you do take him to a new place, let him acclimate himself first—take in the sights and smells. Give him a chance to exercise himself.

Control Position

From leash over the shoulder, you are going to graduate to "Control Position" as part of your distraction training. Control Position makes is easier for you to remind Rascal of his responsibility to pay attention to you and stay in heel position.

Holding the leash in Control Position:

➤ Put the loop of the leash over the thumb of your right hand.

➤ Neatly fold the leash, accordion-style, into your right hand, with the part going to the dog coming out from under your little finger.

➤ Place your right hand against the front of your leg, palm facing your leg.

➤ With your left hand, grasp the leash in front of your left leg, palm facing your leg.

➤ Keep both hands below your waist at all times, and your elbows relaxed and close to your body.

➤ Attach the leash to the live ring of your dog's training collar.

➤ Position both rings of the collar under his chin. Take up enough slack in the leash so that the leash snap is parallel with the ground.

Control Position—note that the leash snap is parallel to the ground.

Heeling in New Locations

In a location new to your dog, and after he has had a chance to look around a bit, do some heeling with particular emphasis on having your dog paying attention to you. Anytime his attention wanders—he may want to sniff or just look around—remind him with a little check that he has to pay attention to you. When he does, tell him what a good boy he is, then release him.

Check in the direction you want your dog to focus—somewhere on you. Depending on his size, this can be your ankle, lower leg, upper leg, torso, or face. Focusing on your face would be ideal, and some dogs pick up on that quickly. Others are structurally not able to do that.

When you release him with OK, take five steps straight forward at a trot. Keep both hands on the leash. You want to get him excited about heeling with you. If he gets too excited, release him with somewhat less enthusiasm. After a check to re-focus the dog's attention on you, release him. Make it as much fun as you can for your dog.

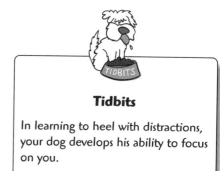

Tidbits

In learning to heel with distractions, your dog develops his ability to focus on you.

The goal of heeling with distractions is for your dog not to permit himself to become distracted. In the process he learns to pay attention to you. It is not so important how he does it, so long as he does.

Our Shepherd, Katharina, as did our Labrador, Bean, usually heeled with her head facing straight forward, seemingly without looking at any part of the handler. Both dogs were very attentive, it just didn't look that way.

Heeling with a Distracter

The next progression in your heeling exercise is to go through the same sequences you did with the sit-stay.

Heel your dog past your helper who can be standing, sitting, or squatting while smiling invitingly at your dog. If your dog is distracted, check, and then praise. Repeat until he ignores your helper.

Next, have your helper talk to your dog; then have your helper offer your dog a treat. You want your dog to ignore your helper and focus on you. When he does, be sure to praise him.

Making the Transition to Heeling Off Leash

To make the transition from heeling on leash to heeling off leash we use a technique called "umbilical cord." Here is how it works.

➤ With your dog sitting at heel and the leash attached to the collar, take the loop end of the leash in your right hand and pass it around behind you into your left hand.

➤ With your right hand unsnap the leash from the collar, pass the snap through the loop of the leash and reattach it to the collar.

➤ Pull on the leash to tighten the loop end around your waist at your left side.

➤ Put your left hand against your belt buckle and let your right hand swing naturally at your side.

Umbilical cord—the transition to heeling off leash.

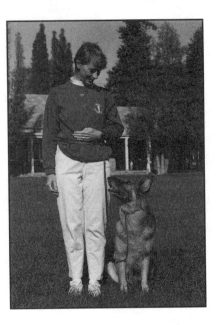

Say "Rascal, heel" and start to walk your normal brisk pace. If your dog deviates from heel position, slowly reach for the collar, put two fingers of your left hand through the collar, back to front, palm facing you, at the side of his neck, and bring him back to heel position. Keep walking, let go of the collar and tell him what a good dog he is.

This maneuver lets you and your dog experience the feeling of heeling off leash while he is still attached.

When you reach for your dog, be sure you do it slowly so as not to frighten him. Remember, he is still on leash and can't go anywhere. If you start snatching at him, he will become apprehensive and try to bolt.

Tidbits

Slow, deliberate movements should be used when training. Just as you should not run toward your dog when he moves out of position, don't grab at his collar when you reach for him when practicing heeling.

For Rascal there is another important lesson. He learns to accept the reinforcement of you reaching for the collar so that you can do it when he actually is off leash. That is why it is so important that you do it slowly so you don't inadvertently teach him to bolt from your side.

If you have difficulty getting two fingers through the collar—your dog may be small or have lots of hair around his neck—use the leash snap to bring him back.

This technique teaches your dog that it is his responsibility to remain in heel position. Unless he learns to accept that responsibility, he will not be reliable off leash. You can help the process by being consistent in reminding him of that responsibility. For example, Rascal deviates, you reach for the collar, but he corrects himself and you do nothing. Unfortunately, Rascal has not learned anything.

Anytime you make a move to bring him back, you must follow through. This principle applies to other situations, as well.

If there is a trick to this exercise, it is to keep it short and sweet. Take 10 steps, then halt, put your right hand against his chest, place him into a sit and stand up. Praise, release, and start over.

This time, go 10 steps, make a right turn, take another ten steps and halt, praise, and release. Remember to say your dog's name before you make the turn. Start over and incorporate an about-turn, using his name before the turn. Also incorporate changes of pace. You get the picture. By keeping the time and distance short, you have a better chance of maintaining your dog's interest and attention.

> **Top Dog Tips**
>
> Keep the time and distance short and you have a better chance of maintaining your dog's interest and attention.

As you and your dog's proficiency increases, add distractions in the order you did before. You also need to gradually increase the time and distance that you heel your dog before a halt. How much total time should you spend on this exercise? After a two-minute warm-up of heeling in Control Position in a large circle or straight line with plenty of releases, no more than one to two minutes per training session.

Heeling Off Leash

You are now ready for heeling off leash. If you have any doubt about what the little fellow will do, practice in a safe area.

> **Tidbits**
>
> In training, success breeds success. Keep your sessions short and interesting for your dog so that he is more likely to succeed.

➤ Start with a two-minute warm-up in Control Position. Walk in a large circle or a straight line. Forget about turns and concentrate on keeping his attention on you. Now is the time to remind him to pay attention to you. Check, if you have to, then praise and release.

➤ Set up for umbilical cord. Heel for 10 to 15 steps and release. Set up again and heel for about the same distance and halt. Just as before, put your right hand against his chest, place him into a sit, and stand up.

➤ Unclip the leash from his collar and put the snap into your left pocket so that a loop dangles on your side.

➤ Say "Rascal, heel" and start at a brisk pace.

➤ Halt after 10 steps and sit your dog.

➤ Put the leash back on your dog and release.

➤ Go on to another exercise, or end your session.

If you need to reinforce, very slowly reach for his collar, bring him back, let go, and praise.

Proficiency comes in small increments and not all at once. Each session add something new to your off-leash heeling, such as a turn—use his name—or a change of pace. Keep it short and snappy. Make it exciting and fun. Over the course of several sessions, both you and Rascal will become increasingly confident and begin to work as a team. Resist the temptation to go beyond his ability to be successful.

Unclip the leash from the dog's collar, and put the leash snap into your pocket.

Off-Leash Heeling with Distractions

When both of you are comfortable doing this exercise in an area relatively free of distractions, you can go on to heeling off leash with distractions. Use the same order as you did before, that is, making it incrementally more difficult as you progress. Use the same reinforcement as you did for "umbilical cord." When you come to a halt, put your right hand against his chest.

Responsibilities During Heeling

Both you and your dog have specific responsibilities for heeling. Notably, yours are far more numerous than your dog's.

Responsibilities for Heeling

Yours	Your Dog's
Leash handling	Paying attention to you
Body posture	Staying in position
Pace and rhythm	
Concentrating on dog	
Use of the leash	
Anticipating when to check	
Direction of check	
When and how to reward	

Your Dog Is Not an Elephant

True or false? Once my dog is trained, I will never have to practice his lessons again.

Answer: False.

Your dog does not have the memory of an elephant, so you will need to review his lessons on a regular basis.

For example, if you have used the Recall Game to teach Rascal to come when called, you need to reward him with a treat on a random schedule when he responds to your call and comes to you. If you get lax, the association between the command and the reward will weaken. You can tell when this begins to happen.

➤ It starts with Rascal not coming immediately.

➤ He may take a detour or lift his leg just one more time.

➤ Then, you have to call him again.

➤ Finally, he ignores you while you implore him to come.

We call this the principle of *successive non-reinforced repetitions*. It sounds more complicated than it is. Think of it in terms of payday, which is your reward for slaving in the pits from nine to five.

Every time your dog responds to a command without a reinforcement it is a *non-reinforced repetition*. The number of these repetitions is finite, and depends on the extent to which the behavior is in harmony with the dog's instincts or drives. A Labrador Retriever, once he has been trained to retrieve, will happily fetch almost indefinitely without any reinforcement. An Afghan Hound will probably retrieve only a few times without reinforcement. The Labrador was bred to retrieve, the Afghan was not.

Just recently we had a wonderful demonstration of this principle. Before tackling this book, we decided we needed a week off. For this vacation we visited friends in Newfoundland, who have two delightful Whippets. Every morning our friends take a short ride to the local park for their own daily walk and to let the dogs run. Naturally, we joined them.

The park covers about 100 acres, with wonderful walking trails, plenty of wildlife and a large pond inhabited by a variety of fowl. Once inside the park, much to our surprise, our friends let the dogs loose. When we say surprise, it is because Whippets are sight hounds, extremely high in prey drive, who love to chase anything that moves. They are also incredibly fast and can cover great distances in seconds. We were wondering how our friends would get these dogs back.

To make a long story short, when the dogs ranged a little too far, or started chasing something, our friends called them back. To our amazement, the dogs came instantly every time, and every time they got a treat. The response was reinforced!

Any taught response needs to be reinforced. You needn't worry about the exact number of *non-reinforced repetitions* your dog will retain of a given behavior. All you need to know is that they are not infinite. To keep him sharp, randomly reinforce—whether you think he needs it or not.

This principle applies to everything you have taught your dog, from the simplest responses to the most complex. The reinforcement can be a treat or a little check on the leash, depending on the exercise, and how you taught him. It is usually the review progression for the particular exercise.

It's easy to make excuses and blame the dog. But your dog is not an elephant and needs occasional reminders.

The Least You Need to Know

➤ Distraction training teaches your dog to concentrate on what you expect him to do.

➤ Distractions are introduced in a structured and orderly way.

➤ When you need to help your dog, approach him slowly to avoid creating anxiety.

➤ It may take your dog several repetitions before he understands what you want.

➤ Successive non-reinforced repetitions weaken the association between the reinforcement and the response to a command.

➤ Be patient and maintain a friendly and positive attitude.

Chapter 13

The Star of the Class— The Retriever

Most of us are not too thrilled about having Rascal lug our possessions about. We would prefer he limited his retrieving instincts to his own things.

Many dogs like to retrieve, or at least chase, a variety of objects. For them, it is a self-rewarding activity. They do it because they enjoy it. Some of them actually bring back the ball, Frisbee, or stick so you can throw it again.

They will continue so long as it's fun. When it's no longer fun, they stop. They will also retrieve only articles they like. For example, your dog may happily retrieve a ball, but turn up his nose when you want him to pick up a glove.

The well-trained dog has been taught to retrieve and has learned to do it for you and not just himself. Of course, he can have fun in the process, so long as he understands that it's not a matter of choice.

Retrieving Basics

As a part of learning how to retrieve on command, your dog learns to take, as well as to give, an equally important lesson. If it hasn't happened to you already, it will. Rascal has picked up something he thinks is edible, but which you don't think is a suitable dietary supplement. Having taught him to retrieve, you will be able to convince him to give it up.

There is another practical side to teaching your dog to retrieve. One of our students wanted her Golden Retriever, Sunny, to bring in the morning paper, preferably in readable condition. So we first had her teach Sunny the formal retrieve. We then told her go out with Sunny, have him pick up the paper, bring it in the house and reward him with a dog biscuit.

It only took Sunny two repetitions until he figured it out and from then on, every morning he dutifully brought in the paper. After several days we got a frantic phone call. It seems that Sunny was somewhat of an entrepreneur. In an effort to garner more biscuits he started retrieving the neighbors' papers as well. Fortunately, that problem was easily fixed—a biscuit only for the first paper. When he realized that, he stopped bringing home other papers.

The retrieve sounds simple, but it consists of many separate behaviors, some or all of which have to be learned by the dog. These are:

➤ going to the object

➤ picking it up

➤ holding it

➤ walking with and carrying the object

➤ bringing it back, and

➤ giving it up

For the dog that already retrieves on his own, teaching him to do it on command will be a cinch. For those who don't, you need to have a little more patience. Your dog's ability to learn to retrieve will depend on what your dog was bred to do and how many prey drive behaviors he has.

The object we use for the formal retrieve is a wooden dumbbell. These are available at your local pet store or through catalogs. You need to get one that is commensurate to the size of your dog and the shape of his mouth. The bells should be big enough so he can pick it up off the ground without scraping his chin, and the diameter of the bar thick enough so he can comfortably carry it. The length of the bar should be such that the bells just touch the side of his face.

Dumbbells can also be made of plastic, and these last a lot longer than wooden ones. They are terrific once the dog has learned how to retrieve. In the teaching process, however, we have found that dogs take more readily to the wooden dumbbells than the plastic ones.

To get started, you need the following equipment:

➤ enthusiastic handler

➤ hungry dog

➤ small can of cat food

➤ metal spoon

➤ wooden dumbbell

➤ chair

Cat food seems to be irresistible to dogs and works well as a reward. Because many dogs are not fond of retrieving metal objects, we use a metal spoon to get them used to the feel of metal. We also let Rascal lick out and play with the empty can.

Word Association

The ideal time to start teaching Rascal to retrieve is when he is hungry, before he is fed. Place food, spoon, and dumbbell on a chair. With your dog sitting at heel, face the chair. Give him a small portion of food with the spoon saying "take it." Give the command in an excited and enthusiastic tone of voice to elicit prey drive behavior. Repeat 10 times or until your dog readily opens his mouth to get the food. Few dogs can resist this treat.

Introduction to the Retrieve

Have your dog sitting at heel, again facing the chair. Put your left palm lightly on top of his muzzle and place your left index finger behind his left canine tooth. Gently open his mouth and with your right hand place the dumbbell in his mouth. Rest the thumb of your right hand on top of his muzzle, fingers under his chin, and cup his mouth shut. Praise enthusiastically, immediately say "give" and take the dumbbell out of his mouth. Reward with food. Repeat 10 times for five sessions.

Hold the dumbbell by the bell so you can easily put the bar in his mouth. After one second take it out with "give."

The goal of this progression is for your dog to accept the dumbbell in his mouth without any resistance. It is only an introduction and you don't want to close his mouth for longer than one second. When your dog readily accepts the dumbbell, you can go on to the next sequence.

With your right hand, gently put the dumbbell into your dog's mouth.

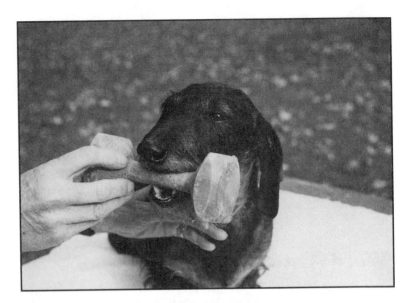

Gently hold the dog's mouth shut for one second with your thumb on top of his muzzle and your fingers under his chin.

Your Dog Still Needs Some Help

With your dog sitting at heel, chair in place, put two fingers of your left hand through his collar, back to front, palm facing you, at the side of his neck. Place the bar of the dumbbell directly in front of his mouth, touching the small whiskers. Say "take it," and when he takes it, briefly cup his mouth shut and tell him how clever he is. Say "give," take out the dumbbell, and reward with food.

At this point in the training, some dogs will not yet take the dumbbell on their own, but will open their mouth. In that case, just put the dumbbell in, cup his mouth shut, etc.

If he sits there like a bump on a log, watch for signs of *intention behavior*. *Intention behaviors* are those actions that tell us what the dog's intentions are. They range from the extremely subtle, such as bringing the whiskers forward as a play invitation to another dog, to the overt, such as sniffing the ground in a circular motion when the puppy is about to eliminate.

Doggy Dogma

Intention behaviors are those behaviors that tell us what the dog's intentions are. They can be quite subtle or quite obvious.

Intention behaviors indicating that he is thinking about taking the dumbbell in his mouth are

➤ licking

➤ nosing the dumbbell

➤ intensely staring at it

When you see *intention behavior*, take your hand out of the collar, open his mouth, put the dumbbell in and briefly cup his mouth shut. Praise, remove the dumbbell from his mouth and reward with food. Repeat until Rascal readily opens his mouth and accepts the dumbbell. It is important that you praise while he has the dumbbell in his mouth.

Be patient. Sometimes it can take several minutes before the dog makes a move. If absolutely nothing happens and the little wheels have come to a grinding halt, go back to the previous step for a few sessions.

Learning to Hold On

Before we go any further with the retrieve part of this exercise, we first want to teach the dog what we want him to do with the object after he has picked it up.

Put the dumbbell into your dog's mouth and say "hold it." Make a fist with your right hand and hold it under his chin. Smile and count to five. Praise, remove the dumbbell, and reward him with food. Repeat 20 times, increasing gradually the time you have him hold the dumbbell in five-second increments up to 30 seconds.

If your dog starts mouthing the dumbbell or looks as though he will open his mouth to drop the dumbbell, give him a gentle chuck under the chin with "hold it." Then remove the dumbbell with "give," praise, and reward.

Your goal is to have the dog firmly hold on to the dumbbell by closing his mouth over it.

Doggy Dogma

We have produced a videotape on teaching your dog to retrieve using this method. See Appendix A for information on where you can obtain a copy.

The Penny Drops

Once Rascal understands that he has to hold the dumbbell, the next sequence is to teach him to reach for it. With two fingers of your left hand through his collar at the side of his neck, back to front, palm facing you, hold his dumbbell two inches in front of his mouth. Say "take it." If he does, cup his mouth shut with "hold it," count to five, praise, remove the dumbbell with "give," and reward with food.

If he does not take the dumbbell, lightly twist his collar by rotating your left hand a quarter of a turn towards you, which will bring his head forward and toward the dumbbell, until he reaches for and takes it. Cup his mouth shut with "hold it," count to five, praise, remove the dumbbell with "give," and reward with food.

Do not twist his collar for more than 30 seconds or try to increase pressure more than a quarter of a turn. Instead, put the dumbbell in his mouth, cup shut with "hold it," praise, remove, and reward. Repeat until your dog voluntarily reaches for and takes the dumbbell.

Should your dog show signs of noticeable stress during this sequence, the following will happen:

➤ If he is a negative stresser, he will clamp his mouth shut and turn inward when you apply pressure on the collar. Pressure on the collar will not make him open his mouth. Stop, put the dumbbell in his mouth, praise, reward and try again.

➤ If he stresses positively, he will engage in *redirected behaviors*, one of which will be to grab the dumbbell, at which point you praise and reward.

Increase the distance Rascal has to reach for the dumbbell in two-inch increments to arm's length. After that, make a game of it by having him chase the dumbbell while you turn in place to your right. Remember to reward him every time he takes the dumbbell.

Walking While Holding

Put the dumbbell in your dog's mouth with "take it," say "hold it," and encourage him to walk two steps forward to the chair with the cat food on it. To give your dog confidence, put your right hand under his chin when he starts to move. Praise, remove the dumbbell, and reward. Repeat until your dog is successful, then gradually increase the distance in five-step increments to 20 steps.

The Pick Up

Review holding on to the dumbbell with your dog. Hold the dumbbell about two inches from his mouth and say "take it." Have your dog take the dumbbell, lowering it in two-inch increments to the ground. Your fingers are still in the collar.

When you get to the ground, place the bell of the dumbbell on the ground and hold it at a 45-degree angle. Say "take it," and when your dog takes the dumbbell, take your hand out of the collar, say "hold it," and back up two steps. He will quickly come to you to get his reward. Praise, remove, and reward. Repeat until your dog is comfortable picking up the dumbbell with you holding it at that angle.

Next, place the dumbbell on the ground but keep your hand on it. Have your dog retrieve the dumbbell several times while you have your hand on it. Then hold your hand first two inches, then six inches, and then 12 inches away from the dumbbell until you can place it on the ground and stand up straight.

Each time back up several steps, praise, remove, and reward.

If your dog does not pick up the dumbbell from the ground, lightly twist the collar until he picks it up. Should this sequence become an issue and your dog continues to refuse to take the dumbbell, review the prior progressions. Be sure you followed them religiously and that your dog has mastered each progression before you went on to the next.

Finally, say "stay," and place the dumbbell one foot in front of your dog. Say "take it," and when he brings it back, praise, remove and reward. Repeat by first placing it three feet and then six feet in front of your dog.

Your dog will tell you how many times in a row you can ask him to retrieve. If he has many prey drive behaviors, you can get in quite a few repetitions. If not, he will quickly lose enthusiasm and you are better off stopping after 5 repetitions and picking the game up again at the next session.

Remember also that for the dog, picking up a dumbbell that you have placed on the ground is not terribly exciting, and if it weren't for the reward, it would be an absolute bore. Still, it is a necessary sequence because you want your dog to learn he has to do it for you and not for himself.

The Fun Part

Now comes the fun part, where you get to throw the dumbbell and Rascal gets to chase it. Throw the dumbbell a few feet and at the same time send your dog with "take it." As soon as he picks it up, tell him how terrific he is. When he gets back to you, take the dumbbell with "give" and reward him with a treat.

Sometimes dogs get carried away by the fun of it all and don't come right back with the dumbbell. They might make a detour, or just run around for the joy of it. Should that happen, say "come" as soon as he picks up the dumbbell, and praise and reward him when he gets back to you.

Gradually increase the distance the dumbbell is thrown. As he gains confidence, introduce the sit in front with "hold it." When he gets back to you say "sit" and "hold it." Since he has not done this before, you may have to hold your hand under his chin to prevent him from dropping the dumbbell. Praise, remove, and reward. From now on make him sit and hold the dumbbell every time he gets back to you.

Making Him Wait

Rascal also has to learn to stay while you throw the dumbbell and until he is permitted to get it. Making him wait will get him all the more excited about getting to his dumbbell.

Start with your dog in heel position. Put two fingers of your left hand through his collar, say "stay" and throw the dumbbell about 15 feet. Very, very gingerly let go of his collar, count to five and say "take it." When he returns, praise, remove, and reward. Repeat until your dog holds the stay without having to hold him by the collar.

Remember to give the command in an excited and enthusiastic tone of voice to put the dog into prey drive. Never use a harsh or threatening tone of voice as that will put the dog in the wrong drive and make it more difficult for him to learn.

If at anytime your dog needs motivation, throw the dumbbell at the same time saying "take it," letting him chase after it.

Training with Distractions

Now that Rascal knows how to retrieve, he is ready for distraction training. During distraction training, you will see the following responses, or variations thereof:

➤ He starts going toward the dumbbell, but then backs off and fails to retrieve, meaning "I don't have the confidence to get close enough to the distracter to retrieve my dumbbell."

Remedy: Without saying anything, slowly approach him, put two fingers of your left hand through the collar, back to front, palm facing you, at the side of his neck and take him to the dumbbell. If he picks up the dumbbell, praise, remove dumbbell and reward; if he does not, put the dumbbell in his mouth, then praise, remove, and reward. The command is not repeated.

Try again. Remember your dog's learning style and how many repetitions it takes before he understands. You may find that you have to help him several times before he has the confidence that he can do it by himself. Once he has done it on his own, stop for that session!

➤ He leaves altogether and does not retrieve, saying in effect "I can't cope with this."

Remedy: Same.

➤ He does nothing, meaning "if I don't do anything maybe all of this will go away."

Remedy: Same.

➤ He permits himself to be distracted, meaning "I would rather visit than retrieve my dumbbell."

Remedy: Same.

➤ He takes the dumbbell to the distracter.

Remedy: Slowly approach your dog without saying anything, put the leash on the dead ring of the training collar and, with a little tension on the collar, show him exactly what he was supposed to do by guiding him to you. No extra command is given.

➤ He anticipates the retrieve, meaning he is catching on and wants to show you how clever he is.

Remedy: Without saying anything, slowly approach him, take the dumbbell out of his mouth, put it down where he picked it up, go back to the starting point and then send him. Whatever you do, don't shout "no," or do anything else that would discourage him from retrieving after you have just worked so hard to get him to pick up the dumbbell.

➤ He does it correctly and that is when you stop for that session.

Introduce your dog to distractions as follows: the distracter stands about two feet from the dumbbell. He assumes a friendly posture, not threatening to the dog. Send him and as soon as he picks up the dumbbell, enthusiastically praise. Look at the exercise as having been completed as soon as your dog picked up his dumbbell.

As he gains confidence, the distracter stands a little closer, and then over the dumbbell.

The distracter also hides the dumbbell by standing directly in front of it with his back to the dog, and then lightly puts his foot on it. You can use a chair as a distraction by putting the dumbbell under the chair and then on the chair.

Continue to use food rewards for Rascal on a random basis, that is, not every time, and not in a predictable pattern but often enough to maintain his motivation.

When your dog confidently retrieves under these circumstances, introduce the next level of distractions. The distracter crouches close to the dumbbell and tries to distract him by saying "here puppy, come visit for some petting." The distracter does not use your dog's name.

Once he has successfully worked his way through that level, favorite object distractions are added, such as offering the dog food or a ball or toy. Of course, the distracter never lets the dog have the food.

Distractions add an extra dimension and take training to a higher level. Distraction training builds your dog's confidence and teaches him to concentrate on what he is doing. This type of training is especially important for the shy dog, providing the confidence he needs to respond correctly under different conditions.

During distraction training, keep in mind that anytime you change the complexity of the exercise, it becomes a new exercise for the dog. If Rascal goes for the food, you would treat his response the same way you did when you first introduced him to distraction training. No, your dog is not defiant, stubborn, or stupid, just confused as to what he should do and has to be helped again.

How Much Help to Give

By challenging Rascal to use his head, you can increase the strength of his responses and increase his confidence in his ability to perform under almost all conditions.

When using distraction training, it is also important to give Rascal a chance to work it out for himself. Don't be too quick to try and help him. Be patient, and let him try to figure out on his own how to do it correctly. Once he does, you will be pleasantly surprised by the intensity and reliability with which he responds.

You are now ready to work with different objects. When you do, you may have to review the first few sequences. Just because Rascal retrieves one object does not necessarily mean he will retrieve others. He may need to get used to them first.

The Least You Need to Know

➤ Many dogs retrieve on their own and for themselves.

➤ Teach your dog to retrieve for you and not just for himself.

➤ Be alert to intention behaviors during the teaching process.

➤ If you get stuck, review the previous sequence.

➤ Dogs who have been taught to retrieve have more fun.

Chapter 14

SLOBBERATORIAN

Graduating from High School— The Canine Good Citizen

In This Chapter

➤ Your dog's first exam—the Canine Good Citizen

➤ Ten tests and he already knows most of them

➤ Practicing with a helper

➤ Tips to help you succeed

To demonstrate that Rascal is ready to graduate from high school and go on to college, you might consider taking the *Canine Good Citizen* test. It is offered by many dog organizations, and your local kennel club will know the particulars. You should be able to locate the kennel club in the Yellow Pages of your telephone directory.

The test is unique in that it is the only AKC-sponsored activity that includes mixed-breed dogs. The concept of a *Canine Good Citizen* is based on the premise that all dogs should be trained. It was also designed as an outreach program—to motivate dog owners and encourage them to go further in training their dogs.

Welcome to the World of Organized Dog Activities

Since its inception on September 1, 1989, the *Canine Good Citizen* has become one of the fastest growing and most popular programs in AKC history. Moreover, other organizations such as the Delta Society and Therapy Dogs International have adopted parts or all of the Canine Good Citizen test into their respective programs.

Doggy Dogma

The *Canine Good Citizen* uses a series of exercises that test the dog's ability to behave in an acceptable manner in public. Its purpose is to demonstrate that the dog, as a companion for all people, can be a respected member of the community and can be trained and conditioned to always behave in the home, in public places, and in the presence of other dogs in a manner that will reflect credit on the dog.

Today, the Canine Good Citizen program is offered by many training organizations and the test itself has become a popular adjunct at dog shows. Dog-related organizations in other countries, notably England and Japan, are becoming interested in using the Canine Good Citizen test.

Join the ranks of those who have obtained their Canine Good Citizen certificates. Ideally, every dog should be trained to become a Canine Good Citizen and the more that are, the better the chances of counteracting the growing anti-dog sentiment in many communities. Irresponsible dog ownership has been the cause for this sentiment and only responsible pet ownership can reverse it. Demonstrate that your dog is a well-trained personal companion and a member in good standing with the community by training him to become a Canine Good Citizen.

A Canine Good Citizen is a dog that is well behaved around people and other dogs, at home and in public. It is the kind of dog that is a pleasure to own, one that is safe with children and one that you would welcome as a neighbor. It is a dog that is a nuisance to no one. To become a Canine Good Citizen your dog must demonstrate, by means of a short test, that he or she meets these requirements.

Bet You Didn't Know

Florida was the first of several states that have passed resolutions endorsing the Canine Good Citizen program as a means of teaching responsible pet ownership, and as a means of teaching dogs Canine Good Citizen behaviors for the community.

Test Requirements

The Canine Good Citizen uses a series of exercises that test the dog's ability to behave in an acceptable manner in public. Its purpose is to demonstrate that the dog, as a companion for all people, can be a respected member of the community, and can be trained and conditioned to always behave in the home, in public places, and in the presence of other dogs in a manner that will reflect credit on the dog.

The examination consists of the following 10 tests, all of which are scored on a pass/ fail system:

Accepting a Friendly Stranger

Demonstrates that the dog will allow a friendly stranger to approach and speak to the handler in a natural, everyday situation.

The evaluator approaches the dog and handler, and greets the handler in a friendly manner, ignoring the dog.

The evaluator and handler shake hands and exchange pleasantries. The dog must show no sign of resentment or shyness and must not break position or try to go to the evaluator.

Accepting a Friendly Stranger.

Sitting Politely for Petting

Demonstrates that the dog will allow a friendly stranger to touch him while he is out with the owner/handler. With the dog sitting at the handler's side (either side is permissible) throughout the exercise, the evaluator pets the dog on the head and body only.

185

The handler may talk to his or her dog throughout the exercise.

After petting, the evaluator then circles the dog and handler, completing the test. The dog must not show shyness or resentment.

Sitting Politely for Petting.

Appearance and Grooming

Demonstrates that the dog will welcome being groomed and examined and will permit a stranger, such as a veterinarian, groomer, or friend of the owner, to do so. It also demonstrates the owner's care, concern, and responsibility.

The evaluator inspects the dog to determine if it is clean and groomed. The dog must appear to be in healthy condition (i.e., proper weight, clean, healthy, and alert). The handler should supply the comb or brush commonly used on the dog. The evaluator then easily combs or brushes the dog and, in a natural manner, lightly examines the ears and gently picks up each front foot.

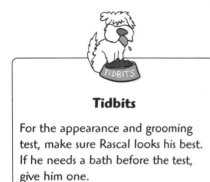

Tidbits

For the appearance and grooming test, make sure Rascal looks his best. If he needs a bath before the test, give him one.

It is not necessary for the dog to hold a specific position during the examination, and the handler may talk to the dog, praise, and give encouragement throughout.

Out for a Walk—Walking on a Loose Leash

Demonstrates that the handler is in control of the dog. The dog may be on either side of the handler, whichever the handler prefers. (Note: The left-side position is required in AKC obedience competition and all activities where the dog is in service to the handler, such as guiding the blind. See Part 4, Turning Pro.)

The dog's position should leave no doubt that the dog is attentive to the handler and is responding to the handler's movements and changes of direction. The dog need not be perfectly aligned with the handler and need not sit when the handler stops.

Top Dog Tips

For the Walking on a Loose Leash test, the dog need not "march in formation" with the handler, but he dog should be attentive and clearly responding to the handler's movements.

The evaluator may use a pre-plotted course or may direct the handler/dog team by issuing instructions or commands. In either case, there must be a left turn, right turn, and about-turn, with at least one stop in between and another at the end. The handler may talk to the dog along the way to praise or command it in a normal tone of voice. The handler may also sit the dog at the halt, if desired.

Walking Through a Crowd

Demonstrates that the dog can move about politely in pedestrian traffic and is under control in public places.

The dog and handler walk around and pass close to several people (at least three). The dog may show some interest in the strangers but should continue to walk with the handler, without evidence of over-exuberance, shyness, or resentment. The handler may talk to the dog and encourage or praise the dog throughout the test. The dog should not be straining at the leash.

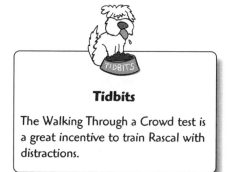

Tidbits

The Walking Through a Crowd test is a great incentive to train Rascal with distractions.

Note: Children may act as members of the crowd in this test, as well as in the Reaction to Distractions test, test 9. However, whenever children participate in a test they must be instructed on their role and be supervised. It is permissible to have one dog in a crowd but the dog must be on lead and well mannered.

Sit and Down on Command—Staying in Place

Demonstrates that the dog has training, will respond to the handler's commands to "sit" and "down," and will remain in the place commanded by the handler (sit or down position, whichever the handler prefers).

Prior to this test, the dog's leash is replaced with a 20-foot line. The handler may take a reasonable amount of time and use more than one command to make the dog sit and then down. The evaluator must determine if the dog has responded to the handler's commands. The handler may not force the dog into either position but may touch the dog to offer gentle guidance.

When instructed by the evaluator, the handler tells the dog to "stay" and, with the 20-foot line in hand, walks forward the length of the line, turns and returns to the dog at a natural pace (the 20-foot line is not removed or dropped). The dog must remain in the place in which he was left (the dog may change position), until the evaluator instructs the handler to release the dog. The dog may be released from the front or the side.

Tidbits

For the Coming When Called test the dog is on a 20-foot leash. Because you have already trained Rascal to come when called off leash, he should not have any difficulty passing this test.

Coming When Called

Demonstrates that the dog will come when called by the handler.

For this test, the dog will remain on the 20-foot line that was used in the Sit and Down on Command. The handler will walk 10 feet from the dog, turn to face the dog, and will call the dog. The handler may use body language and encouragement when calling the dog, and may tell the dog to "stay" or "wait" or just walk away. The dog may be left in the sit, down, or standing position. If the dog attempts to follow the handler, the evaluator may distract the dog (e.g., petting) until the handler is 10 feet away.

The point of the test is to determine if the dog "comes when called" and whether it stays, and the exercise is completed when the dog comes to the handler and the handler attaches the dog's own leash.

Reaction to Another Dog

Demonstrates that the dog can behave politely around other dogs.

Two handlers and their dogs approach each other from a distance of about 10 yards, stop, shake hands and exchange pleasantries, and continue on for about 5 yards.

The dogs should show no more than casual interest in each other. Neither dog should go to the other dog or its handler.

Reaction to Distractions

Demonstrates that the dog is confident at all times when faced with common distracting situations.

The evaluator will select only two of the following list (Note: Because some dogs are sensitive to sound and others to visual distractions, most tests involve one sound and one visual distraction.):

➤ A person using crutches, a wheelchair, or a walker. This distraction simulates a disabled person who requires the use of service equipment.

➤ A sudden closing or opening of a door.

➤ Dropping a large book, pan, folded chair, or the like, no closer than 5 feet behind the dog.

➤ A jogger running in front of the dog.

➤ A person pushing a shopping cart or pulling a crate dolly passing 5 to 10 feet away.

➤ A person on a bicycle passing at least 10 feet away.

During the Reaction to Distractions test, the dog may express a natural interest and curiosity and may appear slightly startled but should not panic, try to run away, show aggressiveness, or bark. The handler may talk to the dog and encourage or praise it throughout the exercise.

Supervised Separation

Demonstrates that the dog can be left with another person and will maintain its training and good manners while the owner goes out of sight. Evaluators will say something like "would you like me to watch your dog?"

The handler will fasten the dog to a six-foot line such as the dog's leash, give the end of the leash to the evaluator, and go to a place out of sight of the dog for three minutes. The dog should not continually bark, whine, howl, pace unnecessarily, or show anything other than mild agitation or nervousness. This is not a stay exercise; dogs may stand, sit, lie down and change positions during this test.

Dogs are tested individually, not as a group, and more than one dog can be tested at a time.

These are practical tests that determine the amount of control you have over your dog and the dog's ability to behave appropriately in public. The evaluators, in addition to deciding the dog's ability to pass these exercises, are asked to consider if this is the kind of dog that:

1. he or she would like to own;

2. would be safe with children;

3. he or she would welcome as a neighbor; and

4. makes its owner happy and isn't making someone else unhappy.

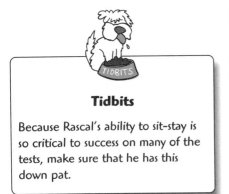

Cramming for the Exam

If you have done the basic training, you are already halfway there. The new exercises you need to teach your dog are:

Tidbits

Because Rascal's ability to sit-stay is so critical to success on many of the tests, make sure that he has this down pat.

➤ Accepting a Friendly Stranger

➤ Sitting Politely for Petting

➤ Appearance and Grooming

➤ Reaction to Another Dog

➤ Reaction to Distractions

➤ Supervised Separation

Four of the tests require a solid sit-stay in the face of a distraction, such as a person, another dog, or an auditory distraction. You have already trained for these except for the distraction of another dog. Even so, you need to practice these tests to make sure Rascal can do them, and to reassure yourself.

Accepting a Friendly Stranger

We suggest that you start by teaching your dog the Sit for Examination and build from there. You will need a helper for these exercises.

Top Dog Tips

The best way to prepare for the Accepting a Friendly Stranger, Sitting Politely for Petting, and Appearance and Grooming tests is to teach your dog the Sit for Examination, and build from there. You will need a helper for these exercises.

With Rascal in heel position, begin as you did for the sit-stay. Say and signal "stay" and have your helper approach your dog from 6 feet at a 45-degree angle to your left. Have the helper approach in a friendly and non-threatening manner, without hovering over the dog. Have the helper show your dog the palm of a hand and continue to walk by. If Rascal stays, praise, and release. If your dog wants to get up, check straight up with your left hand with "stay" and try again.

Remember scoring your dog for fight or flight? This score will determine his response to the helper. For example, if the helper is a stranger and your dog is high in fight, he may show signs of aggression. On the other hand, if he is low in fight and high in flight behaviors, Rascal may try to hide behind you or show signs of shyness when the helper approaches.

Because the Sit for Examination is the cornerstone for all the distraction tests, you need to condition your dog to perform this exercise correctly before you continue.

Rascal's response determines how close the distracter gets in the beginning. If he becomes apprehensive about the helper's approach, we suggest that he or she walk past the dog at a distance of 2 feet without making eye contact with or looking at the dog. As the dog gets used to that maneuver, have the helper offer a treat to the dog, placed on the open palm, as he or she walks by, still without making eye contact with the dog. It does not matter whether the dog takes the treat or not—it's the gesture that counts.

When your dog accepts that, have the helper first offer a treat and then pet the dog on the head, still without making eye contact, as he or she continues past the dog. After that, the helper can attempt to look at the dog as he or she touches the dog and goes past. For this particular test, it is the eye contact in connection with the examination that is the hard part of the exercise, and it may require several sessions before the dog is steady.

The ultimate aim of this exercise is for the dog to allow the approach of a stranger who will also then pet the dog. For the majority of dogs, this is not a particularly difficult exercise, but it does require a little practice.

To prepare for the Canine Good Citizen test, you'll need a helper. Perhaps a neighbor whom your dog does not know well would be willing to assist.

Appearance and Grooming

Appearance and Grooming is a similar test and one that can be introduced as soon as your dog accepts petting by a stranger. Have your helper lightly comb or brush Rascal with you at his side or directly in front. The helper examines the ears and picks up each front foot. If your dog finds this difficult, have the helper give the dog a treat as he or she touches a foot. Condition the dog with praise and treats to accept having the feet handled.

Bet You Didn't Know

The Appearance and Grooming test is one of the most frequently failed tests, and mainly because the dog will not permit the evaluator to handle his feet. If you make a point of handling your dog's feet when he is a puppy (and have your friends do it too), he will not be upset by this as an adult.

Because your dog's profile determines how he reacts to a particular distraction, you need to expose him to different distractions to see how he deals with them. Some dogs take it all in stride and others require several exposures to become accustomed to the distraction. The best foundation is a solid sit-stay.

Reaction to Another Dog

Again, this is a sit-stay exercise, but you should practice this with some one else who also has a well-trained dog. With your dogs at heel position, approach each other from a distance of about 20 feet and stop close enough to each other so you can just shake hands. As you stop, tell Rascal to sit and stay.

Should he want to say hello to the other dog, reinforce the stay command. Be sure you instruct your training partner not to let his or her dog come to say hello to Rascal.

Reaction to Distractions

Take another look at the list of distractions above. If you think that your dog may be unduly startled by any one of them, you need to practice and condition him to ignore that distraction.

The evaluator will pick two distractions, one sound and one visual distraction. During the test, the dog may attempt to walk forward slightly to investigate the distracter but should not pull on the leash. A solid sit-stay is often the answer to an unforeseen reaction.

A dog that growls, lunges, or continuously barks at the distracter will not pass. One bark is acceptable.

Supervised Separation

Although this test does not directly deal with distractions, it does evaluate a dog's response to the unforeseen, and so resembles the tests above. It shows that the dog can be left with someone else, which demonstrates training and good manners. You hand your leash to the evaluator who watches your dog, and in some cases, other dogs may be in the vicinity who are also doing this test or just being walked. The dog should not bark, whine, howl, or pace unnecessarily, or register anything other than mild agitation or nervousness.

You can leave your dog in either the sit or the down position; it is not necessary that he hold that position until you return, only that he does not vocalize or pace unnecessarily. Still, by having Rascal focus on staying in place, you reduce the likelihood that he will bark or howl, or become overly agitated. It can be done as a simple down-stay exercise with the owner out of sight, which is what we recommend.

Taking the Test

Organizations offering the Canine Good Citizen test have considerable leeway in making up the order in which to give the tests. The most common order is the one in which they are listed above. The Supervised Separation test may take place in the presence of other dogs that are also doing this test.

Usually three evaluators conduct the test. The first evaluator conducts tests one through three, the second one tests four through nine, and the third one tests ten. The test is scored on a pass/fail basis and in order to qualify for a Canine Good Citizen certificate the dog must pass each of the ten tests.

An automatic failure results when a dog eliminates during testing, except during test ten, provided it is held outdoors. Handlers are also not permitted to give their dogs food while the dog is being tested.

Any dog that growls, snaps, bites, attacks or attempts to attack a person or another dog is not a good citizen and must be dismissed from the test.

To participate in a Canine Good Citizen test you need to present, at the time of the test, a current rabies certificate and any other state or locally required inoculations and licenses.

All tests are done on leash and dogs need to wear a well-fitting buckle or slip collar made of leather, fabric, or chain. Snap-around collars, prong collars or head halters are not permitted. The leash can be either fabric or leather.

Top Dog Tips

Your attitude and state of mind are the most important influence on the outcome of the test. If you are excessively nervous, your dog will become nervous, too. Handlers under stress sometimes do things they would never dream of doing any other time. If this happens, it will confuse your dog to the point where the dog might fail. Maintain a positive outlook and rely on your training.

Dos and Don'ts of Taking the Test

The following are a few hints that will help you in preparing for and participating in the Canine Good Citizen test.

Do:

➤ practice the entire test with a helper and friends before you actually enter a test. This is more for your benefit than Rascal's. As you become familiar with the test, you will lose some of your nervousness. It will also identify Rascal's weak areas and give you additional time to work on them.

➤ give your dog a bath and thoroughly groom him before the test.

➤ use the correct equipment for the test—a well-fitting buckle or slip collar of either leather, fabric, or chain, and a leather or fabric leash.

➤ exercise Rascal before you take the test. Should your dog eliminate at any time during testing, he must be marked failed.

➤ warm-up your dog before taking the test so that both of you are as relaxed as possible under the circumstances.

➤ use a second command for any exercise, if necessary.

➤ talk to your dog during an exercise to keep attention on you, if necessary.

➤ ask the evaluator for an explanation if you don't understand a procedure or an instruction.

➤ maintain a loose leash throughout the entire test, even between exercises, to the extent possible. While an occasional tightening of the leash is generally not considered a failure, it does become a judgment call for the evaluator in assessing your control over your dog. It is best not to put yourself or the evaluator in that position.

➤ understand that your attitude and state of mind are the most important influence on the outcome of the test. If you are excessively nervous, your dog will become nervous, too. Maintain a positive outlook and rely on your training.

➤ conduct yourself in a sportsmanlike manner at all times.

➤ keep in mind the purpose of the Canine Good Citizen, and become an ambassador of good will and good manners for all dogs.

If you are nervous during the exam, your dog will sense it. He'll get nervous too!

Don't:

➤ lose your temper or attitude should your dog fail an exercise. If you berate your dog, you will sour him on the entire experience. You may feel a certain amount of disappointment and frustration, but those feelings, too, you need to control. The more you work with your dog, the more attuned he is to your feelings. He will associate them with the circumstances and not the failure of an exercise.

➤ change your attitude toward your dog after he has failed an exercise so that the dog is completely unaware that something went wrong. Your remedy is not to make the dog feel stupid or anxious, but to review your training, work on the difficult exercise, and try again. If your dog's confidence is undermined, training will take longer and become a less rewarding experience than if you realize that your job is to help your dog at every step of the way through support and encouragement.

Tidbits

Of course, if you take the time to participate in the Canine Good Citizen test, you obviously want Rascal to pass. Even if he doesn't, you should feel good about yourself and Rascal anyhow. You are making an effort to train your dog to be a model member of the community. In that small way, you are doing a service to all dogs and their owners.

The Least You Need to Know

➤ The Canine Good Citizen is a test to demonstrate your dog's ability to behave in an acceptable manner in public.

➤ The dog that has mastered the sit-stay is half-way home.

➤ You do need to practice with and around distractions, including other dogs.

➤ When taking the test, have confidence in your training and don't confuse your dog.

➤ Maintain an up-beat attitude—here is your chance to show off how well you have trained Rascal.

Going to College—
Tricks 101

For this chapter we are indebted to Mary Ann Rombold Zeigenfuse, one of the lead instructors at our annual dog camps and the trainer of Millie, the White House dog during the Bush administration. She wrote *Dog Tricks: Step by Step* (Howell Book House, Inc., 1997), thereby keeping alive the tradition of anyone who has ever had anything to do with the White House, no matter how remote, becoming an author.

In college we learn the tricks of the trade, and so does Rascal. Every well-trained dog knows a trick or two that will impress friends and family alike. Tricks you can teach your dog can be simple or complex, depending on your dog's drives and your interest.

One of the more astonishing tricks, at least until you know how it works, requires a solid retrieve on command. Others require no more than a simple "stay," but to the uninitiated, they are equally astonishing.

Doggy Dogma

Sequencing means breaking down what you want to teach your dog into components small enough for the dog to master, which lead up to the final product.

Deciding on the Tricks for Your Dog

The trick to teaching tricks is *sequencing. Sequencing* means breaking down what you want to teach your dog into components small enough for the dog to master, which lead up to the final product. For example, if you want to teach your dog to shake hands, also known as high five, you would start by taking Rascal's paw in your hand with the command you want to use and then praise and reward him. Next, you would offer your palm, and so on.

When you decide on the kind of tricks to teach Rascal, keep in mind his personality profile. Tricks like high five or roll over are easiest with dogs high in flight behaviors and not so easy with those high in fight behaviors. A dog high in fight behaviors wouldn't stoop so low—it's beneath his dignity.

Tricks learned quickly by dogs high in flight behaviors:

➤ high five

➤ roll over

➤ play dead

Tricks learned quickly by dogs high in prey behaviors:

➤ find mine, such as keys, wallet, or whatever (dog must know how to retrieve)

➤ jump through arms or hoop

Tricks learned quickly by dogs high in pack behaviors:

➤ don't cross this line or wait until I tell you

➤ you have food on your nose

When you see Rascal do something that could turn into a trick, such as sit up and beg, reward it and work on getting him to do it on command.

Bet You Didn't Know

Dogs, too, are either right or left footed. You can tell by the direction in which your dog turns when he comes to you. If he turns to the right, he is right footed. If he retrieves, you can tell by the directions in which he turns after he has picked up the object to bring it back.

High Five

The object is to teach Rascal to raise one front paw as high as he can on command.

Sequence 1—goal: Introducing your dog to the concept.

➤ Sit your dog in front of you.

➤ Reduce your body posture by kneeling or squatting in front of your dog. You don't want to lean or hover over him.

➤ Offer him at mid-chest level your palm and say "shake" or "gimme five," or whatever command you want to use.

➤ Take the elbow of his dominant front leg and lift it off the ground about 2 inches. (If you don't know your dog's dominant side, he will quickly tell you.)

➤ Slide your hand down to the paw and gently shake.

➤ Praise enthusiastically as you are shaking his paw.

➤ Reward and release him with "OK."

Repeat this sequence 5 times over the course of three sessions to get your dog used to this exercise and to hearing the command.

Top Dog Tips

When teaching your dog to shake and when you offer him your palm, reduce your body posture by either kneeling or squatting so that you don't lean or hover over him.

Tidbits

You will find that as soon as you offer your palm your dog will put his paw in it without waiting for the command. When this starts to happen, teach him to give you the other paw with the command "the other one."

Evo demonstrates how to "give five."

Sequence 2—goal: For your dog to lift his paw.

➤ Sit your dog in front of you and reduce your body posture.

➤ Offer your palm with the command "shake."

➤ Pause. You are looking for some sort of response. If nothing happens, touch his elbow and offer your palm again. Give him the chance to lift his paw.

➤ When he lifts the paw on his own, take the paw, enthusiastically praise, reward, and release.

➤ If nothing happens, take his paw, praise, reward, and release.

Stay with this sequence until your dog is lifting his paw off the ground on command so you can shake it.

Sequence 3—goal: To put his paw into your palm.

➤ Sit your dog in front of you and reduce your body posture.

➤ Offer your palm at mid-chest level and say "shake." At this point, he should put his paw on your palm. Praise enthusiastically, reward, and release.

➤ If nothing happens, go back to Sequence 2.

Stay with this sequence until your dog readily and without hesitation puts his paw on your palm.

Sequence 4—goal: To raise his paw as high as he can.

➤ Sit your dog in front of you and reduce your body posture.

➤ Offer your palm at chin level and say "shake." By now your dog should readily and without hesitation put his paw into your hand. When he does, praise, reward, and release. If not, go back to Sequence 3.

➤ Raise your palm, in 2-inch increments, until you have reached your dog's limit. (If you have a Yorkie, you're done.) After several repetitions, your dog will stretch his paw as high as he can. Praise, reward, and release.

The Other One

This trick is an extension of "shake." It follows the same sequences, except you want your dog to give you the other paw. What you will see happening is that as soon as you offer your palm, your dog will give you his paw without waiting for the command.

You are going to use the same sequences except that you will point directly at the leg you want the dog to lift, that is, the other one and you will use a new command, such as "the other one," or whatever. It is not going to take Rascal long to figure out the difference, because he won't get the treat unless he gives you the correct paw.

You can now impress your friends and neighbors with how clever Rascal is.

Roll Over

Roll over is always a great favorite. It requires the dog to lay on the floor and completely roll over sideways. As a prerequisite, the dog must know how to lie down on command.

Sequence 1—goal: To get your dog to roll over with a little help from you.

➤ Place your dog into the down position, either with a command or a treat.

➤ Reduce your body posture by kneeling or squatting in front of your dog. You don't want to lean or hover over him.

➤ Hold the treat in such a way that your dog has to look over his shoulder while lying on the ground.

➤ Say "roll over" and slowly make a small circle around his head, keeping the treat close to his nose.

➤ With your other hand gently help your dog roll over in the direction you want him to go. When the dog has completely rolled over, enthusiastically praise, reward, and release.

➤ Repeat until your dog is completely relaxed with you helping him roll over.

Tidbits

Roll over is always a crowd pleaser. It can easily be taught to most dogs that know the down command and respond to a treat.

Top Dog Tips

When teaching your dog to roll over on command, reduce your body posture by squatting or kneeling and keep your upper body straight so you are not hovering over the dog.

Sequence 2—goal: Your dog rolls over on his own.

➤ Place your dog into the down position, either with a command or a treat.

➤ Reduce your body posture.

➤ Say "roll over" and get him to follow the treat without any help from you. When he does it, praise, reward, and release. If not, go back to Sequence 1.

➤ Repeat until your dog rolls over with a minimum of guidance on your part.

Sequence 3—goal: Dog rolls over on command.

➤ There is now no treat in your hand, but be prepared to reward the correct response.

➤ Say "down" and then "roll over." The first few times you do this, you may have to use the same hand motion as though you had a treat in it. Praise, reward, and release when your dog does it.

➤ Reduce the hand motion until he does it on command alone. Praise, reward, and release.

Once your dog has learned the trick, you will notice that he will offer this behavior anytime he wants a treat. Unfortunately, you cannot reward him for that for the obvious reason that he is now training you to give him a treat on demand.

Instead, go to random rewards when he does the trick on command.

Play Dead

This trick is an old favorite and a logical extension of roll over. It is easily taught to dogs high in flight behaviors. If your dog is high in fight behaviors, don't waste your time.

It consists of aiming your index finger and "firing" at your dog with a command such as "bang," and your dog falls on his side or back and plays dead.

Sequence 1—goal: Dog lies down on side or back.

➤ Have a treat in your "gun" hand.

➤ Down your dog.

➤ Lean over your dog and in a deep tone of voice say "bang" as you point your index finger at him. If he is high in flight behaviors, he will roll on his side or back.

➤ Praise and give him a treat while he is in that position and then release him with "OK."

➤ If he does not roll on his side or back, use the treat as you did for the "roll over." Then praise, reward, and release.

Repeat this sequence until your dog responds to the "bang" command.

Tidbits

It is generally easier to teach tricks that use Rascal's natural tendencies. If your dog has a quirky habit, you may find that you can turn this into a fun trick.

Sequence 2—goal: Your dog plays dead from the sitting or standing position.

➤ Get your dog's attention by calling his name.

➤ Lean over your dog and in a deep tone of voice say "bang" as you point your index finger at him.

➤ If he lies down and plays dead, praise, reward, and release. If not, show him what you want by placing him in the "dead" position. Praise, reward, and release.

Practice this sequence until he responds to the "bang" command from the sitting or standing position.

Sequence 3—goal: Your dog plays dead at a distance.

➤ With your dog about 2 feet from you, get his attention by using his name and give the "bang" command as you point your finger at him. If he responds, praise, go to him, and reward him, and then release. If not, show him what you want and start all over.

➤ Gradually increase the distance to about 6 feet.

This last sequence will go quickly since your dog has learned to respond to the "bang" command and signal. You can then gradually increase the time between his response and the praise, reward, and release to 30 seconds. After that, start giving the reward on a random basis.

It's a simple trick, but one that will delight friends and family.

Find Mine

The Find Mine trick is one of the most impressive tricks you can teach Rascal. It combines the retrieve with the dog's use of his nose to discriminate between different articles. It's a terrific parlor trick that will astound and amaze your friends.

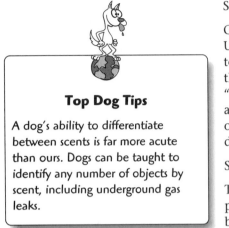

Top Dog Tips

A dog's ability to differentiate between scents is far more acute than ours. Dogs can be taught to identify any number of objects by scent, including underground gas leaks.

Sequence 1—goal: To retrieve your keys.

Get a leather or plastic key fob and put some keys on it. Using a leather or plastic fob makes it easier for the dog to pick up and carry them. Get your dog excited about the keys and throw them a few feet in front of you with "find mine." When he brings them back, praise, reward, and release. If he doesn't, review the first few sequences of teaching the retrieve (Chapter 13). Repeat until your dog readily brings back your keys.

Sequence 2—goal: To find your keys.

Tell your dog to "stay" and with him watching you, place the keys in the corner of an armchair or couch. Go back to your dog and send him with "find mine." Praise, reward and release. Repeat several times, each time changing the location slightly, so Rascal gets used to looking for the keys.

Sequence 3—goal: To find your keys using his nose.

This sequence is the heart of the trick and the real fun part. Tell your dog to stay and without him watching, place the keys on the floor, just inside the doorframe of another room. Go back to your dog and send him with "find mine." What you want him to do is to find your keys by retracing your steps and then using his nose to locate the keys.

Over the course of several sessions, make the game increasingly difficult. For example, a fairly advanced search would involve you going into one room, coming out again and going into another room and putting the keys behind a wastebasket. Or, using two floors. Anytime he gets stuck, help him by showing him where you placed the keys. Remember to praise and reward correct responses, although you no longer have to do it every time.

Sequence 4—goal: To discriminate between objects.

For many years this has been our favorite trick. Like any good trick, it's baffling if you don't understand how it's done, yet childishly simple for the dog.

It starts with the knowledge that a dog's nose is far more powerful than a human's, and that he is able to discriminate between different scents. He can certainly tell the difference between you and anybody else. Armed with this knowledge, you are ready to fleece anyone gullible enough to take on Rascal.

➤ Crumple up a dollar bill, place it on the ground and have your dog retrieve it with "find mine."

➤ Have a helper, and this can be a member of the family, also crumple up a dollar bill. Place the bills on the floor about 6 inches apart and send your dog with "find mine." At this point the odds are better than 50 percent that he will bring back your dollar bill. If he does, praise and reward. If he brings back the wrong one, ignore the response, that is, don't take it from him. Just send him again to get the correct one. Repeat until you are sure he is using his nose to identify your dollar bill.

➤ Have your helper add another bill. Each time your dog is successful, have your helper add another bill, until there are a total of 10 bills from which to choose. While Rascal is learning this trick, he will occasionally make a mistake and bring back a wrong bill. Without taking that bill from him, send him again with "find mine." Reward every correct response. You will need to replace the wrong bill that the dog brought back—it now has his saliva on it.

That is all there is to this trick. The fun part comes when you change the denomination and get other people involved. Say you have a half dozen visitors. During a lull in the conversation you say "did you know that our dog can tell a twenty dollar bill from a single?" Of course, nobody is going to believe you.

So, you take out a twenty and say "anybody have any ones?" Crumple up your twenty and have the others crumple up their singles. Then have Rascal do his number. A variation is to ask for someone else's twenty with the understanding that if your dog retrieves it, you get to keep it. Naturally, you can only handle that twenty and the person who gave it to you cannot contribute any singles. Good luck!

Jumping Through Arms or Hoop

A hula-hoop makes a wonderful prop for this trick in which you first teach your dog to jump through the hoop and then your arms. Start by getting a hoop commensurate with your dog's size.

Sequence 1—goal: Dog jumps through hoop on leash.

➤ Lay the hoop on the ground and take your dog over to examine it.

➤ Put your dog on leash and walk him over the hoop.

➤ Pick up the hoop and let the bottom edge rest on the ground. Thread the leash through the hoop and encourage your dog to jump through with "jump." You can use a treat to get him to walk through the hoop. Repeat until your dog readily goes through the hoop with the command "jump." Praise, reward, and release for successful tries.

➤ Thread the leash through the hoop and raise it a few inches off the floor. If necessary, use a treat to get him through and then enthusiastically praise. As your dog gains confidence begin raising the hoop in two-inch increments until the bottom is eye level in front of him.

Sequence 2—goal: Dog jumps through hoop off leash.

➤ Take the leash off and present the hoop in front of your dog with the bottom no higher than the dog's knees. Say "jump" and let the dog jump through. Praise and reward with a treat. Repeat but change the position of the hoop so the bottom is level with the dog's elbows, then shoulder. How high you can raise it depends on the athletic ability of your dog. Keep in mind that as soon as you get to about shoulder level (the dog's, not yours), you need a surface with good traction on which the dog can take off and land. Wet grass and slippery floors are not good surfaces for this trick.

➤ Teach your dog to jump as you pivot in a circle with the hoop. Pivot slowly at first and then increase speed, but never so fast that the dog loses interest or can't keep up.

Sequence 3—goal: Dog jumps through your arms.

Review having your dog jump through the hoop at his shoulder level several times. Put the hoop away. Squat down and let your dog see you put a treat at the spot where he is going to land. Make a circle with your arms out to the side. Keep the upper part of your body upright. Tell your dog to jump and when he does, tell him how clever he is. Going around you to the treat is considered bad form and you need to pick up the treat before he gets it. Then try again. It will not take him long to figure out the only way to the treat is through your arms. Stop after he has been successful.

Keep working on this trick until your dog jumps through your arms every time you make the circle.

> **Top Dog Tips**
>
> Don't Cross This Line is a good review of door and stair manners. Remember, you have to release your dog to go through doors or up and down stairs. If you get lax about it, your dog will start releasing himself, thereby defeating the object of the training.

Don't Cross This Line

This trick is an extension of door and stair manners. Its most useful application is to keep the dog out of one or several rooms in the house, either temporarily or permanently.

Sequence 1—goal: Review door manners on leash

➤ Use the command "stay" or "wait until I tell you."

➤ Put your dog on leash.

➤ Walk toward the front door, say "wait" and open it. Make sure the leash is loose and that you are not holding Rascal back.

➤ If he starts to cross the threshold, check on the leash to bring him back in.

➤ Close the door and start all over. Because you have already taught him to sit at the door before you release him, this review on leash will go quickly.

➤ Repeat until he begins to hesitate crossing the threshold.

Sequence 2—goal: The dog learns to cross the threshold with your permission.

➤ Walk toward the front door, say "stay" and open it.

➤ Briefly hesitate and then say "OK" and cross over the threshold with your dog.

Sequence 3—goal: You go through the doorway and your dog does not.

➤ Approach the door and open it.

➤ Say "stay" and go through the doorway. If he tries to follow, pull him back by extending your arm through the door and then close the door on the leash.

➤ Open the door, but don't let him come out yet until you say "OK." Then praise.

Sequence 4—goal: Review Sequences 1-3 coming back into the house.

Remember, you have to release your dog to go through doors or up and down stairs. If you get lax about it, your dog will start releasing himself, thereby defeating the object of the training.

You can now apply the same principle to one or more rooms in the house. As a trick, you can teach this to your dog by drawing a line on the ground and using the line as a threshold. Once your dog understands the basic principle, he will catch on to anything you don't want him to cross.

You Have Food on Your Nose

This is a cute trick. It involves balancing a piece of food on Rascal's nose until you say "OK." Some dogs even toss it in the air and catch it on the way down.

Sequence 1—goal: To be able to cup your hand over your dog's muzzle. If you have taught your dog to retrieve, he already knows this.

➤ Sit your dog and pet him for a few seconds.

➤ Cup your hand over his muzzle from the top, just as you did for the retrieve. Kneel or squat in front of your dog and keep your upper body straight. With your other hand hold a treat near your dog's nose and get him to focus on the treat. Release with "OK" and give him the treat. You need to be able to hold his muzzle so you can put a piece of food on his nose.

➤ Repeat until you can cup his muzzle and he focuses on the treat.

Place a treat on your dog's nose, tell him to "stay," and then release him.

Sequence 2—goal: Put the treat on his nose.

➤ Gently hold his muzzle and put the treat on the dog's nose in front of your thumb. Tell him to "stay" or "wait," and then release him. The treat will either fall off or get bounced into the air.

Sequence 3—goal: Increase the time he balances the treat.

➤ Start by holding his muzzle and placing the treat on his nose.

➤ Say "stay" and have your dog balance the treat for 10 seconds, then release him.

➤ Repeat and increase the time to 20 seconds.

Sequence 4—goal: Dog balances the treat without help from you.

➤ Put the treat on his muzzle and then slowly let go of his muzzle, reminding him to "stay." Get him to focus on your index finger by holding it front of his nose.

➤ Wait a few seconds and release your dog.

Sequence 5—goal: Increase time and distance.

➤ Gradually increase the time he holds the treat before you release your dog.

➤ Gradually increase the distance of your finger from the dog's nose.

What if he drops or tosses the treat before you said "OK?" Well, if you can't get to the treat before he does, an unlikely outcome, reduce the time and distance until he is reliable again and you can increase them again.

The Least You Need to Know

➤ The trick to teaching tricks is sequencing.

➤ Make each sequence small enough so it can easily be understood by your dog.

➤ Your dog's Personality Profile will tell you the tricks that are easy for him.

➤ A great tool for tricks is the dog's ability to use his very sensitive nose.

Part 4
Turning Pro

Discover the exciting world of organized dog sports in which anyone can participate. The possibilities are virtually endless and there is a sport for almost every dog, whether he is a purebred or a Designer Dog. The object is to earn a performance title in a given event. Among the many organizations sponsoring such events, the largest is the American Kennel Club. It oversees over 30 performance titles in eight different categories, plus the Canine Good Citizen test.

Agility, obedience and tracking events are for all breeds. Other events are more breed specific and test the dog's ability to perform the function for which he was bred, such as hunting tests and field trials for the hounds, Retrievers, and Sporting dogs. For the small Terriers and the Dachshunds, there are Earthdog trials, which test the dog's ability to go after critters under ground, and now you know why they dig. For the sight hounds, there is lure coursing, incredibly fast paced and exhilarating events.

Many breed clubs have their own performance titles, such as the Newfoundland Club of America, which tests the dog's ability as a water rescue dog and as a draft dog. When you see these majestic dogs working in the water, it brings tears to your eyes.

The darling event of the '90s is agility, designed strictly for the fun of it. You get to huff and puff and your dog gets to jump over obstacles, climb others and go through tunnels. It has experienced phenomenal growth during the last ten years, with good reason—the dogs love it, the handlers love it, and it has enormous spectator appeal.

Enter this world with caution. You can become addicted and it will change life as you know it.

Chapter 16

The Exciting World of Obedience Competition

In This Chapter

➤ An overview of the basic requirements

➤ Why getting and keeping your dog's attention is so important

➤ Learning to dance with your dog

➤ How to make practicing fun for you and your dog

If you and Rascal enjoy working together, the sky is the limit. You can participate in obedience competitions and earn obedience titles. It's a lot of fun and you meet lots of nice people. We must warn you, however: Once you get started, you can become addicted, and your life will never be the same.

Almost every weekend of the year, you can go to a dog show and show off what the two of you have accomplished. Dog shows are either conformation shows, where your dog is judged on his appearance, or obedience trials, where you and he are judged on your ability. They can be held together, or separately.

Bet You Didn't Know

To participate in a dog show you need to enter about three weeks ahead of time.

If you have already been to a dog show and watched the obedience trial, you were probably amazed at the training and maybe thought to yourself, "My dog could never do that." Well, not necessarily so. It all depends on his Personality Profile, and whether the two of you enjoy spending quality time with each other.

Doggy Dogma

At a dog show, the dogs are exhibited in a clearly defined enclosure, often made of baby gates, called a *ring*, which is a rectangular area no less than 30 feet by 40 feet.

What's Out There

Different organizations have licensed shows, including those at which Designer Dogs can participate. We are going to concentrate on those shows held under the auspices of the American Kennel Club (AKC), the oldest and largest organization to license such events.

The AKC awards three basic obedience titles.

➤ Companion Dog, or C.D., from the Novice Class

➤ Companion Dog Excellent, or C.D.X., from the Open Class

➤ Utility Dog, or U.D., from the Utility Class.

The level of difficulty increases with each class, from no more than basic control to retrieving and jumping, to responding to signals and direction. The classes are designed so that any dog can compete successfully for titles. Once your dog has earned a Utility title, you are then eligible to compete for the special obedience titles of Obedience Trial Champion and Utility Dog Excellent.

Top Dog Tips

To participate in an AKC licensed event your dog must be a purebred and registered with the AKC.

All three classes and all levels of competition have one exercise in common and that is heeling. This means that you and Rascal need to have a firm foundation and to keep practicing.

The first class you and Rascal can enter is appropriately called the Novice Class. The required exercises are designed to demonstrate the usefulness of the purebred dog as our companions.

What Is Expected from You and Your Dog

The Novice Class consists of six exercises, each with a specific point value. For a qualifying score you and Rascal have to earn more than 50% of the available points for each exercise and a final score of 170 out of a possible 200.

Required Exercises	Available Points
1. Heel on Leash and Figure 8	40
2. Stand for Examination	30
3. Heel Free	40
4. Recall	30
5. Long Sit	30
6. Long Down	30
Maximum Total Score	200

Doggy Dogma

A qualifying score at an obedience trial is called a *leg*. Your dog needs three *legs* under three different judges to earn the AKC title Companion Dog.

These exercises are always done in the order listed, and they are all pack behavior exercises.

You will notice that the Novice exercises are an extension of those required for the Canine Good Citizen test. But, there are some important differences and additions.

➤ Rascal has to respond to the first command.

➤ Walking on a Loose Leash is now called Heeling and includes a Figure 8; it is also more exacting.

➤ The temperament test requires the dog to stand and is done off leash.

➤ The Heel Free is done off leash.

➤ The Come When Called is now called the Recall. It is done off leash and requires Rascal to come on command, sit in front of you and then go to heel on command.

Tidbits

The Stand for Examination is a form of temperament test similar to the Accepting a Friendly Stranger and the Sitting Politely for Petting in the Canine Good Citizen test.

➤ The Sit and Down-Stay are done off leash for one and three minutes, respectively.

The Novice Class is tailor-made for the dog that is highest in pack drive behaviors. For the dog that is highest in prey drive behaviors, it is a little more difficult because of his distractibility. To help your dog overcome this difficulty you are going to teach him a command that lets him know he has to pay attention to you.

Tidbits

When you look at the Novice Class exercises you will see that 120 points depend on your dog being able to stay—the Stand for Examination, the Recall, and the Sit and Down Stay. So you can see how important that exercise is.

Doggy Dogma

Training collars are used to train your dog and are not permitted at obedience trials. To show your dog in a trial he must wear a well-fitted plain buckle collar, or a slip collar made of leather, fabric, or chain. A slip collar has only two rings and slips over your dog's head.

Are You Ready?

The first exercise in the Novice Class is the Heel on Leash and we like to teach our dogs a command that tells them now the two of us are going to heel together. The command we have chosen is "ready!" Notice that the ready is a command and not a question, and is said in a quiet, yet excited tone of voice, almost a whisper. The reason we have chosen this command is simple. In an obedience trial, the judge will ask you "are you ready?" before he or she gives the order "forward," at which point you give Rascal the command "Rascal, heel!" and start to move.

When the judge asks you the question, naturally you are expected to give some indication that the two of you are ready to go. We use the answer "ready," and Rascal snaps to attention and is all set to go.

No doubt you are wondering by now why all this is necessary when Rascal is supposed to respond to the heel command and move with you when you do. The reason is that you want to make sure Rascal's attention is on you and not something else that may have attracted his attention when you give the heel command. Otherwise, he may just sit there like a bump on a log, totally engrossed in what is going on in the next ring, and while you start to walk, he has to play catch-up.

To avoid this from happening, teach Rascal the ready command. In addition, you are going to decide on your lead-off leg, that is, the one that tells the dog when he is expected to go with you. If you are right handed, you will be more comfortable making your lead-off leg your right, but you can start on either, so long as you are consistent.

Sequence 1—goal: To focus your dog's attention on you.

➤ Put the leash on the live ring of the training collar.

➤ Sit your dog at heel.

➤ Hold the leash in Control Position.

➤ Look at your dog, keeping your left shoulder absolutely straight, and smile.

➤ Say your dog's name and release straight forward.

➤ Release with an enthusiastic "OK" and take five steps straight forward at a trot, keeping your hands in Control Position.

➤ Repeat 10 times.

Sequence 2—goal: To introduce your dog to the ready command.

➤ Start as in Sequence 1.

➤ Quietly and in an excited tone of voice say "ready!"

➤ Say "Rascal, heel," and move out smartly for five paces and release.

➤ Repeat 10 times.

Don't worry about what Rascal is doing. Concentrate on your part, which is making it exciting and fun for your dog, keeping your hands in position, and starting and releasing on the lead-off leg.

Sequence 3—goal: To teach your dog to respond to the ready command.

➤ Start as in Sequence 1.

➤ Quietly and in an excited tone of voice say "ready!"

➤ Say "Rascal, heel," and start at a fast pace as quickly as you can for ten paces and release.

➤ Repeat 10 times.

The first few times you do this, you may feel a little tension on the leash, before Rascal understands you want him to move with you. Do wait until you have finished the command before you start to run. It would hardly be fair to your dog to take off without having told him what you want.

You also need to resist the temptation to let your left hand trail out behind you as you feel a little tension on the leash and to let your left shoulder drop. To prevent this, hook the thumb of your left hand under your waistband and lock it in place, and concentrate on keeping the left shoulder straight.

After four to five tries you will notice that Rascal is actually responding when you say "ready!" and is outrunning you.

Sequence 4—goal: To reward your dog's response.

Not all dogs pick up on this exercise at the same rate of learning. For those that are a little slow, or just to reward those that are doing it, this is a good remedial sequence.

Top Dog Tips

When teaching the ready, hold your hands in Control Position and keep your shoulders absolutely straight. You want to use body language to communicate forward motion to your dog. Dropping your left shoulder or pointing it back communicates just the opposite to your dog.

Top Dog Tips

Wait until you have finished giving the command before you move. Otherwise, you are teaching your dog to move on his name or your motion, not a good idea.

➤ With your dog sitting at heel, neatly fold the leash into your left hand, placed at your belt buckle.

➤ Hold a treat in your right hand and put it at your right side.

➤ Look at your dog, smile and say "ready!"

➤ If he looks at you, tell him how clever he is, give him the treat, and release.

➤ If he doesn't, put the treat in front of his nose and move it in the direction of your face.

➤ When he follows the treat, tell him how clever he is, give him the treat and release.

➤ Repeat until your dog responds without hesitation to the ready command.

Sequence 5—goal: To reinforce the ready command.

There are going to be times when your dog is distracted to such an extent that he will not respond to the treat, much less the command. For those occasions, you need to be able to reinforce the command so that he will learn that when you say the magic word, he has to pay attention no matter what is out there.

Bet You Didn't Know

Nagging your dog with ineffective checks is not a good training technique. Get a response the first time so you can praise and release him. If you repeatedly don't get a response, you are being too feeble or are using the wrong equipment.

➤ Start as in Sequence 1.

➤ Give the ready command.

➤ If he looks up at you expectantly, praise and then release.

➤ If he does not, check in the direction you want him to focus, usually your face. When he looks up, praise and release.

➤ Repeat until he is rock solid on responding to the ready command.

This sequence is the review progression for this exercise.

Sequence 6—goal: To ignore distractions.

You can now start working with a helper who will try to distract your dog. The three main distractions are:

1. Visual, or 1st degree—helper approaches and just stands there.

2. Auditory, or 2nd degree—helper approaches and tries to distract him with "Hello, puppy, want to come and visit?" or whatever comes to mind. The name of the dog is not used.

3. Object of attraction, or 3rd degree—helper approaches and offers him a toy or a treat.

When working on distraction training, have the helper approach your dog at a 45-degree angle and not straight on from the front or the side. The helper starts to approach the dog from 10 feet away and stops 2 feet from the dog.

You set up as in Sequence 1. You give the ready command. Your helper then approaches in a non-threatening manner. If your dog keeps his attention focused on you, praise and release. If he permits himself to become distracted, reinforce, praise, and release.

Practice with 1st degree until your dog ignores the distracter. Then move on to 2nd and 3rd degree, respectively.

Let's Dance—Heeling

Heeling is like dancing with your dog. And, you are going to have to be the leader. If you know anything about dancing, you also know you have the tougher job. The dog will follow only your lead, and you need to give him the necessary cues to change direction or pace.

In Chapter 12 you taught Rascal to heel around distractions and you will need to review that on a frequent basis. In addition, you are going to work on perfecting those turns and changes of pace.

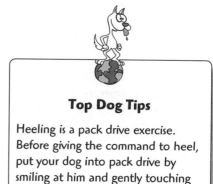

Top Dog Tips

Heeling is a pack drive exercise. Before giving the command to heel, put your dog into pack drive by smiling at him and gently touching him on the side of his face.

Under the AKC Obedience Regulations, the judge will call a heeling pattern for you. The pattern has to include, in addition to normal pace, a fast, a slow, and a right, left, and about turn. That is the bare minimum. A simple heeling pattern might look something like this: forward, fast, normal, left turn, about turn, halt, forward, right turn, slow, normal, about turn, halt.

Tidbits

You can get your own copy of the Obedience Regulations free of charge by contacting the American Kennel Club at 5580 Centerview Drive, Suite 200, Raleigh, NC 27606-3390. It's a good idea to know the rules so you know what is expected from you and your dog.

If you have your dog's attention, and if you don't accidentally confuse him with incorrect cues, everything should go reasonably well. Still, you need to look at each one of these maneuvers as a separate exercise that you and Rascal have to practice. Sort of like the steps of a particular dance.

For the halt, called the automatic sit at heel, put the rings of the training collar on top of your dog's neck. As you come to a halt, check with your left hand straight up. Be careful that you don't inadvertently check toward or across your body as that will cause your dog to sit with his rear end away from you and not in a straight line. It is called the automatic sit because the cue for the dog to sit is that you stop. Under the Obedience Regulations, you are not permitted to use a command or signal to sit. The dog has to do it on his own.

Practice 2 or 3 automatic sits with a check and then try 1 without a check. Your dog will immediately tell you where you stand with that exercise.

For the changes of pace and turns, we train the dog to take his cue from the lead-off leg. We are going to use three techniques to teach him this concept.

1. The Release.
2. An Object of Attraction, which can be a treat or favorite toy.
3. A Check.

Here is an example: You want to teach the dog to stay with you as you change pace from slow to normal.

First, release your dog from a slow walk on your lead-off leg. The idea is to get your dog all excited about accelerating with you from slow to normal.

Second, as you go from slow to normal, use a treat to draw the dog forward as the lead-off leg makes the transition. The leash is held in the left hand and the treat in the right. Show the dog the treat just as you are about to make the change and draw him forward with your right hand as the lead-off leg accelerates into normal.

Third, hold the leash in Control Position and give a little check straight forward at the same time as the lead-off leg makes the transition. The check teaches your dog that ultimately it is his responsibility, on or off leash, to accelerate when you change pace.

Assume that over the course of two or three training sessions you are going to practice this component of heeling 10 times. Out of those 10 repetitions, 4 should be done with a release, 4 with a treat, and only 2 with a check. This is the general rule for any exercise for which you would use these techniques, although your dog's Personality Profile may call for a slightly different mix.

When making turns, keep your feet together so your dog can keep up with you. For the right and about turn Rascal needs to learn to accelerate and to stay close to your side as you make the turn. You can do this by using:

1. the release as you come out of the turn,

2. a treat to guide him around the turn, and

3. a little check coming out of the turn.

When you use a treat,

➤ neatly fold the leash into your left hand and place it against your right hip—this will keep your shoulder facing in the right direction;

➤ hold the treat in your right hand at your side;

➤ just before you make the turn, show your dog the treat and use it to guide him around the turn.

Hold the treat as close to your left leg as you can so your dog learns to make nice tight turns.

For the left turn, Rascal first needs to slow down so you don't trip over him and then accelerate again. Draw back on the leash just before you make the turn, and then use the same techniques as you did for the right and about turns.

Once a week you will want to test your dog's understanding of heeling by doing a little pattern with him, similar to what you would perform in the ring. In the ring you are not allowed to check your dog and there can be no tension on the leash. The only true test is when your dog is off leash, but using Umbilical Cord or Show Position will also give you a good idea of what you need to practice. For Show Position, neatly fold the leash into your left hand and place it at your belt buckle, allowing anywhere from three to eight inches of slack, depending on the size of the dog.

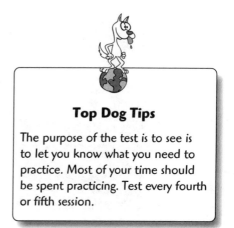

The following chart tells you how to practice the different component parts of heeling. The column "Responses you may see" alerts you to what to watch for so you can work on it in your training. If you need to check your dog, release after the check. When your dog is doing it correctly, or is trying, be sure to reward him with a treat or praise.

> **Tidbits**
>
> A minimum of 1/3 of your repetitions of any of the heeling components should include the release and another third, a treat.

> **Top Dog Tips**
>
> The purpose of the test is to see is to let you know what you need to practice. Most of your time should be spent practicing. Test every fourth or fifth session.

For Show Position, fold the leash into your left hand and place it at your belt buckle.

Component	Dog's responsibility	You have to practice	Responses you may see
Start	Accelerate	Fast starts	Slow start, lags behind
Normal pace	Normal pace	Straight line or large circle. If dog is distracted, check and release.	Lags or forges, crowds or goes wide, sniffs or becomes distracted (prey drive)
Halt	Decelerate	Check into sit, then release.	Forges ahead, sits crooked
Normal to slow Fast to normal	Decelerate	Draw back on the leash as you slow down.	Crowds, forges ahead
Slow to normal Normal to fast Right turn About turn	Accelerate	Alternate between release, treat and check.	Lags, goes wide
Left turn	Decelerate	Draw back on the leash.	Forges or crowds, then lags, goes wide
	Accelerate	Alternate between release, treat and check.	

Let's Do the Twist—The Figure 8

The Figure 8 is a fun exercise. In the ring it is done around two people, called stewards, standing 8 feet apart, and who act as posts. You and your dog start about equidistant from the two posts and walk twice completely around and between them. In practice, you can use chairs as posts. In order to stay in heel position, your dog has to speed up on the outside turn and to slow down on the inside turn, while you maintain an even brisk pace throughout.

Until your dog has learned this exercise, he will have a tendency to forge or crowd on the inside turn and to lag or go wide on the outside turn. In teaching this exercise, you will use your body as your main communication tool. By rotating the upper part of your body back toward your dog, or forward away from your dog, you will cause him to slow down or speed up, respectively. Your left shoulder will be the cue for your dog, indicating what you want him to do. When the left shoulder points back, your dog will slow down; when it points forward, he will speed up. Just as dogs communicate with each other through body language, so can you.

Let's do the twist—practice doing the Figure 8 around two chairs.

Go ahead and try it. It's almost the same motion as the twist, only from the waist up. Rotate the upper part of your body first to the left and then the right. This is the motion you will use to control your dog's momentum.

Sequence 1—goal: To teach your dog to slow down on the inside turn and to speed up on the outside turn.

Tidbits

One lament we frequently hear is "He does fine at home, but take him anywhere and forget it!" Make it a point to seek out new locations, at first without and then with distractions to see how Rascal does. Use your review progressions in new locations before you expect him to do it correctly.

The inside turn:

➤ Start with your dog sitting at heel, leash in Control Position.

➤ Say "Rascal, heel" and walk a circle to the left, about 4 feet in diameter, at a slow pace.

➤ Twist to the left as you walk.

➤ Release your dog after you have completed the circle.

After 2 or 3 tries you will notice how your dog responds to your body cues. If nothing happens, exaggerate your body motion.

The outside turn:

➤ Start with your dog sitting at heel, with the leash neatly folded into your left hand.

➤ Put your left hand against your right hip. This will keep your left shoulder facing forward.

➤ Have a treat in your right hand.

➤ Say "Rascal, heel" and walk in a circle to the right, about 4 feet in diameter, at your normal brisk pace.

➤ Use the treat, which is held just in front of his nose, to guide your dog around, and give him the treat after you have completed the circle.

You are looking for a visible effort on the part of your dog to accelerate. Repeat several times so you become comfortable with the maneuver. Then try going at a trot.

Sequence 2—goal: To teach your dog the Figure 8. This is the review progression for this exercise.

➤ Place two chairs about 12 feet apart.

➤ Start with your dog sitting at heel, 2 feet from the center line, equidistant between the chairs.

➤ Neatly fold the leash into your left hand and place it against your belt buckle, and hold a treat in your right hand.

➤ Say "Rascal, heel" and start to walk at a slow pace around the chair on your left, rotating the upper part of your body to the left.

➤ When you get to the center between the two chairs, show your dog the treat and guide him around the chair on your right at a trot, keeping you left shoulder facing forward.

➤ Stop at the center and sit your dog. Praise and release.

Your success in keeping Rascal at heel position without crowding or lagging depends on how well you use your shoulders to communicate with him.

Sequence 3—goal: The perfect Figure 8.

➤ Practice the review progression making 2 complete Figure 8s.

➤ Start from the center and complete 1 Figure 8 at normal pace, using your shoulders to cue your dog. Stop and sit your dog. Repeat the review progression often to maintain your dog's enthusiasm.

Doggy Dogma

The Obedience Regulations are quite specific about the position of your hands. For heeling on leash, you can hold the leash in either hand, or in both, provided they are in a natural position. For the Heel Free, the hands can hang naturally at your side, or you can move the right hand and arm naturally at your side and place the left hand against your belt buckle, which is the position we use.

Top Dog Tips

Hold the treat at your right side and out of Rascal's sight until you get to the center and want him to speed up. Then hold it as close as you can to your left leg so he learns to stay close to your side. Don't show it to him on the inside turn, or he will try to get to the treat instead of slowing down.

225

➤ Over the course of several sessions, put the chairs closer together in 1-foot increments until they are 8 feet apart.

➤ Do a Figure 8 with Umbilical Cord concentrating on the direction of your shoulders. Keep your left hand on your belt buckle.

➤ Do a Figure 8 off leash.

Although in the Novice Class the Figure 8 is done on leash, practicing it off leash is a good test. You will quickly see where he needs more practice. At one point or another, you may have to use a little check going into the outside turn to impress upon Rascal how important it is to you that he speed up.

In the next chapter, we'll discuss the remaining exercises required for the Companion Dog title.

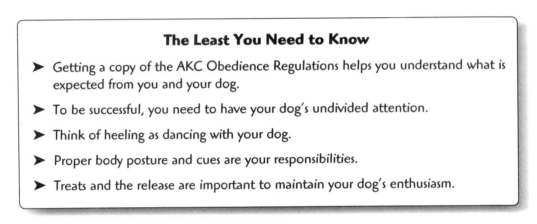

The Least You Need to Know

➤ Getting a copy of the AKC Obedience Regulations helps you understand what is expected from you and your dog.

➤ To be successful, you need to have your dog's undivided attention.

➤ Think of heeling as dancing with your dog.

➤ Proper body posture and cues are your responsibilities.

➤ Treats and the release are important to maintain your dog's enthusiasm.

The Companion Dog

The remainder of the exercises for the Companion Dog title are the:

➤ Stand for Examination

➤ Recall

➤ Group Exercises

The Stand for Examination

While the Stand for Examination is a requirement for the Novice Class, it is also a practical and useful command to teach your dog. It is certainly a lot easier brushing, grooming, and wiping feet, as well as visiting the veterinarian with a dog that has been trained to stand still than with one that is in perpetual motion.

Tidbits

During a training session, practice different exercises and vary the order. Start with some brisk heeling as a warm-up, including fast starts and changes of pace. Keep it interesting and fun for both of you.

Top Dog Tips

When you put Rascal into a stand, watch his front feet—they should remain in place and not move forward. You can lock them in place by applying a little downward pressure on the collar as you stand him.

In the ring it looks something like this: You will give your leash to the steward. Then the judge will say "stand your dog and leave when you are ready." You stand your dog in heel position, say "stay," and walk 6 feet straight forward in front of your dog, turn around and stand facing the dog. The judge will approach your dog from in front, and with one hand touch your dog's head, body, and hindquarters. The judge then says "back to your dog," whereupon you will walk around behind your dog and return to the heel position.

When you begin teaching this exercise to your dog, you can either stand, or kneel on your right or both knees, or have the dog on a table, depending on his size. What you want to avoid is leaning over him because if you do, he will want to move away from you, especially if he is low in defense fight behaviors.

Sequence 1—goal: To teach your dog the command.

➤ Start with Rascal sitting at your left side, off leash, both of you facing in the same direction with your shoulders square and not turned toward him.

➤ Put the thumb of your right hand in the collar under his chin, fingers pointing to the floor, palm open and flat against his chest.

➤ Apply a little downward pressure on the collar, say "stand" and at the same time apply backward pressure on his stifles with the back of your left hand.

➤ Keep both hands still and in place, the right through the collar and the left against his stifles. Count to 10, praise and release.

➤ Repeat 3 to 5 times per session, over the course of several sessions.

Sequence 2—goal: To teach Rascal to stand still.

➤ Place your dog into a stand as in Sequence 1.

➤ With both hands on your dog keep him standing still to the count of 30.

➤ Over the course of several sessions increase the time you keep him standing still to one minute.

Notice the position of the handler's hands as she teaches the dog to stand.

Sequence 3—goal: Your dog stands still without you holding him in position.

➤ Stand Rascal as in Sequence 1.

➤ Take away your left hand.

➤ Count to 30, then praise and release.

➤ If he moves, reposition him.

➤ When he is steady without you holding on to him with your left hand, take your right hand out of the collar. This may take several sessions.

Sequence 4—goal: To teach Rascal the stand and stay.

➤ Stand your dog as in Sequence 1.

➤ Take both hands off, stand up, keeping your shoulders square.

➤ Signal and say "stay."

➤ Count to 30, then praise and release.

➤ Practice until you can stand next to him for one minute without him moving.

Top Dog Tips

Remember, praise is verbal and not petting. When you praise Rascal, be sure he remains in position. Praise tells him he is doing it correctly; it is not an invitation to move. Don't confuse verbal praise with the release.

229

Sequence 5—goal: To leave Rascal on a stand-stay.

➤ Stand next to your sitting dog.

➤ Put your the thumb of your right hand through the collar as in Sequence 1. Depending on the size of your dog, you may have to bend at the knees to avoid leaning over him.

➤ With a little downward pressure on the collar, say "stand." He should now stand without you having to touch his stifles.

➤ Take your right hand out of the collar and stand up straight.

➤ Say "stay" and step directly in front of him.

➤ Count to 30, step back to heel position, praise, and release.

➤ If he moves, reposition him.

➤ Gradually increase the distance you leave him to 6 feet in front.

➤ From now on when you leave him, go 6 feet straight forward, turn and face him—do not back away from him—count to 30, go back, praise, and release.

Sequence 6—goal: Teaching the return behind your dog.

➤ Stand your dog and go 6 feet in front.

➤ Go back to your dog and put two fingers of your left hand on his withers (the highest part of the back at the base of the neck) to steady him, and walk around behind him to heel position. Pause, making sure he doesn't move, praise, and release.

➤ When he understands that you are going to come around behind him, eliminate touching him as you return to heel position.

Sequence 7—goal: Teaching Rascal the examination.

For this sequence you need a helper who can be a member of the family. Eventually, however, Rascal will have to be examined by a stranger, and as the judge can be either male or female you will need to practice with both men and women. To introduce your dog to this exercise, start with the sit for examination, which is almost identical to the Sitting Politely for Petting in the Canine Good Citizen test.

➤ Put the rings of the collar on top of the dog's neck.

➤ Attach your leash to the live ring of the collar.

➤ Sit your dog at heel position.

➤ Neatly fold the leash into your left hand and hold it above his head and say "stay."

➤ Have your helper approach and offer your dog the palm of his or her hand.

➤ If Rascal tries to say hello to the helper, reinforce the stay command with a check straight up.

➤ Have your helper lightly touch Rascal's head and back. Praise and release. Repeat until he readily permits the examination. Practice this examination over the course of several sessions.

➤ Repeat this maneuver with your dog standing at heel, then with you standing directly in front, then 3 feet in front, and finally 6 feet in front.

When Rascal has mastered that part, follow the same progressions off leash. Congratulations!

Doggy Dogma

Dog shows are held either indoors or outdoors and in all kinds of weather conditions. If it is outdoors and it's raining, the judge will have on rain gear, something your dog may not have experienced before. Don't be caught unprepared—practice under those conditions.

The Recall

The recall is different from a traditional "come" where all you are concerned about is the dog coming to you. It consists of four components.

1. Stay
2. Come
3. Front
4. Finish

Top Dog Tips

Before every exercise, the judge will ask you "are you ready?" We answer with "ready" for the heeling exercises and "yes" for everything else.

The recall is performed from one end of the ring to the other. The judge will tell you to leave your dog on a sit-stay and to go to the other side of the ring. He or she will then tell you to call your dog. You give the come command, Rascal comes and is expected to sit directly in front of you. The judge then says "finish" and you say "Rascal, heel," and Rascal goes to heel position.

The Come with Distractions

Even though Rascal already knows the come command, you still need to work on distraction training for which you need a helper. Leave Rascal on a sit-stay and go 20 feet in front. Have your helper position him or herself equidistant between you and Rascal, about 2 feet from Rascal's anticipated line of travel. Facing Rascal, the helper crouches and smiles.

Doggy Dogma

The release backwards is used any time you want to encourage the dog when he is coming toward you. Lean backwards, throw up your hands invitingly and take a few steps back with an enthusiastic "OK."

Call your dog and as he passes the distracter, release backwards with an enthusiastic "OK," and give him a treat when he gets to you. If he goes to the distracter, smile and very slowly approach Rascal, put the leash on the dead ring of the training collar and with a little tension on the leash show him exactly what he should have done by trotting backwards to the spot where you called him. Praise and release backwards. You may have to show him a few times until he catches on. Once he is successful, stop for that session.

Should he veer from the distracter, use two distracters, separated by about 10 feet, and teach him to come between them. As Rascal progresses in his training, work your way through 2nd and 3rd degree distractions.

Now all that is left for the recall is the front and the finish. The object of both is to teach the dog a position, and both exercises can be practiced inside in the form of a game.

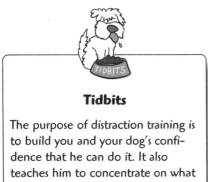

Tidbits

The purpose of distraction training is to build you and your dog's confidence that he can do it. It also teaches him to concentrate on what he is supposed to do. If at any time you feel it is too much for him, stop. Come back to it at another session.

The Front

The front is similar to the automatic sit at heel in that the dog is supposed to come to you and sit in front without a command to sit. We like to use a chute to teach the dog exactly where we want him to sit when he comes to us. For a chute we use plastic rain gutters, commensurate to the size of your dog. They should be about as long as your dog. Place them on the ground, just far enough apart so your dog can sit comfortably in between.

Sequence 1—goal: To get Rascal used to the chute.

➤ Place the chute on the ground.

➤ Walk your dog through the chute a few times.

➤ Heel your dog into the chute and have him sit in it.

➤ Repeat until he readily sits in the chute.

Sequence 2—goal: Teaching your dog to come into the chute.

➤ Heel your dog up to the chute and tell him to stay.

➤ Walk through the chute and face your dog.

➤ Hold a treat in both hands below your waist.

➤ Call your dog and as he comes bring your hands to your waist using the treat to make him sit.

➤ Give him the treat, praise, and release backwards.

➤ Practice this sequence about 5 times.

➤ When he understands this part, leave him on a stay 3 feet from the entrance of the chute and call him.

➤ Increase the distance you leave him facing the entrance of the chute in 2-foot increments until he is 35 feet from the entrance.

You want to teach Rascal to sit as close as possible in front of you without touching you. Using treats you can practice this inside without the chute. Call him to you and use your treat to make him sit. Only give him the treat when he sits straight. If he doesn't, try again.

Ultimately, he has to sit in front of you with your hands hanging naturally at your side, so you need to wean him from having your hands in front of you. You can still reward him in practice when he does it correctly.

The Finish

After your dog has come to you and sat in front, the judge will say "finish." You say "Rascal, heel" and your dog goes to heel position. He can go either to the left or to the right. We like to teach both, just to keep the dog guessing. For the finish to the left, we use the command "heel," and for the finish to the right "place." Actually, we prefer giving a signal because a signal is more readily understood by the dog than a command, and more clearly indicates to the dog the way we want him to go.

> **Top Dog Tips**
>
> When practicing the front keep the upper part of your body erect. If you lean over or toward your dog, he will not come in close enough. If you need to get down to his level, bend at the knees.

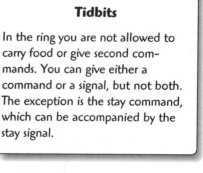

> **Tidbits**
>
> In the ring you are not allowed to carry food or give second commands. You can give either a command or a signal, but not both. The exception is the stay command, which can be accompanied by the stay signal.

Sequence 1—goal: To introduce Rascal to the finish to the left.

➤ Sit your dog at heel, say "stay," and step directly in front of him.

➤ Say "Rascal, heel." Take a step back on your left leg, keeping the right leg firmly planted in place, as you guide him with a treat held in your left hand in a semicircle into heel position. Make the semicircle large enough so he winds up in the correct position. His head has to pass your knee so he can make the turn.

➤ Give him the treat, praise, and release.

➤ Repeat until he enthusiastically and briskly goes to heel.

You will quickly see that the guidance of your left hand becomes his signal to go to heel.

Top Dog Tips

Any time we want the dog to move, we use his name before the command. For example, "Rascal, come." Any time we don't want him to move, we eliminate the name. For example, "stay." We have no idea how much difference it makes to the dog, but it makes us feel better.

Sequence 2—goal: To teach Rascal to finish on command or signal.

➤ Put the leash on the live ring of the training collar.

➤ Neatly fold the leash into your left hand.

➤ Step in front and say "Rascal, heel," and step back on your left leg, using the leash to guide him into heel position.

➤ Reward him with a treat, praise, and release.

➤ Practice until he goes to heel without any tension on the leash.

You can now eliminate the step back on the left leg and experiment using either the command or signal. The signal is the same guiding motion you used in Sequence 1.

The finish to the right uses the same progressions except you step back on the right leg and guide Rascal around behind you into heel position. When you are using a treat, you have to switch it behind your back from the right hand into the left. The same applies to the leash.

Your dog's response to this exercise will tell you which direction is better for him. As a general rule, a long-bodied dog will do better going to the right.

The Group Exercises

The Group Exercises are the last part of the test. They consist of a long sit and a long down for one and three minutes, respectively, and are done off leash in a group not to exceed 12 dogs. The judge will tell where to line up the dogs in the ring, then tell you to leave, and return when the requisite amount of time has expired. When you return you have to walk around behind your dog to heel position.

Look at the stay exercises from the perspective of time and distance. Teach Rascal to stay in place for a specific period of time with you about 3 feet in front. Then, the first time you increase the distance from your dog, decrease the time you are away from him.

Although you can give a command and/or signal for any stay exercise, your dog's Personality Profile will influence whether you want to use a signal. Any stay is a pack drive exercise so you want your dog in pack drive. For dogs low in defense fight behaviors, a stay signal puts them into defense drive where they are uncomfortable. It may cause the dog to break the stay and come to you, or to whine and fidget.

Rascal already knows the basics of the sit and down-stay. You do need to fill in the missing pieces, which are practicing:

➤ with distractions

➤ off leash

➤ at the right distance

➤ the requisite length of time plus one minute

➤ different locations and surfaces

The review progression for any stay is the sit-stay test.

Tidbits

Whenever you approach your dog, do so in a non-threatening manner so he does not become anxious. Your dog should never become frightened when you approach him.

Doggy Dogma

When you are training your dog, change only one variable at a time. When teaching a stay, for example, you can change the distance or the time, but not both together. Increase one and when Rascal is steady, the other.

Introducing Self-generated Distractions

Put the leash on the live ring of the collar, rings under his chin, say and signal "stay," and step 3 feet in front. Place your left hand against your belt buckle and hold your right hand ready to reinforce. Jump to the right, the middle, the left, the middle, forward, and backward. Any time Rascal wants to move, reinforce the stay. How vigorously you do these distractions depends on Rascal's Profile and your physical condition.

Bet You Didn't Know

If you have a dog that appears to be purebred but you don't have papers for him, you may be able to get an Indefinite Listing Privilege (ILP) number from the AKC that permits you to participate in obedience trials.

As he learns, add clapping and cheering. Periodically review the distraction training you did previously.

Increasing the Level of Difficulty

Practice with self-generated distractions off leash from about 3 feet, and then 6 feet in front of Rascal.

When Rascal is off leash and you need to reinforce the stay, slowly approach him, and put him back by placing two fingers of each hand through the collar at the side of his neck. If he is coming to you, put him back from in front, that is, guide him back to the spot where you left him in such a way that you are facing him when you reinforce the stay. The command is not repeated.

You also need to practice the down-stay using the same distractions, on and off leash.

These dogs show how to sit-stay with distractions.

Gradually increase the time to two minutes for the sit-stay, and four minutes for the down-stay. These are boring, though practical exercises for both you and your dog. There is usually no need to practice these every session, and once or twice a week will do. Afterward, reward your dog with something he enjoys.

When Rascal stays for the requisite length of time, gradually increase the distance you are away from him to 35 feet. All of this should go quickly since this is not a new exercise for him. Finally, you need to practice in different locations and on different surfaces.

The Yo-yo Game

Some handlers have taught their dogs, or vice versa, what we call the yo-yo game. It goes something like this:

➤ Rascal is on a sit-stay with his handler standing 30 feet away.

➤ Rascal lies down and handler approaches to reinforce the Stay.

➤ Rascal sits up by himself and handler retreats.

This scenario can, and often does, deteriorate into the yo-yo game. Rascal lies down, handler approaches, Rascal sits up, handler retreats, with Rascal not having learned a blessed thing, except perhaps the rules of the game and trying to figure out how many times he can play it.

Moral of the story: When you make a move, any move, to reinforce a command, any command, you must follow through, even if Rascal corrects himself before you have had a chance to reinforce the command. But always do it with a smile.

The Least You Need to Know

➤ The Stand for Examination is a test of your dog's temperament and his willingness to be touched by a stranger.

➤ The release backwards is used any time you want to encourage your dog when he is coming toward you.

➤ You need to practice with distractions to build your and your dog's confidence, and so that he learns to concentrate on what he is doing.

➤ When you make a move to reinforce a command you must follow through, no matter what the dog does.

Chapter 18

The Companion Dog Excellent

After you have obtained your Companion Dog title you are eligible to enter the Open Class and compete for the Companion Dog Excellent title.

While the Novice Class is tailor-made for the dog highest in pack behaviors, the Open Class is for the dog that also has many prey behaviors.

Required Exercises	Points	Behavior/Drive
1. Heel Free and Figure 8	40	Pack
2. Drop on Recall	30	Pack
3. Retrieve on Flat	20	Prey
4. Retrieve over High Jump	30	Prey
5. Broad Jump	20	Prey
6. Long Sit	30	Pack
7. Long Down	30	Pack
Maximum Total Score	200	

All the exercises are done off leash, and the Group Exercises (Long Sit and Down) are performed with handlers out of sight of the dogs for three and five minutes, respectively. For your dog, the Open Class is the most exciting of the classes.

Bet You Didn't Know

The first obedience trials held under the auspices of the American Kennel Club took place in 1936. The classes were the same as today, but the requirements varied somewhat. For example, the Open Class included "The Speak on Command." Contrary to popular belief, not all dogs are instinctive barkers, and the exercise was subsequently eliminated.

You can either buy the equipment you will need for the Open Class, or you can make it yourself. The specifications are contained in the AKC Obedience Regulations.

Heel Free and Figure 8

What you have no doubt discovered by now is that heeling is not as simple as it looks. You certainly need to keep practicing on a regular basis. Here is food for thought: Heeling is the only exercise that is done as a team; all the other exercises the dog does on his own. Yet, it is with heeling that many handlers have a hard time: Makes you wonder, doesn't it?

Drop on Recall

The Drop on Recall is a combination of the come and the down. As your dog is coming to you, you tell him to lie down and then you call him again. The exercise starts as a recall, except that after you have called your dog, the judge will indicate for you to give the down command or signal, and then for you to call again. The command sequence goes "Rascal, come," "down," "Rascal, come." The dog has to remain in the down position until called. The front and finish are also part of the exercise.

By now, Rascal certainly knows the down and come commands, and the only really new concept he has to learn is to stop immediately the command is given.

Tidbits

Many of us are blissfully unaware of our own body motions. Because they are so important to success in training, it helps to have someone else watch us and then tell us what we are doing. Better yet, we occasionally videotape each other.

Sequence 1—goal: Down on command.

Test Rascal's understanding of the down command. With Rascal sitting at heel and without giving him any visual cues such as pointing to the ground, bobbing your head, leaning over or bending your knees, quietly say "down." If he lies down, praise, count to five and release.

You may not be aware of the visual cues you are giving your dog. Make sure you are not inadvertently moving some part of your body, even as much as a finger, and that you are facing straight forward. You may want to have someone watch you, or stand in front of a mirror and watch yourself.

If Rascal does not respond to the command, or his response is unacceptable, such as not prompt enough, slowly slide your left hand down the leash all the way to the snap and check straight down. Keep your elbow locked and your arm at your side. Avoid checking across your body as that will teach Rascal to curl in front of you. Stand up, count to five, praise, and release. Repeat until your dog lies down on command at your side. This is the review progression for this exercise.

When you are trying to decide what is an unacceptable response, keep in mind that your dog's size and structure determine how he performs this exercise. Some dogs are structurally unable to lie down without first going into the sitting position. Others can only lie on one side or the other, but not square, which is the ideal.

Sequence 2—goal: Response to the down command in motion. Rascal has to learn to respond promptly to the down command while he is in motion.

With Rascal sitting at heel, say "let's go" and start to walk. The heel command is not used because this is not a heeling exercise. After several steps, say "down" as you come to a halt.

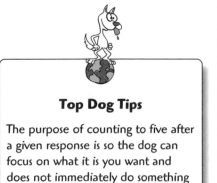

Praise when he does it, count to five and then release straight forward. The release here is the beginning of teaching Rascal to move briskly forward from the down position.

If he does not drop, slowly slide the left hand down the leash to the snap and check straight down, praise and release. Count to five between your praise and the release.

Sequence 3—goal: Down at side from motion, handler continues.

Before you try Sequence 3, review Sequences 1 and 2. Say "let's go" and after having walked for several steps, say "down" and continue walking to the end of the leash, turn to face Rascal, praise, count to five, and release backward. When you release him, remember you are teaching him to come briskly to you after you have dropped him.

If Rascal does not drop, start again. As you give the command, slowly slide your left hand down the leash to the snap and check straight down, then go to the end of the leash, turn, praise, pause, and release. When he responds reliably, go on to the next progression.

Sequence 4—goal: Down from a fast, handler continues.

Before you try Sequence 4, review Sequences 1 and 3. Now, visualize how your dog comes to you on a recall. It is at that speed that he will have to drop on command and without any unnecessary steps. While you may not be able to run as quickly as he can, teach him to drop from a fast pace as you continue to the end of the leash.

Sequence 5—goal: Teaching Rascal to stop and drop from in front.

When Rascal has mastered the drop from a fast, you are ready to try the exercise with him coming toward you. Leave him on a sit-stay and go to the end of the leash, facing him. Call with "Rascal, come" and as he comes to you, take a step toward him on your right foot, keeping the left foot in place, signal by bringing your right arm straight up and say "down." Keep the upper part of your body straight. Stepping toward Rascal will cause him to stop his forward progress.

After he has dropped, bring the right foot back, lower your arm, praise, count to five, and release. Use the release backward to teach him to come again quickly and enthusiastically after you have dropped him. If Rascal does not drop, review Sequence 1 with a check and Sequence 4, then try it again.

A word of caution: Once Rascal is coming toward you, do not check him into a down, or do anything else he may perceive as unpleasant, because it will slow down his recall. What is important here is your dog's view of what is unpleasant and not yours. If he does not drop, or the drop is unacceptable, review the prior sequences from the side.

Bet You Didn't Know

The first obedience test was held in 1933 and consisted of what are now the Open Class exercises. For the Retrieve on the Flat the dumbbell weighed two pounds, the Retrieve over the High Jump was a 3' 6" obstacle, and the dumbbell weighed eight to 10 ounces. The Broad Jump was six feet wide.

Sequence 6—goal: Teaching Rascal to stop and drop from in front, off leash.

Repeat Sequence 5 off leash. You may want to review Sequence 1 with a little check before you try this. As Rascal responds, gradually increase the distance between you and him.

Maintain the "step, command & signal" sequence until he is reliable. After that, first eliminate the step, and then decide whether you prefer voice or signal. You will probably want him to respond to either.

Sequence 7—goal: Teaching Rascal to ignore distractions.

Begin by having a distracter crouch about 2 feet from Rascal's line of travel and where you intend to drop him. Call and give him the command or signal to drop.

He may do one of several things:

➤ anticipate the drop, that is, slow down or drop before you have given the command or signal

➤ drop after he has gone past the distracter

➤ not drop at all

➤ avoid the distracter by arcing away from him or her

➤ not respond to the come command

➤ actually do it correctly—not likely the first time you try this.

1. Rascal anticipates the drop.

   Slowly go to him without saying anything, put the leash on the dead ring of the collar and with a little tension on the collar show him exactly what he should have done by guiding him backward to the spot where you called. Have Rascal sit in front, praise, and release backwards. No extra command is given.

2. Rascal drops past the distracter or does not drop at all. Slowly approach him without saying anything, put two fingers of your left hand, palm facing you,

243

Top Dog Tips

Avoid having Rascal anticipating the drop by randomly alternating between straight recalls and drop on recalls.

through the collar, back to front, at the side of his neck, take him to the spot where he should have dropped and reinforce the command from in front. The command is not repeated. Praise your dog, count to five, and enthusiastically release backwards.

What Rascal is telling you is that he lacks the confidence to drop near the distracter and it is your job to show him that he can do it. His confidence will increase with each successive correct repetition.

3. Rascal arcs away from the distracter. Use two distracters, facing each other about eight feet apart, and teach Rascal to drop between the distracters.

Rascal may also start to anticipate the come from the down. If he does, you should slowly approach your dog without saying anything, put two fingers of your left hand, palm facing you, through the collar, back to front, at the side of his neck, take him back to the spot where he should have stayed and reinforce the down from in front. Do not repeat the command. Praise, count to five, and enthusiastically release backwards.

As Rascal gains confidence and responds correctly, work your way through the different levels of distractions. Since you have already trained him to ignore these distractions for the Novice recall, it will not take him very long to figure out what you want.

At some point you will have to decide whether to use a signal or a command to drop him because you can't use both. Experiment with Rascal to decide whether you should use a signal or a command when in the ring. Rascal's Profile should help you with your decision. If he is weak in Defense (fight), you will be better off using the command rather than the signal. If he is high in prey behaviors, you will be more successful with a signal.

Retrieve on the Flat

For this exercise, the judge will tell you to throw the dumbbell and then send your dog who is expected to retrieve the dumbbell, present to front, give up the dumbbell on command, and then finish on command. Your command sequence is "stay," "take it," "give," and "Rascal, heel." Rascal must do all the other parts of this on his own.

Teaching the retrieve has been discussed in Chapter 13. Many dogs retrieve without having been formally taught. This is called a play retrieve. If you have done your distraction training, your dog will have shown you whether you can rely on his cooperation. Ask yourself: "Is he retrieving for me or for himself?" For greater reliability, teach him to retrieve for you.

You also may need to review the teaching progressions for the front while he is holding the dumbbell. For your dog, a front with the dumbbell is not the same exercise as a front without a dumbbell. It becomes a new exercise.

How quickly Rascal will generalize the front while carrying the dumbbell will depend on the extent to which the exercise is in harmony with his instincts. Retrievers do it almost automatically, whereas other breeds may need a few repetitions.

Retrieve Over the High Jump

The principal features of this exercise are that your dog jumps over the jump, picks up the dumbbell and promptly returns with it over the jump. The judge's commands are "throw the dumbbell," "send your dog," "take it," and "finish." Your commands to Rascal are "stay," "jump," "give," and "Rascal, heel."

To teach this exercise to your dog we are going to introduce you to the concept of target training. As the name implies, we teach the dog to go to a target. Once your dog has learned that, you can then place a jump or other obstacle between your dog and the target. In order to get to the target, the dog has to jump the obstacle.

Tidbits

Anytime you change the content or the complexity of an exercise, it becomes a new exercise for the dog and you will have to go back to the teaching progressions. If he was bred to do it, he should learn quickly. If he was not bred to do it, it will take longer.

Doggy Dogma

We have produced a videotape called "The Motivational Retrieve—Teaching, Practicing, Testing." For information on how to obtain this tape, see Appendix A.

A good way to prepare for the Open Class is to practice retrieving with distractions.

Target Training

The principle is simple, as is the execution. Place a target on the ground, 3 feet in front of you and Rascal, put a treat on the target and send Rascal to the target. The target can be a paper plate, a wooden disk, a square piece of wood, or anything else suitable.

Make it fun and exciting for your dog by using several targets, with the objective that he goes where you tell him to. The progressions are as follows:

➤ Get your dog's attention on the treat, go to the target, say "out," place the treat on the target and let your dog pick up the treat. Repeat 3 times.

➤ Start 3 feet from the target, say "stay," place the treat on the target, go back to your dog, and say "out" as you motion with your left arm and hand in the direction of the target. Praise him when he gets there and call him back to you. Repeat 3 times.

➤ Over the course of several sessions, increase the distance from the target to 50 feet in increments of 2 feet.

➤ Have a helper place a treat and send your dog.

This is an exciting exercise for your dog, especially if he is high in prey behaviors. How many repetitions your dog will perform depends on his Personality Profile and the number of prey behaviors he has.

Sequences to Teach the Retrieve Over the High Jump

Sequence 1—goal: To get your dog accustomed to the jump.

Put your leash on the dead ring of Rascal's training collar and walk him up to the jump, set at teaching height (the dog's height at the elbows). Touch the top board with your left hand and let him examine the jump. Step over the jump and encourage him to follow. You can use a treat to get him to go over. Repeat 3 times or until he goes over the jump without hesitation.

Sequence 2—goal: To teach your dog to jump on his own.

Sit Rascal 3 feet from the center of the jump. Put his target 3 feet from the jump on the other side. Say "stay," step over the jump, place a treat on the target, go back to your dog and send him with "out."

You can also stay with the target, tap it with your fingers and call him over the jump. Repeat until Rascal is comfortable going over the jump.

Repeat five to 10 times per session. Jumping repetitions are necessary not only to teach Rascal the exercise, but to condition him physically as well.

Sequence 3—goal: Dog jumps by himself and from different angles.

Leave Rascal 10 feet from the jump, go to the other side by stepping over the jump, focus his attention on the center of the top board, take three steps backward, pause, and say "Rascal, jump." It is not a good idea to tap the top board as you say "jump," because it teaches your dog to jump on a visual cue instead of on the command. Once you see that he has committed himself to jump, back up to give him enough room to land. Praise as he lands and release backward, giving him a treat.

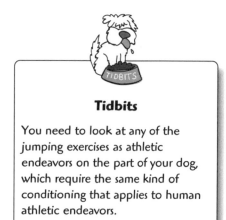

Tidbits

You need to look at any of the jumping exercises as athletic endeavors on the part of your dog, which require the same kind of conditioning that applies to human athletic endeavors.

Few of us can throw the dumbbell so that it always lands in the right spot, and some of us never get it there. So you might as well teach your dog to jump from different angles. Leave Rascal facing the right upright of the jump, 10 feet away, go to the other side by stepping over the jump, focus his attention on the center of the top board, take three steps backward, pause, and say "Rascal, jump."

Sequence 4—goal: Dog jumps while holding the dumbbell.

Repeat Sequence 3 with Rascal holding his dumbbell as he jumps. Here you are teaching the "return over the jump" part of the exercise, which, like any other part of an exercise, has to be taught.

Sequence 5—goal: Teaching the "Motivational Retrieve."

With Rascal at heel, put two fingers of your left hand, palm facing you, through your dog's collar at the side of his neck, back to front. Hold the dumbbell in your right hand and get him excited about retrieving the dumbbell. From 10 feet, say "Rascal, jump" and briskly approach the jump. Two feet before you get to the jump, throw the dumbbell and let go of your dog. Continue to approach the jump, and as he picks up the dumbbell and turns around to look at you, focus his attention on the center of the jump. As he commits himself to jump, back up to give him enough room to land. Praise, take the dumbbell, and release. Repeat until your dog jumps, retrieves, and returns reliably.

Practice this sequence with "bad" throws so your dog learns to come back over the jump from different angles. Picture a 45-degree line from each upright and condition Rascal to return over the jump from anywhere within that area.

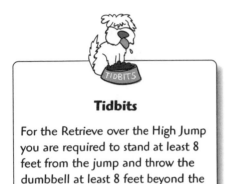

Tidbits

For the Retrieve over the High Jump you are required to stand at least 8 feet from the jump and throw the dumbbell at least 8 feet beyond the jump.

Sequence 6—goal: Teaching Rascal to wait.

From 10 feet, tell Rascal to stay, put two fingers of your left hand through his collar and throw the dumbbell. Very, very gingerly let go of the collar, count to five, and say "Rascal, jump."

After he has jumped, quietly follow him and, after he has picked up and turned to face you, focus his attention on the center of the jump. As he commits himself to return, back up so he has enough room to land, take the dumbbell, and release. Repeat until he stays without two fingers in the collar and returns without any help from you. Position yourself facing the center of the jump, at least 8 feet away and throw the dumbbell at least 8 feet beyond the jump.

Practice "bad" throws as in Sequence 5.

Sequence 7—goal: Raising the jump.

Begin raising the jump in 2- or 4-inch increments, depending on the size of your dog. If the height of the jump becomes an issue, condition your dog at a lower height. Difficulties with jumping are never disciplinary in nature—your dog is trying to tell you something. Your dog's structure may be such that he is unable to do what you ask, or he may experience pain for any number of reasons.

Sequence 8—goal: To ignore distractions.

Follow the program outlined in Chapter 13. In addition, have a distracter stand close to an upright while the dog is jumping, and once he is successful, have the distracter try to get your dog to go around the jump on the return by talking to him or enticing him with food.

Anytime your dog goes around the jump on the return, slowly approach your dog, put two fingers of your left hand (palm facing you), through the collar at the side of his neck, back to front. Take him back to where he picked up the dumbbell, tell him to stay—he can stand, sit, or lie down—go over the jump yourself to the other side, focus his attention on the top board, step back, and tell him to "jump." Praise as he lands and release. Then try it again.

Rascal may also try to go around the jump on the way out, in which case you slowly approach him and, if he has picked up the dumbbell already, take it out of his mouth and put it back where he picked it up. Now return with Rascal to the starting point and send him again.

Under no circumstances say "no," or do anything else that might discourage your dog. You want to put Rascal in a position where he can figure out for himself the desired response. Instead of doing anything that might discourage him, you are going to help him by literally showing him exactly what it is you want, which may include physical guidance. The hardest part for you will be to keep your mouth shut and remain patient.

You know how many repetitions it takes for your dog to figure something out, so there is no need to get impatient. You want him to keep on trying until he has figured it out. This is called the "aha" response. Translated it means: "Aha, now I know what you want." It is a powerful response because the dog has figured it out by himself, albeit with your help, instead of being told what to do. As a result, he responds with great reliability and enthusiasm.

Broad Jump

For the Broad Jump your dog is required to jump a distance equal to twice the height of the High Jump. Depending on that distance, that can be two, three, or four boards. It starts with you lining your dog up in front of and at least 8 feet from the jump. The judge will then say "leave your dog." You say "stay," and go to a position facing the right side of the jump, with your toes about 2 feet from the jump, anywhere between the first and last board.

Tidbits

How high your dog has to jump depends on his breed. Some breeds jump $1\frac{1}{4}$ their height at the withers, some once their height, and some 3/4 their height. The AKC Obedience Regulations specify the height each breed has to jump. The jump height is set at the nearest multiple of 2 inches. For example, Landseer Newfoundlands have to jump 3/4 of their height at the withers. Or, a 27 1/2-inch tall dog would have to jump 20 inches.

The judge will then say "send your dog," and you say "Rascal, over." As your dog jumps, you execute a right angle turn in place. The dog must sit and finish as in the Novice Recall.

Sequence 1—goal: Getting your dog used to the jump.

➤ Set up the jump at twice the height of your dog at the elbows. With a small dog, this means only one board.

➤ Put a target 8 feet from the center of the jump.

➤ Walk Rascal up to the jump and let him examine it.

➤ Position yourself and your dog 8 feet from the center of the jump.

➤ Show him a treat and use it to lure him over the jump with the command "over."

➤ Place the treat on the target and let him have it. Praise and release. Repeat 3 times.

Sequence 2—goal: Teaching Rascal to jump on command.

➤ Put your dog on a sit-stay 8 feet from the center of the jump.

➤ Walk over the jump and place a treat on the target.

➤ Face your dog and attract his attention to the treat by tapping the target.

➤ Call him over the jump with "Rascal, over." Repeat 10 times.

249

This Briard shows off his broad jump skills.

To save time and steps, you can do this in either direction.

Sequence 3—goal: Teaching your dog to make the turn.

Start as in Sequence 2. Then take a step away from the target and send your dog over the jump. In increments of 8 inches, begin moving to the position you will have to assume in the ring, calling Rascal to you after he has picked up his treat. After you have called him, make sure he sits in front. Praise and release backwards.

As Rascal becomes proficient with this exercise, eliminate the come command and introduce the "finish." For most of your repetitions you want him to sit in front. For the finish, you want to keep him guessing, so you do that only infrequently.

Doggy Dogma

We have authored a training book on the Open Class, as well as produced a videotape. For information on where to obtain these, see Appendix A.

Dogs learn very quickly what the end product is supposed to look like and begin taking short cuts. For example, instead of first sitting in front, Rascal will go directly to heel. You can forestall that by varying your routine and making sure that no matter what, he has to sit in front before he gets to finish.

Sequence 4—goal: To ignore distractions.

Practice with a distracter about 2 feet from the target and work your way through 1st, 2nd, and 3rd degree distractions. Remember to stop for that session after the correct response. That is the one you want Rascal to remember. Resist the temptation to do it just one more time. Your dog just may become creative in which you may be there for a long time until you get another correct response.

Out of Sight Stays

Top Dog Tips

So that the dog does not always turn to the right, we also like to practice this exercise from the opposite side of the jump, so the dog has to turn to the left.

As an introduction to "out of sight stays," leave Rascal on a sit-stay and go 6 feet in front of him. Pause for 10 seconds, walk past him and stand 6 feet behind him with your back to him. Practice with distractions and have your helper tell you when Rascal moves and you have to reinforce the stay. At this stage that would be highly unlikely.

When you are ready to go out of sight, gradually increase the length of time you leave Rascal, starting with 10 seconds and over the course of several sessions work up to the full time. Should you experience difficulties, such as breaking the stays, shorten your time and rebuild the exercise. Nine out of 10 times it is caused by lack of confidence on the part of the dog, and that is what you have to work on.

The Least You Need to Know

➤ When teaching your dog the drop on recall, don't do anything the dog could perceive as unpleasant as he comes to you.

➤ Target training is a simple and effective way to teach complex exercises to your dog.

➤ The jumping exercises are athletic endeavors for your dog and you need to condition him accordingly.

➤ Your dog's refusal to jump is never a question of disobedience—he is trying to tell you something.

➤ When you start practicing the out-of-sight stays, increase the time away from your dog gradually to four and six minutes, respectively.

Chapter 19

The Utility Dog

In This Chapter

➤ The intricacies of hand signals

➤ The power of the dog's nose

➤ The subtleties of direction

➤ The exercise that makes no sense

➤ The fun of jumping

After you have obtained your Companion Dog Excellent title you are eligible to enter the Utility Class, which is intended to be the most difficult and challenging. Curiously, what makes it difficult is not the exercises themselves, but the order in which they are done.

Your dog does not look at all exercises in the same light. Some he considers more fun than others. By observing the impact an exercise has on the psyche of your dog, you will be able to keep him enthusiastic and motivated.

The required exercises in the Utility Class are:

1. Signal Exercise
2. Scent Discrimination, Article No. 1
3. Scent Discrimination, Article No. 2
4. Directed Retrieve
5. Moving Stand and Examination
6. Directed Jumping

Bet You Didn't Know

Each year the American Kennel Club awards approximately 10,000 Companion Dog, 3000 Companion Dog Excellent, and 600 Utility Dog titles.

The Signal Exercise

The components of the Signal Exercise are the correct responses to the signals to heel, stand, stay, drop, sit, and come. The exercise starts with a regular heeling pattern, after which the judge says "stand your dog," whereupon you come to a halt and signal your dog to stand at heel. The position is the same as the automatic sit at heel except the dog has to stand at heel. The judge then tells you "leave your dog," and you give the stay signal and go to the other side of the ring and face your dog, whereupon the judge will then signal you to drop, sit, call, and finish your dog. You are not allowed to use verbal commands and the entire sequence is done with signals.

The Hand Signal to Heel

The heel hand signal is given with the left hand, which moves from left to right, palm down, in front of the dog's eyes. Give the signal together with the command and after several repetitions eliminate the signal.

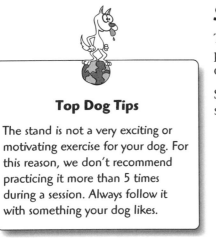

Top Dog Tips

The stand is not a very exciting or motivating exercise for your dog. For this reason, we don't recommend practicing it more than 5 times during a session. Always follow it with something your dog likes.

Stand at Heel on Signal

The signal is given with the left hand, from right to left, palm down and parallel to the ground, above and ahead of the dog's eyes.

Sequence 1—goal: Introducing your dog to the stand signal.

➤ Review standing your dog at heel (see Chapter 17).

➤ Put the thumb of your right hand through the collar under the dog's chin. Stand your dog with command and signal.

➤ Make sure his front feet remain in place. Praise and release.

➤ Repeat 10 times, not necessarily at one session.

Sequence 2—goal: To teach your dog to stand at heel from motion.

➤ With Rascal in heel position, leash in control position, say "let's go" and start walking.

➤ As you come to a halt, and before you have brought your feet together, put the leash in your right hand, place it against your dog's chest, give the signal with your left hand, and say "stand."

➤ Make sure you stop him standing in heel position. Praise and release with a treat.

➤ If necessary, prevent him from sitting by placing your left hand against his right thigh.

Concentrate on putting your right hand against his chest so that Rascal cannot advance past heel position. If you bring your right hand forward, Rascal will follow it and stand wherever you hold it. Repeat 5 times per session over the course of several sessions. After each stand, praise and release enthusiastically with a treat. The object is to have Rascal stand at heel without any tension on the leash.

Sequence 3—goal: Teaching the stand out of turns.

Repeat Sequence 2 after a right turn, about turn, and left turn. In the ring, you will get a stand right after a turn, so this is the maneuver you want to practice most.

Sequence 4—goal: Teaching the stand from a fast.

Teach Rascal Sequence 2 from a fast pace. While not absolutely necessary, it is a good indicator of how well he knows this exercise; it is also a fun way to practice.

At some point, you may have to use a check to stop Rascal's forward momentum. If this becomes necessary, put the rings of his collar on top of his neck. Just before you give the command, check straight back. Be sure the check is straight back. If you check up, you are telling him to sit.

Sequence 5—goal: Practicing the stand off leash.

➤ Review Sequences 1, 2, 3, and 4 off leash.

➤ Review Sequence 2, eliminating the verbal command.

Drop from a Stand and Sit from a Down

Use the same signal as you did for the drop on recall by bringing the right arm straight up above your shoulder as though you are reaching for the ceiling.

Sequence 1—goal: To teach your dog to drop from a stand.

➤ Stand your dog at heel.

➤ Neatly fold the leash into your left hand.

➤ Say "stay" and step in front of your dog.

Doggy Dogma

We have authored a training book on the Utility Class, as well as produced a videotape. For information on where to obtain these materials, see Appendix A.

Tidbits

Play sit from a down, and down from a sit as a game with your dog. Hold the treat in your signal hand and randomly reward correct responses. Be sure to count to five after every change in position so your dog can focus on what you want. Play only as long as Rascal is an enthusiastic participant.

➤ Kneel down and place two fingers of your left hand, palm facing down, through his collar, under his chin.

➤ Signal and say "down," at the same time pushing against his chest with your left hand, and then apply downward pressure on his collar. Tell Rascal to "stay," stand up, praise, and release with a treat.

The purpose of the pressure against the chest is to prevent Rascal from moving his feet forward as he drops, the natural tendency for most dogs. You want to teach him to collapse in place because that is what the Obedience Regulations require. Look at his feet as you drop him. With pressure against his chest, they will not move forward.

The downward pressure on the collar reinforces the drop. Be careful that you do not inadvertently pull him toward you, as that would make him move his feet forward. Practice until he lies down in place without any pressure on his collar, and with the signal only.

Sequence 2—goal: To teach your dog to sit from a down.

The signal is given with the right hand. With your right arm hanging naturally at your side, the back of the hand facing the dog, turn your hand so the palm faces your dog, bring your arm out and away from your body, no higher than your waist, keeping your elbow locked. The object is to train your dog to respond to the turning of your hand. In the teaching phase, the arm moves in front of your body so you can lure Rascal into a sit with a treat.

➤ Down your dog from a stand as in Sequence 1.

➤ Say "stay" and stand up.

➤ Put your left hand, which holds the leash, against your right hip.

➤ Have a treat in your right hand, held naturally at your side with the back of your hand toward the dog.

➤ Say "sit," turn your right hand so that the palm faces your dog, and lure your dog into a sit with the treat.

➤ Praise and release backwards.

Bring the treat to a point directly above his head so your dog sits straight up by bringing his front feet under him instead of moving forward. Practice this maneuver until the dog sits as soon as you turn your right hand. That is what you want, so be sure you reward that response with a treat.

Sequence 3—goal: Teaching the reinforcement of the sit.

➤ Start as in Sequence 2, but without a treat in your hand.

➤ Give the command and signal, at the same time give a little check on the leash straight up, palm up, to a point directly above his head.

➤ Bring your hand back to your side.

➤ Praise and release with a treat.

Reinforcing the sit signal.

This is the review progression for this exercise. Alternate on a random basis between using a treat and a little check. Eliminate the command and practice until your dog responds reliably to the signal.

Sequence 4—goal: To increase distance.

➤ Down and sit your dog, from 3 feet in front, on leash.

➤ As you give the signal, take a step toward Rascal with your right foot, keeping the left leg in place.

➤ Bring your leg and arm back to their original positions.

➤ Praise and give him a treat for every correct response.

The step toward your dog reinforces the response by keeping your dog in place and stops him from moving forward. As you increase the distance, you may need to reinforce the sit with a little check.

Once Rascal has mastered this exercise from 3 feet, increase the distance to 6 feet. As you increase distance, it is important to continue with the step. Remember, Rascal's natural tendency is to come to you and you want him to drop and sit in place.

It is at this point in the training that we introduce distractions, beginning with 1st degree. The distracter stands 10 feet from the dog, at a 45-degree angle. After you have left Rascal on a stand, the distracter approaches in a non-threatening, benign manner to within 2 feet of him. Give the signal to drop, with the step toward your dog. If he does, praise and enthusiastically release. If he does not, slowly go to him and reinforce the down by putting two fingers of your right hand, the one that gave the signal, through his collar, under his chin, and place him down. When he does it correctly, praise, release with a treat, stop, and go on to something else.

Carefully work your way through the three levels of distractions from 6 feet in front off leash. After that, take the leash off and gradually increase distance until Rascal does the exercise with you standing 40 feet in front of him.

The Come and Finish Signal

➤ Leave your dog on a sit-stay and go to the end of the leash.

➤ With your left hand holding the leash at your left side, say "come" and give the signal by bringing your right arm shoulder high and then to the center of your chest.

➤ Praise and release. When you release your dog there is no front or finish.

After five repetitions, not necessarily in a row or during the same session, eliminate the command. If Rascal does not respond to the signal, give him a little tug on the leash. Praise and release. Practice until your dog responds reliably to the signal.

Try the exercise off leash from 6 feet in front. Praise and release. From 6 feet away you cannot expect much speed. There is little motivation to come quickly for such a short distance. As soon as you increase distance, Rascal will pick up speed. Keep making it exciting for him by using a treat and the release.

For the finish use the same signal as you did for the Novice and Open classes. Remember, you don't want to front or finish the dog every time he comes to you. Use the release as an alternative.

Scent Discrimination

Perhaps you have already taught your dog the "find mine" trick with dollar bills, in which case this exercise should go quickly. The only difference between the two is that the Scent Discrimination exercise is done with metal and leather articles, usually dumbbells, five of each. Rascal is required to retrieve first one and then the other, metal or leather, which you have scented, from among the remaining eight.

Sequence 1—goal: Teaching your dog to retrieve leather and metal articles.

You may have to review the teaching progressions for the retrieve, depending on how your dog responds. Leather items are rarely a problem, but metal items can be. He must retrieve either reliably before you can go on.

Sequence 2—goal: Teaching Rascal to use his nose.

To teach your dog that you want him to use his nose, introduce him to the game of "find." For example, when training outside, hide the article around a corner. Let him see you take the article and return. Send him with "find it," and when he brings it back, release him backward with great enthusiasm and reward him with a treat. The first time you try this you may have to show him where you put the article. As he catches on, increase the difficulty so that he has to use his nose to find the article.

Sequence 3—goal: Introducing Rascal to the articles.

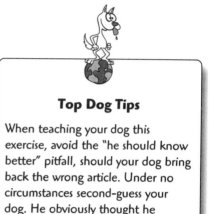

Top Dog Tips

When teaching your dog this exercise, avoid the "he should know better" pitfall, should your dog bring back the wrong article. Under no circumstances second-guess your dog. He obviously thought he retrieved the right one.

Tidbits

Tying the article to a board prevents the dog from picking up the incorrect article and encourages him to keep looking for the right one. We like the board better than a carpet. We tried the carpet and our Newfoundland brought back the entire carpet.

For this purpose we use a scent board. This is a piece of pegboard commensurate with the size of your dog and large enough to accommodate all eight articles placed 6 inches apart. Accustom Rascal to walking on the board by heeling him over it several times and having him sit on it. Then have him retrieve an article from the board, first by throwing it on the board, and then by placing it. Release backward and reward. It is important that your dog is comfortable retrieving from the board before you begin to add other articles.

Top Dog Tips

Some handlers make an effort to give the dog their scent by briefly holding their hand in front of the dog's nose. We have always felt that by now our dogs should know our scent and considered the effort superfluous. It also loads up the dog's nose with scent just when you want it to be clear.

Prepare the board for the next sequence by tying one of each article on the board, with the tie underneath, and anywhere from one half to six inches of slack. Let the board air out for 24 hours.

Sequence 4—goal: Teaching your dog the concept of scent discrimination.

➤ Make sure your hands are clean and free from chemicals and perfumes.

➤ With you and Rascal facing the board from 10 feet away, scent a metal article by slowly rubbing the bar for 20 seconds.

➤ Say "find it," and let him briefly hold the article.

➤ Say "stay" and place the article on the board, letting him watch you place it on the board.

➤ Go back to heel and send him with "find it."

If Rascal tries to pick up an incorrect article, encourage him to keep looking with "you can do it," in an excited tone of voice, or anything other than the original command. When he picks up the correct one, quietly say "that's it," with a big smile on your face, release backward and reward.

Repeat by placing the scented leather article in a different location on the board until you are sure Rascal is using his nose to find the correct article. At the same time, gradually increase the distance you stand from the board to 20 feet. During this sequence stop the praise for picking up the correct article, but continue to smile. You don't want Rascal to become dependent on praise and wait for it before he returns, so eliminate it as soon as you can. Release and reward Rascal after he has returned. Stop after two successive successful responses, that is, one metal and one leather.

Tie two more articles on the board, varying the length of slack for each article. After each successful round, tie two more articles on the board until all eight articles are tied on the board.

Sequence 5—goal: Teaching your dog discrimination.

Up until now, Rascal has only learned to find your article among unscented ones. The object of the exercise is to teach him to find your article among those that have been touched by someone else. Before you send your dog, have a helper briefly touch the articles on the board, then place yours. You and Rascal are still facing the board.

Some dogs catch on quickly and others need to go back to the beginning with two articles tied down. You will have to experiment with Rascal to see how he does. Try it with all eight articles tied down. If he gets hopelessly confused, start at the beginning.

When your dog is reliable at this step, introduce distractions the same way as you did for the retrieve.

Sequence 6—goal: To wean your dog off the board.

Reverse the procedure and untie two articles. After each successful round, stop. Over the course of several sessions, repeat until all the articles are loose on the board. Should he come back with the wrong article, don't take the article from him and send him again. Under no circumstances should you ever do anything that might discourage your dog.

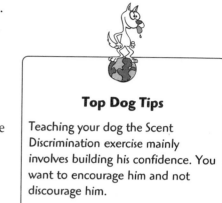

Top Dog Tips

Teaching your dog the Scent Discrimination exercise mainly involves building his confidence. You want to encourage him and not discourage him.

Doing this exercise on the board and doing it on any other surface is not the same. You can work with the board and place two articles on the ground and, as Rascal is successful, place the remainder, two at a time, on the ground in front of the board. You can also start again with just two articles on the ground and build from there. Once he is proficient at this part of the exercise, use the same procedure to move the articles from the board onto grass and rubber matting.

Right after it looks as though Rascal has finally gotten the hang of it, he may go through one or more regressions—he gives the appearance of not having the foggiest idea of what this exercise is all about. You can recognize it by the number of successive incorrect responses. He brings back the wrong article, you send him again and he brings back another incorrect article, and so on. This is normal and you should expect it. The best advice we can give you is to put him back on the board for several days as a form of review.

Sequence 7—goal: Teaching the turn and send.

For the finished product, you and Rascal will have your backs turned to the articles as your article is being placed by the judge. The judge will then say "send your dog." You can then make a right about turn in place, at the same time sending your dog, or you can have him sit at heel and then send him.

Unless there is a compelling reason to have your dog sit at heel, we suggest you send him as you make the turn—it's more motivational.

Directed Retrieve

This particular exercise requires Rascal to retrieve one of three gloves, which are placed at the unobstructed end of the ring about 15 feet apart. You are required to give your dog the direction to the designated glove and the command.

The exercise starts with you and Rascal in the center of the ring with your backs to the gloves. The judge will say something like "glove number one," which designates the glove behind you on your right. Glove number two is the one directly behind you, and number three is the one to your left.

Other than knowing how to retrieve a glove, the only "new" maneuver you have to teach Rascal is the turns in place, with the emphasis on place. When working on the turns in place, keep in mind that the more accurate your dog is on heel position, the less likely he is to make a mistake.

All turns in place start with Rascal at sitting at heel, leash in control position.

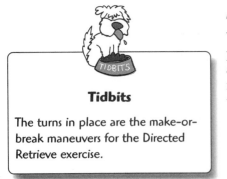

Right Turn in Place

You can teach this turn in three progressions, first placing your right leg, then taking a step on the right leg and finally, making the turn in place by turning your right foot at a 90 degree angle to the right, closing with the left foot.

1. Place your right foot at a 90-degree angle one large step to the right. With "Rascal, heel," close with your left foot and guide your dog into heel position. Praise and release. Repeat 25 times.

2. Say "Rascal, heel," then take a step to the right, close with the left and guide your dog into heel position. Praise and release. Repeat 25 times.

3. Say "Rascal, heel," and turn in place to the right, heel to heel closing with the left. Praise and release.

Right About Turn in Place

1. Say "Rascal, heel," take two steps forward, turn around to your right, keeping your feet together, take two steps forward and guide your dog into heel position. Praise and release. Repeat 25 times.

2. Say "Rascal, heel," take one step forward, turn around, take one step forward and guide your dog into heel position. Praise and release. Repeat 25 times.

3. Say "Rascal, heel," make two right turns in place, and guide your dog into heel position. Praise and release.

Left Turn in Place

1. Place your left foot directly in front of your dog's front feet. Say "Rascal, heel" and take a large step with your right foot, past the left and close with the left, guiding your dog into heel position with slight backward pressure on the leash. Praise and release. Repeat 25 times.

2. Place your left foot directly in front of your dog's front feet. Say "Rascal, heel" and take a small step with your right foot, past the left and close with the left,

guiding your dog into heel position with slight backward pressure on the leash. Praise and release. Repeat 25 times.

3. Say "Rascal, heel," put your right foot at a 90 degree angle directly in front of your left (in a "T" position) and guide your dog into heel position with slight backward pressure on the collar. Praise and release. Repeat 25 times.

4. Say "Rascal, heel," and make two left turns in place, guiding your dog into heel position with slight backward pressure on the collar. Praise and release.

Teaching the Gloves

Give the direction by holding your left arm at the side of the dog's head, with the hand and fingers pointing straight toward the glove, held ahead of his nose. Immediately following, give the command to "take it." What you may not do is give your dog the direction and then pump your left arm as you send him for the glove.

For the center glove, the arm is stretched out so that the elbow is in line with the dog's nose. You may bend your body and knees to the extent necessary in giving the direction to your dog. When giving the direction make sure your fingers are indeed pointing at the designated glove.

Top Dog Tips

Although the Obedience Regulations permit you to send your dog as you give the direction, they also permit you to mark the direction and then send your dog for the glove. This is the method that we teach.

Before you start on this exercise, you may want to review the retrieve with a glove.

1. With your dog sitting at heel, and a glove in your left hand, held between thumb and fingers, get him excited about the glove. Throw the glove, holding your arm as you would if you were to mark the glove, and say "take it." After he has picked up, praise, and release. If he does not retrieve, review teaching him to retrieve the glove.

2. Once your dog retrieves the glove and you have introduced him to the direction, place a glove 15 feet to your right, 15 feet to your left, and 15 feet in front of you. Say "Rascal, heel," and make a right turn in place. Rascal now faces the glove on your right. Mark the direction with your left arm—you may have to hold on to your dog by placing two fingers of your right hand through his collar. Send your dog with "take it." Praise and release after he has picked up the glove.

Repeat for the glove on the left, and the center glove. After three successful repetitions, move the gloves on your right and left, 2 feet straight ahead and start all over. After each set of 3 successful repetitions, move the gloves on your right and left two feet

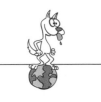

Top Dog Tips

Every time you help your dog, you are assuming the responsibility for his behavior. You want him to learn it is his responsibility to make the right decision. To do that you have to give him a chance to work it out for himself.

straight ahead until they are in line with the center glove. Send your dog to different gloves in a random pattern.

What if he goes to the wrong glove? We let him try to work it out for himself by maintaining the signal. For example, Rascal goes to number two instead of number one. Hold the signal facing number one. When Rascal returns to you he immediately notices something is wrong—you are not standing up straight but are still pointing to the glove. He may try to do one of several things, such as,

➤ insist on giving you the glove, which you do not take,

➤ give up and do nothing, or

➤ go for another glove, probably the correct one.

If he retrieves the correct glove, stand up, praise, and release. If he does nothing, approach the number one glove still holding the signal, and get him to pick it up, preferably just by pointing at it and without an extra command. When he does, praise and release. If he does not, reinforce the retrieve.

Once Rascal has learned the direction portion of the exercise, you can introduce the turn and send. The Obedience Regulations permit you to turn either to the left or to the right, and you will have to experiment to discover what is best for you and your dog.

Tidbits

For the Moving Stand the dog must stand and stay on command without taking any steps forward while you keep walking.

Moving Stand and Examination

For this exercise you are required to heel your dog for about 10 feet when the judge tells you to "stand your dog." Without pausing or breaking your stride, you give the command and or signal to stand and continue walking 10 to 12 feet, turn and face your dog. The judge examines your dog, a little more thoroughly than he did in the Novice Class, and then says "call your dog to heel," and you give the command and or signal for Rascal to go to heel.

1. With your dog on leash and at heel, say "let's go," and start walking. After several steps, give the signal to stand, say "stay," and continue walking. When you get to the end of the leash, turn and face your dog. Tell him what a clever fellow he is, count to five and release. Practice 10 times over the course of several sessions.

If Rascal needs help, use the same technique to teach him to stand and stay that you used to teach him to stand at heel. After that, try it off leash.

2. Start again with your dog on leash, take several steps, stand your dog and go to the end of the leash and face him. Count to five, then signal and say "Rascal, heel," guiding him into heel position. Praise and release. The Regulations permit you to give both the signal to heel and the command for this exercise.

When Rascal correctly goes to heel on leash, try it off leash. Then gradually increase the distance you leave him on a stand until you can go about 10 to 12 feet, as required by the Regulations, before you turn and face him.

Finally, you do need to practice the examination part of the exercise with a helper.

Directed Jumping

For this exercise your dog has to go, on command, from one end of the ring to the other, between the bar and the high jump. The bar and the high jump are in the center of the ring about 18 feet apart. You then give him the command and or signal for one of the jumps, after which he has to front and then finish. The entire procedure is then repeated for the other jump.

Tidbits

The go-out takes a little time to teach because the dog can see absolutely no rhyme or reason for this exercise.

We approach this exercise in three parts: the go-out, the jumps, and putting the two together. To start, the go-out is taught without reference to the jumps. When Rascal has learned the go-out and the directed jumping parts, we then put them together.

Teaching Your Dog the Go-Out

1. To teach Rascal to leave, we use food or an object such as a stick or a toy. To teach him where to go, we use a box, made from PVC pipe and commensurate to the size of the dog. We then put the box in front of a barrier, such as a section of fencing, a fence or the side of a house.

➤ Get your dog used to the box by heeling him into the chute and then calling him into it.

➤ Put a target, commensurate with the size of your dog, inside the box.

➤ With Rascal on leash, show him a treat and say "out," as both of you go into the chute.

➤ Place the treat on the target and let him pick it up. Praise, encourage him to turn around in the chute and release backwards. Repeat until Rascal is comfortable with going into and turning in the chute.

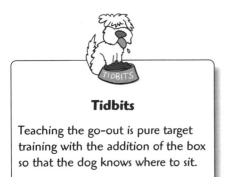

Next, leave Rascal on a sit-stay 10 feet in front of the target, let him see you place a treat on the target, go back to heel position and send him with "Rascal, out." You may signal him at the same time with the left hand in the direction you want him to go. When he gets to the target, let him take the treat, praise, and call him back. With each successive repetition, increase the distance to the target by two feet until you are 75 feet from the target. Repeat at that distance 50 times over the course of several sessions.

2. Remove the target. Leave Rascal on a sit-stay, 10 feet from the barrier, go into the box, face your dog, point to the ground and go back to heel position. Send your dog and after he has left, quietly follow him so that when he gets to the spot you indicated, you are in front of the box. Say "Rascal, sit," using the sit hand signal and a step forward to make him sit in place. Reward him with a treat, held in the hand that gave the signal. From now on, Rascal is only rewarded for going to the designated spot and he has to learn that the reward comes from you.

With each successive repetition, increase the distance to the target by 2 feet until you are 75 feet from the target. Repeat at that distance 50 times over the course of several sessions.

Bet You Didn't Know

The Obedience Regulations do not specify the commands you have to use, nor do they have to be in English. However, excessively loud commands, as in yelling at the dog, are not permitted.

It is during this progression that Rascal learns to turn and sit in the box. Continue to follow him and use the step and signal so that he understands you want him to turn and sit immediately. The step and signal prevent him from getting into the habit of taking several steps toward you, which you don't want.

If Rascal does not leave or only goes part of the way, without saying anything, slowly approach him, put two fingers of your left hand through the collar, back to front, palm facing you, at the side of his neck and take him to the spot you indicated. Reinforce the sit with "sit," let go, give him a treat and release. Send him again.

3. Send your dog 2 times in a row. Leave Rascal on a sit-stay, go into the box, point to the spot, and go back to heel position. Send him and when he gets to the spot, say "Rascal, sit." Praise, count to five, release, and call him back to you. Line him up at heel position, send him again, when he gets there have him sit, then go to him, praise, reward, and release. Repeat this sequence 50 times.

If he does not leave you or does not go to the designated spot, show him where you want him to go.

Introduce distractions as you have for previous exercises by having the distracter first stand midway between you and the designated spot, 2 feet from Rascal's line of travel, and then 2 feet from the designated spot. Work your way through 1st, 2nd, and 3rd degree distractions. If Rascal veers away from the distracter, use two distracters, starting at 8 feet apart, and teach him to go straight through.

Directed Jumping

1. Introducing your dog to the bar jump.

   Introduce Rascal to the bar jump, set at teaching height (the height of your dog at the elbows), by walking him up to the jump, on leash, dead ring, and touch the bar with your left hand. Let him investigate the jump.

   Start from 10 feet away, say "bar," and briskly walk toward the jump. Let him jump as you go over with him or around the jump. Repeat until he jumps without any hesitation.

2. Introducing your dog to direction.

   Set up the high and the bar jumps at teaching height, 18 feet apart.

   ➤ Place your target 10 feet from the center of the high jump.
   ➤ Leave your dog on a sit-stay facing the high jump.
   ➤ Go over the jump to the target and place a treat on the target.
   ➤ Stand 2 feet behind the target facing your dog.
   ➤ Say "jump," and give the signal by bringing your arm up from your side, shoulder height, pointed toward the jump.

   Rascal should go over the jump to reach the target and his treat. Praise and release.

   Repeat for the bar jump with the command "bar," and using your other arm to signal.

   Gradually work your way to the center and increase the distance from the jumps to 20 feet. You should always be in the mirror position to Rascal. Always step over the jump and place your treat. Then test Rascal's understanding by eliminating the treat. This is the review progression for this exercise, so don't hesitate to use the treat on a random basis.

Sophisticated competition is not restricted to big dogs. This Dachshund is a bar-jump master!

Begin raising the jumps in 2 or 4-inch increments, depending on the size of your dog. Difficulties with jumping are never disciplinary. If your dog is having a problem with a jump, he is trying to tell you something—so listen to him!

3. Putting it all together.

You are now ready to combine the go-out with the Directed Jumping.

> ➤ Put your box in front of the fence.
> ➤ Leave Rascal midway between the two jumps.
> ➤ Go to the box and point to the spot where you want him to go.
> ➤ Return to heel position, and send him and tell him to sit and stay.
> ➤ Go back to the spot from which you are going to send him.
> ➤ Give the command and signal to jump.
> ➤ Praise as he lands, and release. Repeat for the other jump.

Now start with Rascal at heel position, 2 feet back from the center line between the jumps, and follow the same procedure. Repeat in 2-foot increments until you stand at the appropriate spot for the exercise before sending your dog. This procedure is a precaution for the first few times you put the go-out together with the Directed Jumping. It should prevent Rascal from coming up with the idea, as he otherwise might, that he has to jump on the way out.

After every two go-outs, reinforce that exercise with 5 repetitions into the box, the first, third, and fifth are rewarded by a treat.

What if Rascal makes a mistake and goes over the wrong jump? Try letting him work it out. Maintain your signal and wait. The response you want to see is Rascal going back into or near the box without any help or command from you. When he does, lower your arm, tell him to sit, and repeat the signal.

Top Dog Tips

Give your dog a chance to work out on his own what it is you want. Before you jump in to help him, see what he does. He may surprise you. Be patient and keep your mouth shut.

Suppose he does nothing and just sits in front of you not knowing what to do. Give him a chance until you are absolutely certain that he has stopped trying, then take him back to where he started, leave him, return, and send him again.

Seeing a dog have the "aha" response—that is, Rascal shows you that the penny has dropped and he has figured out what you want—is perhaps one of the most exciting aspects of training a dog. To get there, you must never discourage your dog from trying, even if the response is incorrect. Permit and encourage your dog to solve these training problems and you will have a motivated student.

Not All Exercises Are Created Equal

We characterize the exercises the dogs are required to do into two categories:

➤ action, and

➤ control.

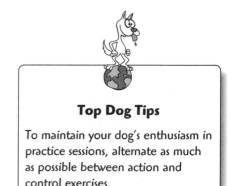

Top Dog Tips

To maintain your dog's enthusiasm in practice sessions, alternate as much as possible between action and control exercises.

Action exercises tend to be motivational for the dog, something he enjoys. Examples of action exercises are heeling, retrieving, jumping, and coming. Control exercises are de-motivational, not something that is fun and exciting. Examples of control exercises are the sit and down-stay, the drop for the drop on recall, and the Stand for Examination. The front and the finish can be either, depending on the dog's perception.

With that in mind, let's take a look at the Utility Exercises.

Required Exercise	Behavior/Drive	Category
Signal Exercise —		
Dog first heels,	Pack	Action
then stands at heel,	Pack	Control
lies down on signal,	Pack	Control
sits on signal,	Pack	Control
and comes on signal	Pack	Action
Scent Discrimination —		
The dog is required to	Prey	More Control than action,
select by scent one		because the article is
article out of eight,		placed and the dog has
retrieve it, and		to discriminate.
bring it back to the	Pack	
handler.		
Directed Retrieve —		
The dog is sent to	Prey	
retrieve one of	Pack	Action
three articles.		
Moving Stand and		
Examination —		
Dog first heels,	Pack	Action
then has to		
stand on command,	Pack	Control
be examined by		Control
the judge, and	Pack	
then go to heel.	Pack	Action
Directed Jumping —		
Dog has to leave	Prey	Action
the handler, then jump.	Prey	Action

You can quickly see that the potentially most devastating impact on the dog's motivation comes from the Signal Exercise, which is immediately followed by another control exercise. It is not until the Directed Retrieve that the dog starts to have any fun.

Obviously the dog can learn the Signal Exercise and even do it with some degree of verve, provided that you don't turn him off in the teaching and practicing phases. When you see that an exercise has a dampening effect on your dog, immediately follow it with something he likes, such as a retrieve. You may have to split up the Signal Exercise into its component parts to keep your dog motivated, and only once or twice a week practice it the way it is supposed to be done.

The Least You Need to Know

➤ Target training is an easy way to introduce your dog to fairly complex exercises.

➤ To maintain your dog's enthusiasm, alternate between control and action exercises.

➤ Don't second-guess your dog's use of his nose, even if he is wrong.

➤ Whenever you can, give your dog a chance to work it out himself.

➤ Expect to spend some time teaching your dog the go-out because it makes absolutely no sense to him.

➤ You need to continue to practice heeling.

Chapter 20

Agility and Other Dog Sports

In This Chapter

➤ A veritable plethora of doggie activities

➤ The exciting world of agility

➤ The origins of dog sports

➤ The most rewarding activity of them all

In addition to obedience competition, there are numerous other competitions and events in which you and your dog can participate. Some are for specific breeds, such as herding trials, and others are for all dogs, such as agility. Many are conducted under the auspices of the American Kennel Club, and some are not, such as Schutzhund trials. Still, others are for one breed, such as the Newfoundland Club of America's Water Rescue and Draft Dog competitions.

The AKC alone has over 30 different performance titles that can be earned, albeit not all by the same dog, in the following categories:

➤ Obedience Titles—5

➤ Hunting Test Titles—4

➤ Field Trial Titles—2

➤ Herding Titles—6

➤ Tracking Titles—4

➤ Agility Titles—9

➤ Earthdog Titles—3

➤ Lure Coursing—3

Bet You Didn't Know

The American Kennel Club awards over 30 different performance titles in eight different categories. And, there are other organizations that have an almost equal number of titles.

You will note that with the exception of Obedience, Tracking, and Agility, these activities roughly correspond to the seven groups (see Chapter 6), although there is some overlap. The intent of many of these events is to demonstrate the dog's ability to perform the function for which it was bred.

This Landseer Newfoundland puppy is getting a head start on learning to master the A-frame, an agility exercise.

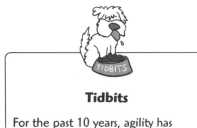

Tidbits

For the past 10 years, agility has been the fastest growing dog sport. It is an exciting and exhilarating sport for both handler and dog, and it has great spectator appeal.

Agility

Agility is one of the AKC's newest events. It has experienced a phenomenal growth over the last 10 years, and with good reason. The dogs love it, the handlers love it, and it has enormous spectator appeal. Agility competitions began in England and now enjoy worldwide popularity.

The AKC is not the only organization that sponsors agility trials, but it now has the largest number of trials. There are also international agility competitions.

The dogs, under the direction of their handlers, negotiate a complex obstacle course that includes walking over a 3- or 4-foot-high plank, weaving in and out of a series of poles, jumping over and through objects, and going through tunnels. To compensate for the size differences among dogs and make the competition fair, there are four height divisions. You and Rascal can earn nine agility titles. The original four titles are:

Title	Requirements
Novice Agility (NA)	Three legs under two different judges
Open Agility (OA)	Same
Agility Excellent (AX)	Same
Master Agility (MX)	Must have earned the AX title and then qualify 10 more times

Other than the exercises themselves, there are some significant differences between agility trials and obedience trials.

Agility	Obedience
Your dog has to be able to work on both your right and your left side	Your dog always works on your left side
Minimum time limits during which you and your dog have to complete the course	No time limit (within reason)
The order in which the obstacles are to be negotiated varies, as do the obstacles	The exercises and the order of the exercises are always the same
You can encourage your dog while he is working, and give second commands	During an exercise you cannot talk to your dog and can only give one command

As with obedience, the level of difficulty increases with each higher class, as does the number of obstacles.

No doubt, part of the appeal of agility competition is its seeming simplicity. Almost any dog in reasonably good physical condition quickly learns the rudiments of the various obstacles. And, almost any handler who is also in reasonably good physical condition can compete in agility. But few things are ever as simple as they appear.

Because the courses you and your dog have to negotiate are never quite the same, there is a premium on your ability to communicate with your dog. Any lapses in communication invariably result in Rascal's failure to complete the course correctly. You are also competing against the clock and have to make split-second decisions. In addition, you are required to memorize the course before you and your dog compete.

Top Dog Tips

Beginning agility is deceptively simple, but it's not as easy as it looks. There is a premium on being able to communicate with your dog and the two of you really have to be in tune with each other.

You can see what makes agility so exciting. The two of you really have to be able to work as a team and keep your wits about you. We highly recommend that you try it. You will be amazed how your dog will take to it. We are not suggesting that you try to set up an agility course in your backyard—few of us have the wherewithal to do that. Find out from your local dog organizations where agility trials are being held and then take a look. In almost every community there will be a group or an individual who has classes that meet on a regular basis where you and Rascal can get started. Even if you are not interested in competing, it's good mental stimulation for Rascal, as well as good exercise for both of you.

A Landseer Newfoundland completes the weave pole exercise in an agility competition.

Tracking

The dog's fabled ability to use his nose and follow a scent is the basis for this activity. Any dog can participate, and if you enjoy tromping through the great outdoors in solitude with your dog, tracking is for you. Tracking is also the potentially most useful activity you can teach your dog. Many a tracking dog has been credited with finding a lost person, or lost article, not to mention the dogs that are used with much effectiveness in law enforcement.

Doggy Dogma

Your dog's sense of smell is almost infallible, and dogs are used by various law enforcement agencies to sniff out bombs, drugs, and other contraband. They are even being used in cancer research to detect cancer in a person.

There are three titles Rascal can earn:

➤ Tracking Dog (TD)

➤ Tracking Dog Excellent (TDX), and

➤ Variable Surface Tracking (VST).

The principle differences between the classes are the age of the track and the surface.

Title	Basic Requirements
TD	The track has to be at least 440 yards, but not more than 500 yards in length. The track shall be laid by a person 30 minutes to two hours before the event. It has to have three to five turns. There are no cross tracks and no obstacles.
TDX	The track has to be at least 800 yards, but not more than 1,000 yards in length. The track has to be not less than three hours and not more than five hours old. It has to have five to seven turns. It has two cross tracks and two obstacles, such as a different surface or a stream.
VST	The track has to be at least 600 yards, but not more than 800 yards in length. Age of track is the same as for the TDX. It has to have four to eight turns. It has to have a minimum of three different surfaces, such as concrete, asphalt, gravel or sand, in addition to vegetation.

Your dog has to complete only one track successfully to earn its title, unlike obedience or agility titles, for which three qualifying performances are required. You can also continue to compete at any level, even if you have earned your VST.

Tidbits

Hunting tests and field trials are popular and test your dog's ability to demonstrate the function for which he was bred.

Field Trials and Hunting Tests

Field trials and hunting tests rival obedience and agility competitions in popularity. These events are for the pointing breeds, retrievers, spaniels, Beagles, Basset Hounds, and, you would never guess, Dachshunds. The tests are divided by type of dog and sometimes by specific breeds. Some of them, such as Beagles, work in groups of two, three, and seven or more.

The performance requirements vary, depending on the specific breed and the particular event. If Rascal is a Labrador Retriever, you and he can participate in both field trials and hunting tests, and the sky is the limit.

Earthdog Trials

These tests are for dogs bred to retrieve critters that live in tunnels or dens. The Dachshund, which translated means Badger Hound, and the smaller terriers are eligible to participate in these competitions.

Tidbits

The instinct of some dogs is to discover and root out the critters that live underground. This can lead to monumental "landscaping." Our Dachshunds are forever digging for moles or anything else that might be under the ground. Of course, anything recently planted must be immediately dug up just to make sure nothing edible has been buried.

The object is to locate the quarry in a tunnel or a den. In the tests, either rats, caged for their protection, or a mechanical, scented device, are used.

Tests are conducted at four different levels:

1. An introductory test to see if the dog has any aptitude for this sort of thing. There is no title for this test, but it is a prerequisite for a title.

2. After the dog has passed the introductory test, he is eligible for the Junior Earthdog (JE) title.

3. Next is the Senior Earthdog (SE) title.

4. Lastly, there is the Master Earthdog (ME) title.

Naturally, the level of difficulty increases with each title. As the levels progress, the distance from which the dog has to locate the den is increased and the tunnels that the dog has to encounter become more complex.

Earthdog trials are quite a specialized activity and explain the penchant these dogs have for redesigning the backyard.

Lure Coursing

An equally specialized activity is lure coursing, which is for the sight hounds. These dogs were bred to run down game over great distances. If you have ever seen a sight hound running flat out, you can appreciate how fast-paced and exciting lure coursing is.

In an AKC test an artificial lure is used, which the dogs follow around a course in an open field. Scoring is based on speed, which is blazing, enthusiasm and endurance. Of course, it helps if the dog is actually chasing the lure and is not off on a frolic of his own.

Again, there are three titles the dog can earn:

1. Junior Courser (JC)
2. Senior Courser (SC), and
3. Field Champion (FC).

Schutzhund Training

The word schutzhund means "protection dog." After field trials, schutzhund training is probably the oldest organized competition. It originated in Germany and is the progenitor of our obedience exercises, tracking, and, to some extent, agility. It is hugely popular in Europe and there are worldwide competitions. Although schutzhund is not an AKC performance event, it enjoys an avid following in this country.

Bet You Didn't Know

Schutzhund training is the progenitor of many of our training activities today. It dates back to the early 20th century, and many of its exercises have been incorporated into today's performance events.

It all began when the German Shepherd came to be used as a police dog. Billed as the only true multi-purpose dog, he was expected to guard and protect, herd, track, be a guide dog for the blind and, of course, be good with children. Rigorous breeding programs were designed to cement these traits into the breed. Behavior was bred to behavior, so that only those dogs with demonstrated abilities procreated. Looks were not considered as important as ability.

As a police dog, a dog's main responsibility is to protect his handler. He also has to be able to pursue and capture suspects, or track them down. Building searches required great agility, perhaps jumping into windows, negotiating stairs, even ladders. Naturally, he has to know all the obedience exercises.

It wasn't long before competitions began among and between police units to see who had the most talented and best-trained dog. Dog owners like you became interested and the sport of Schutzhund was born.

Schutzhund training consists of three parts:

➤ protection

➤ obedience, and

➤ tracking.

To qualify for a title, the dog must pass all three parts. When obedience and tracking were introduced in this country, they were patterned on the requirements for the Schutzhund dog. Agility competitions derived in part from the Schutzhund obedience exercises, which include walking over the A-frame as well as different jumps.

Schutzhund training is not limited to German Shepherds and can be done by any dog of the guarding breeds that has the aptitude. Even some of the non-guarding breeds can do it, although you won't see them at the upper levels of competition.

It is a rigorous and highly athletic sport and the skills required are all-encompassing. It is also one of the most time consuming of dog sports.

Can There Be More?

For you and Rascal there are plenty of other dog activities you can enjoy.

Search and Rescue

There are search and rescue groups all over the country that train dogs to find people that are lost or injured in the woods or similar terrain. One of our Landseer Newfoundlands was a search and rescue dog. The dogs are trained to locate the victim by air scenting, which is different from tracking or trailing a scent. Once the dog has found the victim he returns to the handler and leads him or her to the spot. This training, too, is quite rigorous. The dogs have to have great stamina and persistence, and may have to ride in a helicopter to get to the designated search area. You have to learn how to read a compass and other survival skills.

A dog hones his water rescue skills.

Therapy Dogs

Therapy dogs visit nursing homes and hospitals, accompanied by their handlers. The dogs' power to cheer and comfort is legendary. This activity requires a special dog, a dog that is a natural, one that can deal with people on medication, people that are not rational, people who don't act quite right, people in wheelchairs, with walkers and on crutches.

Tidbits

Undoubtedly, the most rewarding dog activity is having a Therapy Dog. A dog's ability to cheer up and comfort a person in distress or need is legendary.

The Least You Need to Know

➤ Agility is great fun for you and your dog, and it is the fastest growing dog sport.

➤ No matter which kind of dog you own, there is an activity out there for you.

➤ Schutzhund training is the father of most of our training today.

➤ With a Therapy Dog you can make a real contribution.

Part 5
Reform School

Is it a question of training or one of management? Some of the things your dog does that you consider objectionable, such as pulling on the leash and jumping on people, can be fixed by training. Others, such as barking, chewing, or digging are more a matter of management.

One management technique is to provide an outlet for the behavior. Another management approach is to find out what turns the behavior on, so you can eliminate the cause. For example, isolation and boredom are the causes for many undesirable behaviors. With a little effort on your part, you can eliminate these causes.

You may want to get outside help, either with your basic training, or with a particular problem, and there you have a number of options. We recommend, as our first choice, an obedience-training class, which can be lots of fun for you and your dog.

How about a vacation for you and your dog where you can learn and have fun at the same time? Dog camp is the best way to meet these objectives.

Not as easily managed are undesirable behaviors that are due to a physical cause. Finding the cause and curing the dog are sometimes not that simple. You will need to think like a detective and also enlist the help of your veterinarian.

Chapter 21

In the Dog House

In This Chapter

➤ Behavior problems—what are your options?

➤ Landscaping, unnecessary vocalizing and rampant destruction

➤ Please, don't leave me

➤ Oops, I made a mess

➤ Cars make me sick

One of the favorite pastimes of our Dachshunds is digging, or landscaping as we call it. They will engage in this activity at every opportunity and with great zest. Since Dachshunds were bred to go after badgers, this behavior is instinctive, and trying to suppress it would probably make a neurotic nuisance out of the dog. It is unrelated to the fact that ours are obedience trained, housetrained, crate-trained, come when called (mostly), and stay when told.

Does that mean we have to put up with a yard that looks like a minefield? Not at all, but we do have to assume the responsibility for:

➤ expending the "digging" energy, or

➤ providing an outlet for it, or

➤ supervising the little darlings to make sure they don't get into trouble.

The Dachshund is a breed that likes to dig.

Expenditure of the energy involves exercise, and providing an outlet means taking them for walks in the woods where they can dig to their little hearts content. Of course, you can always cover your yard with Astroturf or green cement!

So, the good news is that most so-called behavior problems are under your direct control; the bad news is that you have to get involved.

What Are Your Options?

Anytime you experience objectionable behavior on the part of your dog, you have several options:

➤ You can tolerate it.

➤ You can spend more time with your dog in an effort to solve the problem.

➤ You can find a new home for the dog.

➤ You can take your dog for a one-way trip to the shelter or veterinarian.

Tolerate the Behavior

Simply putting up with annoying behavior may not seem like much of an option. Then you begin to consider the amount of time and energy that could be involved in dealing with your dog's annoying antics and you decide that you can live with them after all. You tolerate him the way he is, because you do not have the time, the energy, or the inclination to put in the required effort to change him.

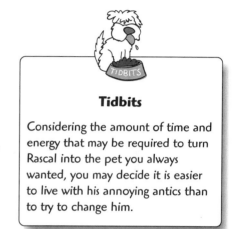

Tidbits

Considering the amount of time and energy that may be required to turn Rascal into the pet you always wanted, you may decide it is easier to live with his annoying antics than to try to change him.

Try to Solve the Problem

You have decided that you cannot live with such a dog and that you are going to work with him to be the pet you expected and always wanted. You understand this will require an investment of time and effort, perhaps even seeking expert help. But you are willing to work to achieve your goal—a long-lasting, mutually rewarding relationship. Good for you!

Obedience training, in and of itself, is not necessarily the answer. Still, when you train your dog, you are spending meaningful time with him, which in many cases is half the battle. Much depends on the cause of the problem.

For most of us, dog ownership is a compromise between tolerating and working with our dogs. There are certain behaviors we find objectionable, but realistically can't do anything about. As long as the joys of dog ownership outweigh the headaches, we put up with these behaviors.

Find a New Home for Your Dog

Your dog's temperament may be unsuitable to your life-style. A shy dog, or a dog with physical limitations, may never develop into a great playmate for active children. A dog that does not like to be left alone too long would not be suitable for someone who is gone all day. While some behaviors can be modified with training, others cannot, or the effort required would simply be too stressful for the dog.

In some instances the dog and the owner are mismatched and they need to divorce. The dog may require a great deal more exercise than the owner is able to give him and as a result is developing behavior problems. Whatever the reason, under some circumstances, placement into a new home where the dog's needs can be met is advisable and in the best interest of both dog and owner.

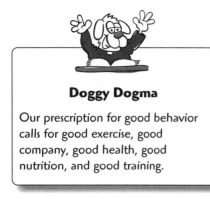

Doggy Dogma

Our prescription for good behavior calls for good exercise, good company, good health, good nutrition, and good training.

The One-Way Trip

If all reclamation efforts have failed, you can't live with this dog and he can't be placed because he is dangerous or for some other reason, your final option is to put him to sleep. It is not something to be considered lightly and only when you have really tried to work it out and there are truly no other alternatives.

Incidentally, don't kid yourself about taking your dog to a shelter. Most are overwhelmed by the number of unwanted dogs, and are able to find new homes for only a small percentage of these orphans. The sad fact is that we live in a throwaway society. Far too often, when the dog outgrows that cute puppy stage, out he goes.

A General Prescription

Many behavior problems have a common cause, or a combination of causes. In order of importance, these are:

1. Boredom and frustration due to insufficient exercise.
2. Mental stagnation due to insufficient quality time.
3. Loneliness.
4. Nutrition and health-related problems.

Before addressing behavior problems specifically, we will give you our general prescription for good behavior, which is:

➤ sufficient exercise

➤ good company

➤ good health

➤ good nutrition

➤ good training.

You will notice that exercise is at the top of the list. Exercise needs vary, depending on the size and energy level of your dog. Many dogs need a great deal of exercise. Bull Terriers are a good example. If a Bull Terrier lives in an apartment in a large city, and doesn't get enough free running exercise, he is bound to develop behavior problems. These can range from tail spinning, which is a neurotic behavior, to ripping up furniture. This kind of dog would show none of these behaviors if he were living in a household where adequate exercise, both mental and physical, were provided. The rule of thumb is tired dogs are happy dogs.

When your dog engages in behaviors that you consider objectionable, it can be a vexing problem. Sometimes the behavior is instinctive, such as digging, sometimes it occurs out of boredom, but never because the dog is ornery. Before you attempt to deal with the behavior, you need to find out the cause.

The easiest way to stop a behavior is by addressing the need that brought it about in the first place, rather than by trying to correct the behavior itself. If there is one single cause for behavior problems, it is the lack of adequate exercise. Another important cause is a physical problem (see Chapter 23).

Mental stagnation can also be a cause of unwanted behavior. Training on a regular basis, or doing something for you, makes your dog feel useful and provides the mental stimulation he needs. You can have your dog help you carry in groceries, take out the dirty laundry to the washing machine, carry your golf clubs to the car, bring them back into the house, pick things up off the floor that you have dropped, anything to make him feel useful.

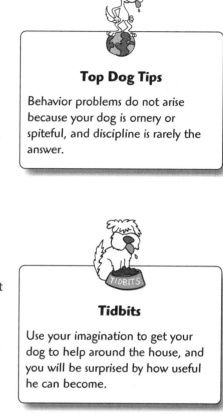

Top Dog Tips

Behavior problems do not arise because your dog is ornery or spiteful, and discipline is rarely the answer.

Tidbits

Use your imagination to get your dog to help around the house, and you will be surprised by how useful he can become.

Landscaping

Although some breeds, such as the small terriers, have a true propensity for digging, all dogs will do it to some extent at one time or another. Let's take a look at some of the more common and sometimes comical reasons for digging.

➤ Allelomimetic behavior, or mimicking. In training this is useful, but it may spell trouble for your gardening efforts. You plant, you dog digs up. Maybe you should do your gardening in secret and out of sight of your dog.

➤ Female dogs make nests for real or imaginary puppies.

➤ To bury a bone and to dig up a bone.

➤ To see what's there, because it's fun, or to find a cool spot.

➤ Boredom, isolation, or frustration.

The cure to digging is rather simple: Don't leave your dog unattended in the yard for lengthy periods.

Barking

On the one hand, few things are more reassuring than knowing the dog will sound the alarm when a stranger approaches. On the other hand, few things are more nerve-wracking than the incessant barking of a dog.

Bet You Didn't Know

Dogs bark in response to a stimulus or because they are bored and want attention, any attention, even if it involves the owner being nasty to the dog.

Therein lies the dilemma: We want the dog to bark, but only when we think he should.

Dogs bark in response to some stimulus, or for no apparent reason.

Barking in Response to a Stimulus

Your dog is outside in the yard and some people walk by, so he barks. It is a natural response of defending his territory. Once the potential intruders have passed, he is quiet again. People passing are the stimulus that causes barking and once it has been removed, your dog stops.

If the people had stopped by the fence for a conversation, your dog would have continued to bark. To get him to stop you have to remove your dog, or the people have to leave. Remove the stimulus from the dog or the dog from the stimulus. If you live in a busy area where this happens frequently, you may have to change your dog's environment. You may not be able to leave him in the yard for prolonged periods.

Your dog will also bark when he is in the house and someone comes to the door. After he has alerted you, tell your dog "thank you, that's enough," and have him sit at your side as you answer the door. If necessary, put him on leash so you can control him.

He may also rush to the window, stand there and bark because he sees or hears something. Again, thank him for letting you know what's going on and tell him "that's enough." If he does not stop, go to him, take him away from the window and have him lie down in his corner.

Barking for No Apparent Reason

Your dog has a reason for barking, but it is not apparent to you. It can be due to:

➤ anxiety,

➤ boredom, or

➤ seeking attention because he is lonely.

Theoretically, none of these are difficult to overcome, if you work to eliminate the potential causes. Spend more time exercising your dog. Spend more time training your dog. Don't leave your dog alone so long, and don't leave him alone so often.

As a practical matter, it's not that easy. Most people work for a living and the dog is left at home alone for prolonged periods. If you live in an apartment, your dog certainly can't bark all day. The stress on the dog is horrendous, not to mention the reaction of your neighbors.

Tidbits

Whatever you may think, Rascal does what he does for a reason. While the behavior may be unacceptable to you, to him it is the only way he can express his unhappiness. When he barks, or digs, or chews, the behavior in and of itself releases the stress that he is feeling, and is self-rewarding.

The most effective and least stressful method for the dog that we know of is an electronic bark collar (see Appendix A). It takes the decision whether to bark or not to bark away from the dog. He no longer has to worry and can relax. Sounds contradictory, but it works.

Chewing

The principle reasons dogs chew are physiological and psychological. The first passes, the second does not, and both are a nuisance.

The Physiological Need to Chew

As part of the teething process, puppies need to chew. They cannot help it. To get through this period provide your dog with a soft and a hard chew toy, such as a hard rubber bone or a real bone, and a canvas field dummy. Don't give him anything he can destroy or ingest, except food items. Carrots or apples, dog biscuits or ice cubes, are great to relieve the monotony.

Make sure your dog does not have access to personal articles, such as shoes, socks, towels, and the like. Do not give him an old sock of yours as a toy—he can't tell the difference between an old and a new pair. Think of it as good training for you not to leave things lying around the house.

A lonely dog will chew up anything in his path. Make sure that your dog gets enough attention from you (and that he gets some strong chew toys)!

The Psychological Need to Chew

Chewing after the dog has gone through teething is usually a manifestation of anxiety, boredom, or loneliness. It is an oral habit that has nothing to do with being spiteful. Should your dog attack the furniture, baseboards and walls, tip over the garbage can, or engage in other destructive chewing activities, use a crate to confine him when you can't supervise him. It will save you lots and lots of money, and you won't lose your temper and get mad at the poor fellow. Even more important, he can't get into things that are a potential danger to him.

We want to emphasize that confinement is a problem-solving approach of last resort. Ideally, the dog is not left alone so long and so often that he feels the need to chew in order to relieve his boredom.

Top Dog Tips

Rather than becoming angry at your dog for chewing up your prized possessions, give him some good solid chew toys. Use a crate or other means of confinement when you need to limit access to your personal items.

Your dog doesn't need you to entertain him all the time, but extended periods of being alone can make your pet neurotic. All of the above problems fall under the category of too much isolation.

Separation Anxiety

Separation anxiety is just that—your dog becomes anxious when you leave him. It is an emotional response to being left alone.

Dog's that experience it are usually high in pack and low in defense (fight) drive.

All of the behavior problems we have discussed so far can be the direct result of separation anxiety. To make matters worse, all too often the owner feeds into the behavior by making a big fuss before leaving the dog, who is left in an empty house in a state of high excitement.

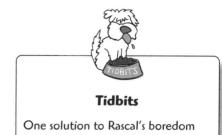

Tidbits

One solution to Rascal's boredom and loneliness is to get another dog. They can keep each other amused, and two dogs are more than twice the fun of one dog.

If you have such a dog, get him accustomed to the routine of your arrivals and departures. Ignore the dog and without saying or doing anything walk out the door—just leave. Stay away for a short period of time. Return the same way, without saying anything, ignoring the dog for the first five minutes. What you want to accomplish is to take the emotional element out your going and coming.

Bet You Didn't Know

Many owners exacerbate the dog's separation anxiety by making a big fuss when they leave him, saying things like "Now don't worry. Mommy/Daddy is going to be right back. You be good, blah, blah, blah."

As your dog becomes used to being left for short periods, increase the time. Before long, your dog will view the separation as a normal part of a day and nothing to get excited about.

House Soiling

House soiling, after your dog has been housetrained and that is not marking behavior (see Chapter 4), can have a variety of causes. It is rarely a behavior problem, but is most frequently a result of one or more of the following:

1. You have left your dog too long without giving him a chance to relieve himself. As the saying goes, "accidents will happen," and that's just what it was, an accident. You know his endurance and his schedule, so don't blame the dog when you for some reason are unable to adhere to it. You may have had to work late or some other unforeseen event prevented you from getting home on time. As long as it doesn't become a regular occurrence on your part, it will not be a problem.

2. Your dog may have eaten something that disagreed with him and he has an upset stomach. Abrupt dietary changes, such as changing dog foods, are the most common cause for an upset tummy. Anytime you change your dog's diet, do it gradually, over a period of several days, so his system can get used to the new food.

3. Giving treats at holiday times that your dog ordinarily doesn't get, such as turkey and gravy, or pizza, can create havoc with his digestive system.

4. Cystitis, a bladder infection, is more common among female dogs than male dogs, and may cause dribbling. You need to consult your veterinarian.

5. As your dog ages, urinary incontinence may develop. It can be treated with medication and homeopathic remedies.

6. Eating chocolate, which can make your dog really sick.

Submissive Wetting

Dogs that are high in defense flight and low in defense fight drives are notorious for this behavior. It usually occurs upon first greeting the dog. He will either squat or roll over on his back and dribble. It dates back to his days as a puppy, when his mother would clean him.

Fortunately, submissive wetting is not difficult to solve.

1. Do not scold the dog, as that will only reinforce the behavior and make it worse.

2. Do not stand or lean over the dog, or try to pick him up.

3. When you come home from work, ignore the dog. Don't approach him and let him come to you instead.

4. Greet him without making eye contact, and by offering the palm of your hand. This is important. The back of the hand transmits negative energy, and the palm of the hand transmits positive energy.

5. Keep your mouth shut and let him sniff your palm, then gently pet him under the chin, not on top of the head.

6. Absolutely do not reach or try to grab for the dog.

7. When friends come to visit, tell them to ignore the dog and let him come to them. Instruct them about the palm of the hand and not grabbing for the dog.

By following this routine, the dog will stop the dribbling.

Car Sickness

Car sickness, which manifests itself in excessive drooling or vomiting, can be attributed to either:

➤ true motion sickness, or

➤ a negative association with riding in a car.

For obvious reasons, dogs that have a tendency to get car sick usually aren't taken for a ride very often. And when they are, it's to the veterinarian. You can compare his reaction to that of a child who, every time he or she gets in the car, goes to the doctor for a shot. It doesn't take many repetitions before an unpleasant association with the car has been made.

> **Top Dog Tips**
>
> Some dogs get sick in vans because they can't see out of the window, and others get sick in cars because they can see out of the window. Whatever the reason for the dog's reaction, you can create a pleasant association with the car.

Some dogs get sick in vans because they can't see out of the window, and others get sick in cars because they can see out of the window. Whatever the reason for the dog's reaction, you can create a pleasant association with the car. You can tell how well he is taking to the car and how much time you need to spend at each sequence.

What, us get car sick? No way!

Throughout this remedial exercise maintain a light and happy attitude. Avoid a solicitous tone of voice and phrases like, "It's all right. Don't worry. Nothing is going to happen to you." These reassurances validate the dog's concerns and reinforce the behavior.

1. Open all the doors and with the engine off, coax your dog into the car. If he doesn't want to go in, pick him up and put him in the car. Give him a treat and tell him how proud you are of him and immediately let him out again. Repeat until he is comfortable getting into the car on his own.

2. Once your dog willingly gets into the car, close the doors on one side, engine still off, and repeat Step 1.

3. When he is comfortable with Step 2, tell him to get in the car, give him a treat and close the doors. Let him out again and give him a treat. Repeat until he readily goes into the car and you can close the doors for up to 1 minute.

4. Tell your dog to get into the car, get in yourself, close all the doors and start the engine. Give your dog a treat. Turn off the engine and let him out.

5. Now it's time for a short drive, no more than once around the block.

6. Increase the length of the rides, always starting and ending with a treat.

7. Ginger cookies are an excellent treat. Ginger calms your dog's stomach.

Eating Stools (Coprophagy)

Halitosis is one thing, but no one wants to be greeted by a canine companion who is in the habit of eating stools. Some dogs eat their own, those of other dogs, or those of other animals such as cats, horses, and cows. Cat stools seem to be especially attractive, and are particularly enticing when frozen.

Without doubt, this is a decidedly undesirable behavior. It, too, can be caused by boredom or, as is more often the case, by dietary deficiencies. Unable to assimilate protein because his food is lacking the correct digestive enzymes, vitamins, and minerals, he eats stools that contain these ingredients (see Chapter 9).

Bet You Didn't Know

Eating stools can be caused by boredom or dietary deficiencies. As unappealing as this behavior may be, it is something that dogs will do—don't freak out that your dog is wacko.

To solve the problem, experiment by adding some raw food to your dog's diet, as well as digestive enzymes. Better yet, try feeding the "Healthy Dog Diet," described in Chapter 9, and the behavior should disappear. If it persists, consult your veterinarian.

Early on in our career we received a call concerning coprophagy that went something like this: "My dogs are eating their stools. I have consulted my veterinarian, and the food supplements he prescribed did not work. I then consulted a dog behavior counselor and he told me to sprinkle Tabasco sauce on the stools. That stopped the dogs for a while, but now they have developed a taste for Tabasco and are right back at it again. Can you help?"

We advised the individual that while he was out in the yard sprinkling Tabasco on the stools, it would probably be just as easy to clean up after the dogs, thereby precluding them from doing their own cleaning up. Two weeks later we got another call. "It works! They are no longer eating stools."

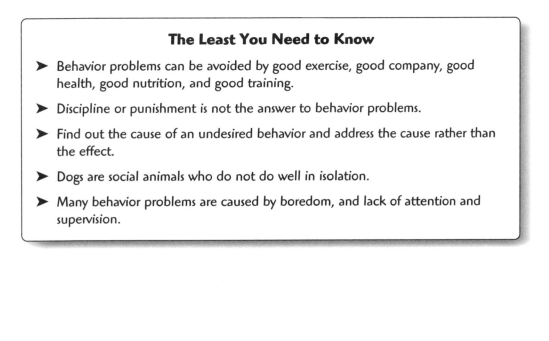

The Least You Need to Know

➤ Behavior problems can be avoided by good exercise, good company, good health, good nutrition, and good training.

➤ Discipline or punishment is not the answer to behavior problems.

➤ Find out the cause of an undesired behavior and address the cause rather than the effect.

➤ Dogs are social animals who do not do well in isolation.

➤ Many behavior problems are caused by boredom, and lack of attention and supervision.

Chapter 22

Aggression— Causes and Cures

In This Chapter

➤ What *is* aggression

➤ Why *is* my dog aggressive

➤ What triggers aggression?

The term aggression means different things to different people. For example, a dog in a fenced yard that runs along the fence barking furiously at a passerby, might well be considered aggressive by the passerby. If it's your dog, you would consider it a perfectly normal reaction. The dog is defending his territory, which is what you would expect from him.

Many dog owners expect a certain amount of protectiveness, or "aggression," from their companions, but only at the right time and under the right circumstances. For the dog, that can be a tough call.

Once Bitten, Twice Shy

Aggression is a natural and even necessary phenomenon. Only when we are unable to manage it, or don't understand its origin, does it become a problem. Two main "causes" of aggression are:

➤ the "aggressive" behavior is actually misunderstood, and

➤ a physical reason, that is, the dog may be sick, or have some other condition making him feel grouchy (see Chapter 23).

Top Dog Tips

Keeping your dog at home until he has had all his vaccinations at 6 months of age prevents proper socialization with people and other dogs, which can be a cause for aggression.

Tidbits

Suppressing a behavior can be an effective momentary solution, provided the dog also has the chance to expend the energy of that behavior on a regular basis.

A rather typical scenario looks something like this: Rascal growls at a person or another dog. Rascal's owner tries to defuse the situation by stroking him, soothingly saying something like "There, there, now be nice." The stroking and soothing voice are interpreted by Rascal as "There's a good boy. That's exactly what I want you to do."

A few years ago, it was brought to our attention that a number of Rottweilers, when taken for their six-month check-ups, had bitten the veterinarian. Apparently, it got so bad that many veterinarians didn't want these dogs as clients anymore.

It was at this point that we were consulted by the Rottweiler Club of England. We learned that the very veterinary community who now didn't want these dogs as clients anymore, had advised their owners not to let the dogs out in public before they had all their vaccines, that is, until they were six months of age. Those who followed this advice ended up with completely unsocialized dogs. Here you have a classic case of aggression on a grand scale caused by a lack of understanding of behavior. Socialization is a continuing necessity throughout your dog's life. If you don't socialize Rascal, you *will* have problems as he grows up. Take this very seriously and get Rascal out into a good puppy class as soon as you can. Continue to take him out so that he can mix with other dogs as he continues to mature.

We are going to examine the triggers of aggression in the context of the three drives—prey, pack, and defense. The triggers are different in each drive, and so is the management, or the cure. Your dog's Personality Profile will tell what the likely triggers are going to be, so you can predict what Rascal will do under certain circumstances.

Your ability to predict your dog's behavior is part of the management. Other than ignoring or putting up with the behavior, you have three basic options.

1. Expending the energy. Each behavior has a time frame, or energy, and can be managed by expending that energy. This means exercise specifically focused on that energy. It can be playing ball, jogging, tug-of-war games, or whatever. Training is always a good idea.

2. Suppressing the energy. The dog is not given an outlet for the energy. Suppression can be an effective temporary solution, provided the dog has periodic opportunities to expend the energy. Absolute, or long-term suppression, is not a good idea. The energy will only redirect itself into another undesirable behavior.

3. Switching the drive. When Rascal growls at another dog, he is in fight drive. To manage the situation, switch him into pack drive. Cheerfully say something like "You must be joking," and walk away in the opposite direction.

Top Dog Tips

Learning to anticipate your dog's reaction under certain situations is part of managing his behavior.

Depending on the circumstances, you are going to use a combination of the three in your management program.

Let's take a look at some of the triggers in each of the drives, and what we can do to manage the behavior.

Aggression from Dogs High in Prey Drive

It should not come as a surprise to you that prey behaviors, those associated with chasing and killing prey, are one of the leading causes for aggression. In a sense, aggression coming from this drive is the most dangerous because it can be triggered by so many different stimuli. Dogs high in prey drive are stimulated by sounds, smells, and moving objects.

Triggers

Anything that moves will trigger prey behaviors. These are the dogs that chase cars, bicycles, joggers, cats, other dogs, squirrels, bunnies, you name it. And, should they catch up with whatever they are chasing, that's when the problem starts.

Management

Play retrieve games on a regular basis and make sure the dog gets plenty of exercise. When you take him for a walk and he spots a cat or a squirrel, give him a check on the leash to refocus his attention on you, and then go in the opposite direction.

Tidbits

Anything that moves will trigger prey behaviors. These behaviors are those associated with chasing and killing prey, and are one of the leading causes of aggression.

If he doesn't reliably respond to the come command, don't let him loose in situations where he might take off. Better yet, train him to come reliably on command. Whatever you do, don't let Rascal chase cars, joggers, or cyclists.

Taxing your dog's mental faculties also expends this energy. We use a very simple game to keep this drive under control with our Landseer Newfoundland, Evo. He loves to retrieve, and on our daily walks he has ample time to play. But he is rarely satisfied, always wanting to do it "one more time." So in the evenings we play the "find it" game. We hide his favorite toy in different parts of the house. We then tell him to find it and he will search until he does.

There are lots of ways to stimulate your dog. Make him feel useful by letting him help you out.

Doesn't sound like much of a game, but since he has to use the little gray cells, after four to five retrieves he is mentally wiped out and peace reigns.

Top Dog Tips

If a puppy is allowed to grow up doing anything he likes and is not given parameters of what he can and can't do, he will assume that you are not strong enough to be the pack leader.

Aggression from Dogs High in Fight Drive

Once they understand who is in charge, these dogs are terrific companions and protectors, great competition and show dogs, and a joy to own. As young dogs they will start bucking for a promotion. You may see signs of aggression toward you when you want the dog to get off the furniture or in similar situations, that is, when he doesn't want to do what you tell him.

If a puppy is not given strong, consistent guidance as to what he may and may not do, he will develop a sense that you are push-over. He will try to take over. Full-fledged signs of aggression don't just suddenly occur. There will have been many warnings, from growls, to lip lifting, to staring at you. If you condone these behaviors and don't deal with them, your dog is on his way to becoming aggressive.

Rascal may also be aggressive toward other dogs. When meeting another dog, he will try to lord it over him. The classic sign is putting his head over the shoulder of the other dog. The dog of lesser rank will lower his body posture signaling he recognizes the other dog's rank.

When two dogs meet who perceive each other of equal rank, a fight may ensue. Left to their own devices, most often, both will decide that discretion is the better part of valor. Both know that there are no percentages to fighting. They will slowly separate and go their own way.

A true dog fight is a harrowing and horrifying experience, and most of us would prefer not to take this chance. We learn to read the signs and take the necessary precautions by keeping the dogs apart. Dogs are no different than people—not all of them get along.

Some owners inadvertently cause dog fights by maintaining a tight leash on the dog. A tight leash alters your dog's body posture, thereby giving an unintended signal to the other dog. Maintain a loose leash when meeting another dog so you don't distort Rascal's body posture. At the slightest sign of trouble, such as:

➤ a hard stare from the other dog,

➤ a growl, or

➤ snarl,

Tidbits

When out enjoying a stroll with Rascal, or on a trip to the dog park, keep him on a loose leash. A tight leash will manipulate his body posture so as to give an unintended signal to other dogs that you meet.

Doggy Dogma

When a female tells off a male dog making unwanted advances, she is entitled. This is not aggression, but perfectly normal dog behavior.

happily call your dog to you and walk away. The "happily" is important because you want to defuse the situation and not aggravate it by getting excited. What you want to accomplish is to switch the dog from fight drive into pack drive.

When a male dog makes unwanted advances to a female dog, she doesn't file a lawsuit. She tells him off in no uncertain terms. She is not being aggressive, she is simply conveying her wishes. This is perfectly acceptable and normal dog behavior.

Signs of aggression are:

➤ low-toned, deep growling,

➤ showing of teeth, and staring,

➤ ears and whiskers pointing forward with the dog standing tall, and with hackles up from his shoulders forward, and, of course,

➤ actual biting.

When this behavior is directed toward you, the owner, ask yourself whether the question of who is number one has been resolved. Usually, it has not, and the dog is convinced he is number one, or thinks he can become number one.

It's not that he is a bad dog, it's just because he is a pack animal, and is looking desperately for leadership. If that leadership is not forthcoming on your part, he will fill the vacuum. Dogs are very happy and content when they know their rank order.

Top Dog Tips

Each behavior has a time frame and a certain amount of energy inherent in that behavior. This energy can be exhausted by providing your dog with the appropriate outlet.

Triggers

There can be a variety of triggers, and some of the more common ones are:

➤ trying to take something out of his mouth,

➤ telling him to get off the couch,

➤ hovering or looming over the dog,

➤ staring at the dog,

➤ approaching the dog in a threatening manner,

➤ teasing the dog.

You can avoid some of these triggers altogether, such as teasing the dog, staring at him or hovering over him. Don't do it! Other triggers you need to deal with.

Management

1. Exercise and training.

   This dog needs lots of exercise and training. Exercise physically tires the body and training tires the brain. In this situation, it is lack of mental stimulation that gets the dog into trouble. Aim for two training sessions a day, each at least 10 minutes long. If you keep to the same time schedule, you'll have a happy puppy.

2. Tug-of-war.

   The energy in this drive needs to be expended by a good game of tug-of-war. This game allows the dog to use up his time frame of wanting to growl and tug and bite. At one point we believed that tug-of-war games would cause aggression and that aggressive behaviors should be suppressed. We are no longer of that view.

Just as we expend the energy in prey drive through retrieve games, so do we expend in fight drive with tug-of-war games. It is the same principle at work. The absence of an outlet for that energy, or efforts to suppress it, will only make matters worse.

Dogs with a strong fight drive can burn off some of that energy by playing tug-of-war.

➤ Put aside 10 minutes a day; it should be the same time every day.

➤ Take a pull toy, a piece of sacking, or a knotted sock and play tug-of-war with your dog.

➤ Allow him to growl and bite the object and shake it.

➤ Let him bring the object back to you to play again.

➤ Let him win each and every time.

➤ When the dog has had enough, or the 10 minutes are up, walk away from this session with the dog in possession of the toy.

The game effectively discharges the energy and the time frame in that drive. The game should be removed from regular training sessions and done when you and your dog are alone with no distractions. It is his time and his only. You will be amazed how satisfying the game is to your dog, and the calming effect it has on him.

Doggy Dogma

Some dog trainers discourage playing tug-of-war with dogs because they believe that it causes aggressive behavior. We used to agree but now think that quite the opposite is the case: playing tug-of-war helps to dissipate aggressive behavior.

When we came up with this concept, we were teaching a class of students who were very advanced in their training. Many of them were training their second or third dog, and all were experienced competitors. They had chosen dogs with a relatively high fight drive, because they knew how well they trained and how good the dogs looked in the show ring—the bold and the beautiful. But they had to live with the tendency towards aggressive behavior and always had to be careful in a class or dog show situation, when their dog was around other dogs.

For the entire eight-week session, they were told to put time aside daily to play tug-of-war with their dogs. By the third week, we already noticed a big difference in the dogs' temperaments. When together in class, the dogs became friendly toward each other, played more and trained better, and were perfectly well behaved when away from home.

3. The Long Down.

We cannot emphasize the importance of this exercise too often. It is a benign exercise and establishes quite clearly who is in charge in a non-punitive way. For dogs that express any kind of aggressive behavior, go back to that exercise and do a 10-minute down, last thing at night, for five out of seven days. It reinforces in your dog's mind that you are in charge. Combined with the tug-of-war game, these are simple solutions for the good dog that gets too pushy.

If it has gotten to the point where you are afraid of the dog, or where he tries to bite you, or you can't get him into the down position, use a muzzle. You may also require outside help (see chapter 24).

4. The Use of a Muzzle.

When you are nervous or anxious about what your dog might do if he encounters another dog or person, your emotions go straight down the leash, which can cause your dog to react in an aggressive manner. In a sense, your worries become a self-fulfilling prophecy. You can solve this dilemma with the use of a muzzle.

A muzzle allows you to go out in public with your dog without having to worry about him. A strange thing happens to a dog while wearing a muzzle—once you have taken away his option to bite, he doesn't even try. It's almost as if he is relieved that the decision has been taken away from him. Even better, it allows you to relax.

Training to a muzzle should be done slowly and gently, as at first many dogs panic having something around their faces. But with diligence, common sense, and some compassion for the dog, he can be trained quite easily to accept it.

➤ Put the muzzle on for a few minutes and take it off again.

➤ Give him a treat and tell him what a good boy he is.

➤ Repeat over the course of several days, gradually increasing the length of time your dog wears the muzzle.

➤ When he is comfortable wearing it at home, you can use it when you take him out in public.

Tidbits

The use of a muzzle is a simple solution to a complex problem. It takes the decision whether or not to bite away from your dog, and gives you peace of mind.

In some European cities, ordinances have been passed that require certain breeds to wear muzzles. We saw many of these dogs happily accompanying their owners on walks. They were well behaved and seemed to be quite comfortable with their muzzles.

Many owners are reluctant to use a muzzle because of the perceived stigma attached to it. You have to make a choice—stigma or peace of mind. Or, another choice—suppose your dog actually bit someone. When you have such a simple solution, why take the chance?

Feeding and Aggression

Your dog may growl when you get close to his food bowl. From his point of view he is guarding his food, an instinctive, and not uncommon reaction. The question becomes "should you try to do anything about it, and if so, what?"

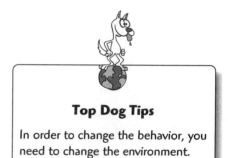

Top Dog Tips

In order to change the behavior, you need to change the environment.

We have never been particularly concerned by food possessiveness in a dog, provided it is the only time we see him act aggressively. Sometimes owners unwittingly exacerbate the behavior by trying to take the dog's food bowl from him while he is eating. This is definitely not a good idea. Why create unnecessary problems?

Make sure Rascal is fed in a place where the children or other dogs cannot get his food. Do not attempt to practice taking food away from him and putting it back. Imagine if someone kept taking away your dinner plate and putting it back. In no time at all would you become paranoid at the dinner table. That sort of thing creates apprehension and makes the guarding and growling worse.

➤ Feed your dog in his crate,

➤ give him his bone in his crate, and

➤ give him peace and quiet while he is his crate.

While Rascal is in his crate, everyone leaves him alone.

Taking Something Out of Rascal's Mouth

There will be times when you have to take something out of Rascal's mouth. It could be a chicken bone from the garbage or anything else inappropriate. Don't yell at him or chase him. He will redouble his efforts to eat whatever it is. A great solution is to get Rascal to "trade." Offer him a piece of cheese or raw meat. As he reaches for it, of course the chicken bone drops out, you pick it up and throw it away.

Bet You Didn't Know

You can negotiate with your dog. If you want to take something out of his mouth, offer him something more desirable. A piece of raw meat will get you the raunchy chicken bone every time.

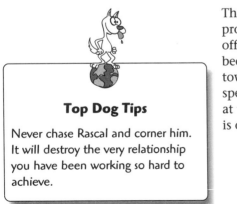

Top Dog Tips

Never chase Rascal and corner him. It will destroy the very relationship you have been working so hard to achieve.

The trade is an easy and simple way to work out the problem. We've always trained our dogs to accept treats off a spoon (see Chapter 13). This works really well because when they see us holding a spoon and coming toward them, they immediately think they are getting a special treat. No matter what they have in their mouths at the time, they will spit it out in favor of getting what is on the spoon.

Dogs with More than 50 Flight Behaviors

The term aggression for these dogs is actually a misnomer. They don't aggress, only defend. When they do bite, it is out of fear, and hence they are called fear-biters.

Triggers

Anytime this dog feels that he is cornered and unable to escape, he may bite. Biting to him is an act of last resort. He would much rather get away from the situation.

Management

Avoid putting this dog in a position where he thinks he has to bite. Use a similar approach to the one described in Chapter 21 for submissive wetting.

Dogs with a strong flight drive can appear shy around strangers, other dogs or new situations. They may hide behind their owners and need space. Keep them a good distance away from people and other dogs, and don't corner them for any reason. Use your body to reassure these dogs, bending down and coaxing them to you with some food. Be patient to gain their confidence and never, ever grab for them.

> **Tidbits**
>
> Fear-biters are most comfortable when they know what is expected of them, as in training. Timid behavior can resurface when left to their own devices and not given clear instruction how to behave.

What this dog needs is confidence building. Training with quiet insistence and encouragement is one way to achieve a more comfortable dog. To get the dog used to people and other dogs, enroll him in an obedience class. You need to be patient with this dog and learn to go slowly. If you try to force an issue, you may wipe out whatever advances you have made.

This dog needs a structured and predictable environment. Walk, feed, and play at certain times of the day, so the dog knows what is coming. Dogs have a phenomenal biological clock, and deviations from the time of walking and feeding can make undesirable behaviors resurface.

Rescue dogs, in particular, those that have gone from pillar to post, often have large numbers of flight behaviors. A tightly controlled schedule greatly helps in their rehabilitation.

Aggression from Pack Drive

It's hard to believe that a dog high in pack behaviors could be aggressive. This dog may:

➤ show signs of aggression toward people,

➤ attack other dogs with no reason,

➤ not give up biting when another dog submits.

Triggers

The problem with this kind of aggression is that there do not seem to be any obvious triggers. It can be observed in those dogs that are taken away from their litter and mother before seven weeks of age. It is between five and seven weeks when a puppy learns to inhibit his biting (see Chapter 3—Your Dog's Growth Stages). Also learned at this time is canine body language. In short, your puppy learns he is a dog.

Puppies that have not learned these lessons tend to be overly protective of their owners and may be aggressive to other people and dogs. They can't interpret body language and have not learned bite inhibition. The result can be a fight.

Lack of adequate socialization with either people or other dogs can be another cause for aggressive conduct. We remember several instances when a female owner came to us because her dog was aggressive toward men. The cause in each case was lack of socialization, or exposure to men. As long as the dog did not come in close proximity with men, it was not a problem. A change of circumstances, such as a boyfriend, however, now made it a problem.

Management

Lack of socialization with other people can be solved with a program of gradually getting the dog used to accept another person. Let's take the case of the man-aggressive dog. As always, the job is made easier when the dog has some basic training, and knows simple commands such as sit and stay.

➤ Begin with Rascal sitting at heel position, in control position (no tension on the leash and only 1/2 inch of slack).

➤ Have the person walk past the dog from a distance of 6 feet, without looking at the dog.

➤ Just before he passes the dog, the person throws Rascal a small piece of a hot dog, or another treat.

➤ Repeat 5 times per session, but no more.

➤ When Rascal shows no signs of aggression at 6 feet, decrease the distance.

➤ Keep decreasing the distance until Rascal will take a treat, open palm, from the person. The person does not look at the dog and pauses just long enough to give the dog the treat and then passes.

➤ Once you have gotten to this point, follow the procedure outlined for submissive wetting.

Aggression to other dogs, especially if the aggressor has had a few successes in his career, is not so simple. Prevention here is the best cure—keep your dog on leash and don't give him a chance to bite another dog.

Walking in the Neighborhood

What do you do when you are walking your dog down the street on leash and another dog comes out of nowhere and attacks your dog?

1. Whatever you do, *don't* yell or scream. Remember, prey drive is stimulated by sound, especially high-pitched sounds.

2. While you have a hold of the leash, your dog is at the mercy of the other dog. Let go, so he can either retreat or fend for himself.

Top Dog Tips

Screaming just escalates the intensity of a dog fight. Try to keep calm at all times.

3. For your own safety, don't try to separate the dogs, or you might get bitten. In the vast majority of incidents like this, one dog will give up, whereupon the other one walks away.

4. Find out to whom the loose dog belongs so you can take appropriate action.

When we trained and exhibited our Yorkshire Terrier, Ty, we got into the habit of being ever vigilant about the intentions of other dogs. We learned to position ourselves between Ty and other dogs so that they could not make eye contact with each other. Fortunately, we never had any untoward incidents with him.

Electric Fences

The current fad in new housing developments is covenants against fences. That's a problem when you have a dog and you want to keep him confined. Tying a dog out on a line, except for brief periods, is not a humane option.

Never fear, technology is here, and the electric fence is the answer. A wire is buried around the perimeter of the property, where a fence would normally be. The dog wears a collar, which serves as a receiver. If he tries to cross the invisible fence, he receives an

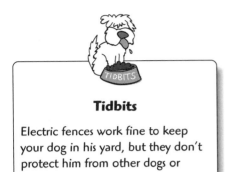

Tidbits

Electric fences work fine to keep your dog in his yard, but they don't protect him from other dogs or children coming into his yard.

electric shock. The dog, being no dummy, figures this out very quickly and stays in the yard, well away from the fence.

Sounds too good to be true, and it is. In the heat of chasing a cat, some dogs, those high in prey drive with a high discomfort threshold, don't honor the fence. When the fence does work as it is intended to, it will keep your dog in the yard, but it doesn't keep other dogs out. It is no protection against bullies coming into your yard and picking on your dog, or for a female in season. It may make your dog fearful of other dogs or aggressive toward them. Keep an eye on him when he is out there, and don't leave him for prolonged periods without supervision.

The Least You Need to Know

➤ A certain amount of aggression in dogs is normal and necessary to cope with the stresses and strains of living with us in our world.

➤ Redirecting aggression works better than trying to suppress it.

➤ Prey behaviors, those directed to the chasing and killing of prey, are the most dangerous.

➤ Motion and sounds, such as high-pitched screaming, stimulate prey behaviors.

➤ Yes, you can negotiate with your dog and get what you want.

When It's Not in His Head

A dog that is fed correctly, given enough exercise, and mental stimulation rarely exhibits behavior problems. He deals well with stress, hardly ever gets sick, and keeps his youthful characteristics into his teens.

In Chapter 9, we talked about the influence of nutrition on health and behavior. In this chapter, we will cover some of the more common health concerns and how they can affect the behavior of your pet. It doesn't take a genius to figure out that when a dog does not feel quite right, he will also not act quite right.

Here Comes That Needle Again

Over the past 20 years we have seen a steady increase in the number of vaccinations that dogs receive. Sadly, instead of improving the dogs' health and longevity, the practice has had the opposite effect.

Doggy Dogma

Vaccinosis is the term used to describe undesirable reactions to vaccines.

Tidbits

Too many vaccinations too close together can cause a puppy's immune system to break down and can result in serious health problems.

Over-vaccinating has created unintended and undesirable reactions to vaccinations, which result in *vaccinosis*. Reactions can range from none or barely detectable to death. These reactions may occur as a result of:

➤ one vaccine,

➤ several vaccines given at the same time, or

➤ repeated vaccinations given in a relatively short time frame.

We recall one consultation involving a four-month old Great Dane puppy, Caesar. When he came to us, he was virtually paralyzed. The veterinarian had told the owners that Caesar probably had contracted some spinal disease, not uncommon in giant breeds, and that nothing could be done.

The owners came to us as a last resort. By that time, Caesar did not want to eat, had become urine incontinent, and was constipated. Our first step was to take Caesar to our own veterinarian. After a blood test and X-rays, a number of diagnoses were considered, but nothing definitive could be determined.

In the meantime, we examined Caesar's history with the owners, and here is what we learned:

➤ The breeder gave Caesar distemper and parvo vaccines at six weeks of age.

➤ Caesar was picked up by new owners at seven weeks of age.

➤ Under the terms of seller's guarantee, Caesar was taken to the owners' veterinarian within 48 hours of purchase for a health evaluation.

➤ On that visit, Caesar was wormed and given a 5 in 1 vaccination.

➤ These vaccinations were repeated at nine, 11, and 13 weeks.

➤ During that time span, Caesar was wormed two more times as a "precautionary matter," even though no fecal sample was taken to see if he actually had worms.

➤ At 15 weeks of age, Caesar received another set of shots, to which the rabies vaccine had been added.

➤ Two days later Caesar collapsed, having received 23 vaccines in nine weeks.

At this point in our narrative we want to make it clear that we are not against vaccinations. What we are against, is random, repetitive, routine, and completely unnecessary vaccinations.

The story does have a happy ending. Through acupuncture, chiropractic, dietary, and homeopathic remedies, we managed to piece Caesar back together into a normal dog.

Aside from too many vaccinations too close together, where do the annual booster shots fit in? Actually they don't. According to Kirk's *Current Veterinary Therapy*, the textbook used in veterinary schools, there is no scientific basis or immunological reason that would necessitate annual re-vaccinations. Immunity to viruses can last for many years, or even for the life of the dog.

When your dog already carries the antibodies against a particular virus, a re-vaccination can cause havoc with his immune system. The many adverse reactions to unnecessary vaccinations have caused breeders, dog owners, and veterinarians to begin questioning the need for boosters and become more cautious in the way vaccines are administered. By law, your dog only needs a rabies vaccination, and the rabies booster only every three years. A rabies shot should never be given before the dog is six months of age.

Some breeds of dogs have extreme, even fatal, reactions to vaccines that are tolerated by other breeds of dogs. Some develop odd behaviors such as:

➤ aggression,

➤ epilepsy and other seizure disorders,

➤ excessive licking,

➤ anxiety or fear,

➤ insomnia, and

➤ snapping at imaginary flies.

How do you know if your dog will have a reaction? You don't, and therein lies the problem. Fortunately, you don't have to take the chance. When you take Rascal in for his annual physical check-up, you can ask your veterinarian to do a titer test. This is a blood test, which will tell you if Rascal has antibodies (or resistance) to the diseases for which he has already been vaccinated. If he has a high titer or level of antibodies to the disease, there is no point in re-vaccinating him. This process of titering is becoming more and more popular.

Bet You Didn't Know

A rabies vaccine given in conjunction with other vaccines can be responsible for aggression, epilepsy, and other seizure disorders.

Immunologists are discovering a direct correlation between the increase in auto-immune and chronic disease states with the increased use of vaccines. Many holistically trained veterinarians now believe that the benefits of many vaccines are outweighed by the risks and that dogs are better off either:

➤ not being vaccinated, except for rabies;

➤ only being vaccinated once for parvo and distemper as young dogs; or

➤ using a homeopathic alternative to vaccines.

To work out a vaccination schedule for a puppy, consult *The Holistic Guide for a Healthy Dog* (Howell Book House, 1995).

Before vaccinating your dog, discuss the safety with your veterinarian if Rascal:

➤ is on any kind of medication;

➤ is not perfectly healthy;

➤ has any skin, eye or ear infections;

➤ has recently been treated for fleas or ticks;

➤ has had prior reactions to vaccines;

➤ has not been supplemented with vitamins and minerals; and

➤ is scheduled for teeth cleaning, or spaying or neutering, or any other surgical procedure.

In the literature that they supply to veterinarians, vaccine manufacturers specifically indicate that no dog should be vaccinated unless in perfect health.

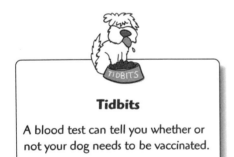

Tidbits

A blood test can tell you whether or not your dog needs to be vaccinated.

When You Have to Vaccinate

Sometimes you have to vaccinate your dog. Many boarding kennels require proof of vaccination, as do obedience schools.

If you have to leave Rascal at any time in such a boarding kennel, make sure that his vaccine has been given a minimum of three weeks before you board him. Vaccinating even a healthy dog stresses his immune system, whether or not you see a reaction. It takes 21 days to build up resistance to the disease. If you vaccinate Rascal and immediately take him to a boarding kennel, you may be exposing him to the risk of the very diseases that the vaccine is supposed to protect him against. Boarding a dog is stressful, even at the nicest boarding kennels. Under stress, Rascal is vulnerable to picking up disease.

Before you vaccinate, call the facility. Some boarding kennels are now recognizing titer tests.

If you cannot find a boarding kennel that will honor your wishes, and your Rascal is one of those dogs who has adverse side effects from vaccinations, you will have to find someone to come in and dog sit for you while you are away. And if the local obedience organization doesn't accept you, then you may have to get a private trainer who comes to your home (see chapter 24).

Doggy Dogma

Immunity to disease develops about 21 days after your dog has been vaccinated against the disease.

Hypothyroidism

The combined effect of poor nutrition, over vaccination, and neutering or spaying a puppy at too early an age, can cause a disease called *hypothyroidism*. Rarely seen in the 1970s, it has become more prevalent as our way of managing dogs has changed in the last 30 years. Over 50 percent of all dogs today show some signs of this disease.

Hypothyroidism is partially hereditary in nature. If your dog's parents had the disease, then the chances of him getting it are quite high.

The physical manifestations of *hypothyroidism* can be:

Doggy Dogma

Hypothyroidism refers to an under-active thyroid gland, which causes physical, as well as behavioral abnormalities.

➤ lack of control over body temperature,

➤ weight gain,

➤ oily, scaly skin, blackened skin on belly,

➤ auto-immune diseases,

➤ heart disorders,

➤ some kinds of paralysis,

➤ abnormal reaction to stressful situations, and

➤ seizures.

Behavioral manifestation may include:

➤ aggression to people or other dogs,

➤ fear and anxiety, separation anxiety, and fear of thunderstorms,

➤ obsessive-compulsive behavior, such as spinning and extreme hyperactivity,

➤ lick granulomas, and

➤ difficulty learning.

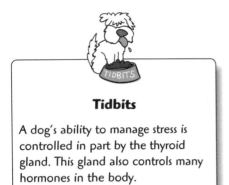

The thyroid gland is part of the endocrine gland system. This system not only controls many of the hormones in the body, but also the brain's ability to deal with stress. The above behaviors were reported in a 1997 English study. Nearly all the abnormal behaviors disappeared when thyroid medication was administered.

How can you tell if Rascal has a thyroid-related problem? If he is exhibiting any of the behaviors listed above, make an appointment with your veterinarian as soon as possible. If you wish to reassure yourself that Rascal does not have hypothyroidism, have your veterinarian do a blood test and ask for a thyroid panel.

The results will tell you whether or not Rascal needs medication. All laboratory reports indicate a low and high normal reading for each test done. Most veterinarians believe that when a dog shows a low normal reading, it should be on medication. High readings are uncommon in dogs.

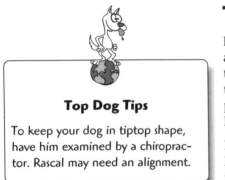

The Bone Crusher

Performance events, especially agility, are athletic activities for the dog. It is not uncommon for these dogs to require chiropractic adjustments to various parts of the body that have gone out of whack. Because the dog's performance is affected, many competitors routinely have their dogs adjusted.

Performance aside, misalignments of your dog's musculoskeletal system can also affect his behavior. Our own introduction to a veterinary chiropractor came through our Briard, D.J. While he was growing up, D.J. was quite unpredictable when meeting new people or new dogs. His first reaction was to lunge and bark, and show typical signs of aggression. We didn't take it too seriously, attributing it to his lack of maturity. With training and gaining confidence, we figured he would grow out of it.

Although the behavior diminished to a certain extent, it did not disappear. At that point we decided to have him examined. We learned that one of the vertebrae in his neck was impinging on the optic nerve and that he had never been able to see properly. Once adjusted, he was a different dog.

After that experience, we had all our dogs examined. These examinations disclosed a number of weaknesses that we had been aware of, but didn't know how to address. For example, one of our Dachshund's jaws was out, which caused him discomfort and affected his behavior and performance. With treatment he became a much happier dog.

It's a good idea to have puppies looked at by a chiropractor to make sure everything is in order. Vigorous play, especially with other dogs, can cause all manner of misalignments, which then may interfere with proper growth.

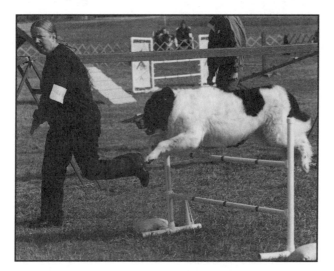

If you participate in performance events with your dog, have him periodically examined by a chiropractor. An adjustment may work wonders!

Sugar Pills

Many dogs experience anxiety under different conditions. This can occur when:

➤ taken on a trip away from home,

➤ before and during thunderstorms,

➤ going to the veterinarian, or

➤ encountering other situations they perceive as stressful.

We have been quite successful in dealing with this sort of anxiety with homeopathic remedies. We carry a small homeopathic emergency kit with us wherever we go, just in case (see Appendix A).

Tidbits

Homeopathic remedies are effective in dealing with anxiety reactions caused by thunderstorms and similar situations your dog perceives as stressful.

More Needles

Many veterinarians today use acupuncture for a variety of chronic conditions. Among its many applications, we have found it particularly effective with allergies, skin disorders, and the aches and pains that come with age.

> ## The Least You Need to Know
>
> ➤ Too many vaccinations over too short a period of time can cause serious health problems.
>
> ➤ Thyroid dysfunction is quite common in dogs and can be successfully treated.
>
> ➤ A chiropractic adjustment can work wonders on your dog.
>
> ➤ Homeopathic remedies work well in a variety of circumstances where your dog may experience anxiety.

Chapter 24

Getting Outside Help

In This Chapter

➤ You pays your money and takes your choice

➤ When you want a job done right ...

➤ Going to obedience school

➤ Yes, you can outsource the job

➤ And a camping we will go

You have a number of choices when it comes to Rascal's education. You can:

➤ train out of a book, such as this one, or

➤ participate in group classes, or

➤ you can have someone else do the training.

Each one has its own pros and cons, and your own personality and life-style will determine your choice.

Doggy Dogma

"The trouble with dog training is not that it is a completely unregulated activity and that anyone, regardless of experience, can set up shop as a dog trainer, but that so many actually do." Jack Volhard

Moreover, there are enormous quality differences, not only in terms of effectiveness of the training, but also in how the dogs are treated. Dog training is a completely unregulated area and anyone, yes, anyone, can proclaim himself a trainer.

When you attempt to make a rational choice, remember that there are many ways to skin a cat. Beware of anyone who says there is only one way to do the job. Successful dog training depends not so much on the "how," but on the "why." Dogs are not a homogeneous commodity and the approach to training has to take into account the dog's Personality Profile, as well as your own personality.

Available Choices

Choice	Pros	Cons
Training out of a book	Least expensive. You can train how you want, what you want, and when you want. You are not tied to a regular schedule. Location is not a problem.	You need to be highly self-motivated or training will fall by the wayside. You have no one to critique you. Possibly not enough exposure to other dogs.
Group Classes	Very economical. There is someone who can tell you what you may be doing wrong. Opportunity to meet people of like mind. Keeps your training on track with weekly sessions. Continuous socialization with other dogs.	Schedule and location may be inconvenient. Instructor dictates how, what, and when. Training method may not be right for you or your dog.
Having someone else do the job	Very expensive. Little time commitment required from you.	Training method may not be how you would want your dog trained.

Within these three major categories, there are additional options. You can take private lessons from an instructor, either at your house, or some other location. Under such an arrangement, the instructor teaches you what to do, and you are then expected to practice with your dog between sessions. In terms of cost, time, and effort, this is one of the most efficient arrangements.

Rascal and You Go to School

Having taught obedience classes for 30 years, we are naturally biased in favor of this choice. A basic class usually addresses your most immediate concerns, such as: not pulling on the leash, the sit and down-stay, and coming when called.

The purpose of the class is to show you what to do, have you try it a few times to make sure you've got it right, and then send you home to practice. You should be prepared to practice at least five times a week. Most classes are sequential in nature, so if you fall behind, you may have a hard time catching up. When you go to a class, do not expect the instructor to train your dog. That is not his or her job.

We think taking Rascal to school is perhaps one of the best things you can do for both of you. It gets you out of the house into an atmosphere where you can spend quality time together. Both of you have fun while learning useful things that make living together that much easier.

Classes can be found in most communities. Until quite recently, the majority of classes were conducted by obedience or kennel clubs. Today, many classes are taught by schools or private individuals. The difference has nothing to do with the quality of the training, but relates solely to profit motive. Clubs are not-for-profit organizations and the instructors, usually members who have trained and shown their own dog, generally volunteer their services. Training schools and individuals who hang out their shingles are for-profit organizations.

Tidbits

Teaching skills are not the same as training skills. To teach people, the instructor needs good communication and people skills, as well as a thorough knowledge of dog training.

Top Dog Tips

Word of mouth is often the best way to find a trainer. Ask your veterinarian, friends, and acquaintances for recommendations.

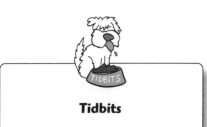

Tidbits

Obedience classes are conducted in almost every community and are an excellent way for you and Rascal to learn together.

Working together in an obedience class can be great fun for you and your dog.

Top Dog Tips

To participate in performance events, you will be best served by joining an organization that offers training for that goal. You will be coached on the intricacies of the various requirements.

Choosing a Good Training Class

To locate a class, look in the Yellow Pages under "Pet & Dog Training" and see what is offered in your community. Chances are you will have several choices.

Call one and find out where and when the class meets and whether you can observe a beginner class. If you can't observe a class, which would be very unusual, forget that one. When you find one where you can observe, leave Rascal at home so you are not distracted.

➤ Notice your first impression of the class. Is it positive or negative?

➤ Do the dogs seem to have a good time?

➤ Is the class atmosphere a pleasant one?

➤ How does the instructor deal with the class participants?

➤ How does the instructor deal with the dogs?

➤ Does the instructor appear knowledgeable?

➤ What is the ratio of instructors to students? We always aimed for a 1:5 ratio, with a limit of 15 students for one instructor with two assistants.

➤ Is the space adequate for the number of dogs? Insufficient space can be a cause for aggression in a class situation.

If you don't like what you see, find another organization. If you like what you see and hear, then this might be the class for you and Rascal. While you are visiting find out:

1. The cost of the class and what is included. For example, our basic training course, or Level 1 as we call it, consists of eight 50-minute sessions and includes a training collar and leash, weekly homework sheets, and a copy of our book *What All Good Dogs Should Know* as part of the fee.

2. What is the goal of the program, that is, what can be expected from your dog upon completion of the class?

3. The schedule of classes, the level of classes and the length of the program.

4. Does the organization offer puppy classes? The ideal age to start training Rascal is around eight to 10 weeks. His brain is fully developed, but he has not acquired any bad habits.

Puppy Classes

The joy of taking a puppy to class is that he can socialize with other young dogs, have fun, yet be taught manners and how to interact with his own kind. Rascal's brain at this point in his little life is just like a sponge, and everything you teach him now, will be remembered for the rest of his life. He will learn all those lessons that will make him an ideal pet.

Look for an organization that offers puppy classes, preferably one that teaches basic control to puppies, rather than just socialization and games. There is nothing wrong with socialization and games; both are necessary, but at the right time and in the right context.

You want Rascal to associate meeting other dogs as a pleasant, but controlled experience, not one of playing and being rowdy. As he grows older playing and being rowdy is no longer cute and will make him hard to manage around other dogs.

The ideal puppy class allows the puppies to interact with each other for up to three minutes before the class starts for the first two classes only. After that the puppies are allowed to play for three minutes after class. This way Rascal learns that he must be obedient to you first, and the reward is playing after he has worked, a lifetime habit you wish to instill while he is young.

Top Dog Tips

Taking Rascal to an obedience class as a puppy is the best investment in his future you can make.

Top Dog Tips

Look for a class where the people are having fun with their dogs, and where the instructor is pleasant and professional to the students. Above all, you want to see happy dogs.

Stay away from the classes where you are told that Rascal is too young to learn obedience exercises. This shows a lack of knowledge of dog behavior.

You can expect that your puppy will learn to sit, down, and stand on command, come when called, stay when told, and walk on a loose leash. An excellent program, with well-trained instructors, will also have Rascal doing the same exercises off leash, as well as on signal. For Rascal, this is easy stuff.

Advanced Classes

Many organizations also offer classes at higher levels, as well as for different activities, such as agility. You might get bitten by the training bug, and if you and Rascal enjoy what you are doing, go for it.

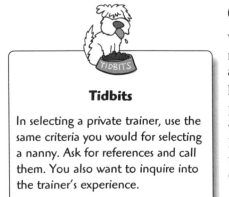

Tidbits

In selecting a private trainer, use the same criteria you would for selecting a nanny. Ask for references and call them. You also want to inquire into the trainer's experience.

Getting Rascal a Private Tutor

You may have serious time constraints, and so you might want to consider a private trainer. Private trainers are not cheap, but it's better than not training at all, provided the trainer doesn't ruin your dog.

In selecting a private trainer, be choosy. This individual will have a great impact on shaping your dog's skills. Don't be afraid to ask for references and to grill the trainer on his experience. Remember, anyone can declare himself a dog trainer!

Once you have found a trainer, he or she usually does the training at your residence. This is an advantage because the trainer gets to see where and how Rascal lives, and can tailor a program to meet your special needs.

At some point you will have to become involved and learn the various commands Rascal has learned and how to reinforce these commands. After all, the object is for your dog to obey you, not just the trainer. You will be expected to work Rascal under the direction of the trainer so that you can learn what and how he was taught.

Sending Rascal to Boarding School

When you outsource the job, Rascal will typically be boarded at the training facility for a specified period, such as three to six weeks. This is our least preferred option. We are not too thrilled about the idea of leaving one of our dogs somewhere to be trained. For us, at least, it seems to conflict with why we have a dog in the first place.

We view this option as one of last resort, when you absolutely cannot make any other arrangements. Before you take this step, inspect the facility.

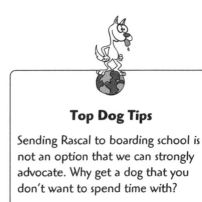

➤ How are the dogs housed?

➤ Is it clean?

➤ How do the other dogs look?

➤ Ask for a demonstration.

➤ Trust your instincts—Rascal is your dog!

Top Dog Tips

Sending Rascal to boarding school is not an option that we can strongly advocate. Why get a dog that you don't want to spend time with?

After your dog has completed the program, the trainer will then work with you for several sessions to show you how to get Rascal to respond to you. It is then your responsibility to keep up the training.

Don't overlook day care as another alternative. Many of these facilities also offer basic training while looking after Rascal.

The Great Vacation—Taking Rascal to Dog Camp

Dog camps have been around ever since we can remember. When we became serious about training and competing with our dogs, that is where we went. They were great fun and invaluable learning experiences. In 1977, we started our own camps, and since then have conducted almost 60, in the U.S., Canada, and England.

Bet You Didn't Know

There are dog camps, just like tennis or computer camps, for you and Rascal. They can be great learning experiences and are a wonderful way of getting closer to your dog.

Most dog camps last from four to five days, and the number of participants can range from 20 to over 100. A few of the distinguishing features are:

➤ Some are highly structured, with each hour of the day filled with specific activities, while others are more loosely organized.

➤ Some camps are program driven, where you learn a particular approach to training, and others are activity driven, where you are exposed to a variety of things you and Rascal can do together.

➤ Some are designed for a particular activity, such as agility or obedience competition, and others are more general.

➤ Some require prior training experience, and others do not.

➤ Some include room and board in the tuition, others only the camp itself.

➤ Some are held in full-fledged conference centers offering every conceivable amenity, others in more Spartan settings.

Summer camp may be one of your best memories. Why not share the experience with Rascal?

All camps combine a vacation element, where you and Rascal can enjoy each other. If you feel you would like to take a week's vacation with Rascal, where you can go have fun and learn more about dogs, training, or a particular activity, then dog camp is the place for you. A good starting point for more information about dog camps, including ours, is the Internet (see Appendix A).

Our own camps are held twice a year, in April and July, and require no prior training experience. They are five days long, tuition is all-inclusive, and they are held at a YMCA Conference Center. For maximum individual attention, participation is limited. Activities include

➤ obedience training at all levels,

➤ problem solving,

➤ understanding and dealing with aggression,

➤ refinements of "drives,"

➤ understanding dog behavior,

➤ nutrition and health,

➤ complementary sources of health care,

➤ agility,

➤ tracking, and

➤ water rescue work.

Because few dogs can maintain an entire day's worth of activity, the training sessions alternate with lectures on a variety of subjects so the dogs can rest.

Current and past participants have given us a slogan for our camps: for the best time with your dog you have ever had!

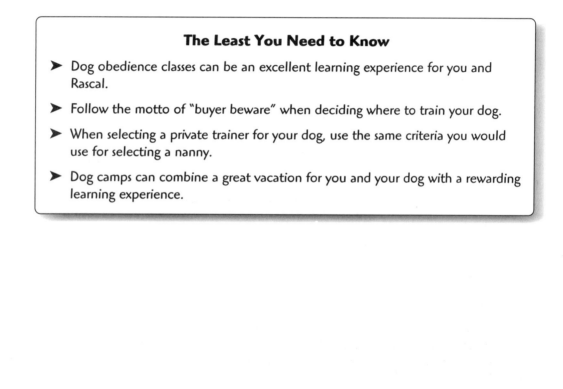

The Least You Need to Know

➤ Dog obedience classes can be an excellent learning experience for you and Rascal.

➤ Follow the motto of "buyer beware" when deciding where to train your dog.

➤ When selecting a private trainer for your dog, use the same criteria you would use for selecting a nanny.

➤ Dog camps can combine a great vacation for you and your dog with a rewarding learning experience.

Recommended Reading and Resources

Books

American Kennel Club. *The Complete Dog Book.* New York: Howell Book House, 1998.

Behavior Problems in Dogs. Santa Barbara, CA: American Veterinary Publication, Inc., 1975.

Campbell, William E. *Owner's Guide to Better Behavior in Dogs & Cats.* Loveland, CO: Alpine Publications, Inc., 1989.

Coren, Stanley. *The Intelligence of Dogs.* New York: The Free Press, 1994.

Fox, Dr. Michael, W. *Understanding Your Dog.* New York: Coward, McCann & Geoghegan, Inc., 1974.

———. *Understanding Your Pet: Pet Care and Humane Concerns.* New York: Coward, McCann & Geoghegan, Inc., 1978.

Frost, April & Rondi Lightmark. *Beyond Obedience: Training With Awareness For You and Your Dog.* New York: Harmony Books, 1998.

Holmes, John. *The Farmer's Dog.* London: Popular Dogs, 1975.

Kirk, Robert W. *Kirk's Current Veterinary Therapy X1 – 205.* Philadelphia: W.B. Saunders Co., 1989.

Lorenz, Konrad. *Man Meets Dog.* New York: Penguin Books, 1964.

——— *On Aggression.* New York: Harcourt, Brace & World, Inc., 1966.

Most, Konrad. *Training Dogs.* London: Popular Dogs, 1954.

Mech, David L. *The Wolf.* New York: The Natural History Press, 1970.

O'Driscoll, Catherine. *Who Killed the Darling Buds of May: Vaccination.* Derbyshire, England: Abbeywood Publishing, Ltd., 1997.

Pfaffenberger, Clarence J. *The New Knowledge of Dog Behavior.* New York: Howell Book House, 1963.

Pryor, Karen. *Don't Shoot the Dog!* New York: Simon and Schuster, 1984.

———*Lads Before the Wind.* New York: Harper & Row, 1975.

The Monks of New Skete. *How To Be Your Dog's Best Friend.* Boston: Little, Brown and Company, 1978.

———. *The Art of Raising a Puppy.* Boston: Little, Brown and Company, 1991.

Tossuti, Hans. *Companion Dog Training.* New York: Howell Book House, 1973.

Volhard, Jack & Melissa Bartlett. *What All Good Dogs Should Know: The Sensible Way to Train.* New York: Howell Book House, 1991.

Volhard, Jack & Wendy. *The Canine Good Citizen: Every Dog Can Be One.* New York: Howell Book House, 1994, 1997. Named Best Care & Training Book for 1994 by the Dog Writers' Association of America.

———. *Open and Utility Training: The Motivational Method.* New York: Howell Book House, 1992.

Volhard, Jack & G.T. Fisher. *Teaching Dog Obedience Classes: The Manual for Instructors.* New York: Howell Book House, 1986.

———. *Training Your Dog: The Step-by-Step Manual.* New York: Howell Book House, 1983. Named Best Care & Training Book for 1983 by the Dog Writers' Association of America.

Volhard, Wendy & Kerry Brown, DVM. *The Holistic Guide for a Healthy Dog.* New York: Howell Book House, 1995.

Weber, Josef. *The Dog in Training.* McGraw-Hill, 1939.

Zeigenfuse, Mary Ann Rombold. *Dog Tricks: Step by Step.* New York: Howell Book House, 1997.

Catalog

Direct Book Service's Dog & Cat Book Catalog
P.O. Box 2778
701B Poplar
Wenatchee, WA 98807-2778
For orders: (800) 776-2665
Fax: (509) 662-7233
E-mail: comments@mail.dogandcatbooks.com
Web site: www.dogandcatbooks.com
Direct Book Service carries the largest selection of dog and cat books available, including our books and videotapes.

Dog Camp

Jack & Wendy Volhard's Training Camps
Innovative training with a purpose.
Top Dog Training School
30 Besaw Road
Phoenix, NY 13135
E-mail: topdog@aiusa.com
Web site: www.volhard.com

Magazines

AKC Gazette: The Official Journal for the Sport of Purebred Dogs
American Kennel Club
260 Madison Avenue
New York, NY 10016
Web site: www.akc.org

Dog Fancy
P.O. Box 53264
Boulder, CO 80322-3264
Web site: www.dogfancy.com

Dog World Magazine
500 N. Dearborn, Suite 1100
Chicago, IL 60610.
312-396-0600
Web site: www.dogworldmag.com

Front & Finish
The Dog Trainer's News
PO Box 333
Galesburgh, IL 61402-0333

Off-Lead Magazine
The Dog Training Instructors Magazine
204 Lewis Street
Canastota, NY 13032

Organizations

American Holistic Veterinary Medical Association
2214 Old Edmorton Road
Bel Air, MD 21015
(410) 569-0795
Write for a list of holistically trained veterinarians in your state.

American Kennel Club
260 Madison Avenue
New York, NY 10016
(212) 696-8200

APDT
Association of Pet Dog Trainers
1-800-PET-DOGS
Web site: www.apdt.com

Delta Society (Therapy Dogs)
Web site: www.deltasociety.com

Homeopathic Educational Services
Dana Ullman, President
2124 Kittridge Street
Berkely, CA 94704
(800) 359-9051

NADOI
National Association of Dog Obedience Instructors
729 Gragevine Hwy, Suite 369
Hurst, TX 76054-2085

UKC
United States Kennel Club, Inc.
325 West 29th Street
Hialeah, FL 33012
(305) 885-3008
Web site: www.uskennelclub.qpg.com

Suppliers of Dietary Supplements

Dr. Goodpet
322$^1/_2$ E. Beach
Inglewood, CA 90302
For orders: (800) 222-9932
Homeopathic Remedies.
Scratch Free, Calm Stress, Diarrhea Relief, Flea Relief, Ear
Relief, and Digestive Enzymes.

Moss Nutrition
2 Bay Road, Suite 102
Hadley, MA 01035
For orders: (800) 851-5444
Specialized food supplements, glandulars.

Naturmix US Inc
PO Box 682
Cummings, GA 30128
For orders: (800) 825-1669
Web site: www.naturmix.com
Natural Neem Flea and Tick products.
Food supplements.

PHD Products
PO Box 8313
White Plains, NY 10602
Phone: (800) 743-1502
Fax: (800)743-6234
Web site: http://phdproducts.com
Vitamin/mineral mix, enzyme supplements, homeopathic emergency kit, natural dog
foods we recommend.

Training Equipment

Handcraft Collars, Inc.
4875 Camp Creek Road
Pell City, AL 35125
For orders: (800) 837-2033
Fax: (205) 338-0439
Web site: www.handcraftcollars.com
This is the supplier of the collars and leashes we use.

J-B Wholesale
5 Raritan Road
Oakland, NJ 07436
(800) 526-0388
All manner of pet supplies and training equipment, including electronic collars.

Max 200
114 Beach Street, Bldg. 5
Rockaway, NJ 07866
(800) 446-2920
Web site: www.max200.com
All manner of training equipment.

Sylvia's Tack Box
4333 11th St. A
Moline, IL 61265
(309) 797-9060
Handmade prong collars for small dogs.

Glossary

Agent   see **professional handler.**

Agility titles

- ➤ Novice Agility Dog—NA
- ➤ Open Agility Dog—OA
- ➤ Excellent Agility Dog—AX
- ➤ Master Agility Dog—MX
- ➤ Novice Jumper with Weaves—NAJ
- ➤ Open Jumper with Weaves—OAJ
- ➤ Excellent Jumper with Weaves—AXJ
- ➤ Master Jumper with Weaves—MXJ
- ➤ Master Agility Champion—MACH

AKC   American Kennel Club. Keeps records of purebred dogs and oversees performance events.

Automatic failure   of the Canine Good Citizen for dogs that eliminate, and handlers who give food during the test.

Bench show   a dog show at which dogs are required to be displayed on "benches" except when in the ring for judging.

Best in Show (BIS)   the dog judged best of all the dogs at a particular show.

Brace   two dogs of the same breed exhibited at the same time in either conformation or obedience.

C.D.   Companion Dog. An obedience title awarded by the AKC for dogs that have qualified in three Novice classes. The exercises are Heel on Leash and Figure 8, Stand for Examination, Heel Free, Recall, 1-minute Sit, and 3-minute Down.

C.D.X. Companion Dog Excellent. An obedience title awarded by the AKC for dogs that have qualified in three Open classes. Dogs must have earned a C.D. to enter the Open Class. The exercises are Heel Free and Figure 8, Drop on Recall, Retrieve on the Flat, Retrieve over High Jump, Broad Jump, 3-minute Sit, and 5-minute Down with handler out of sight.

Ch. Champion. An AKC conformation title.

Check a quick tug on the collar with an immediate release.

Conformation a dog's form, structure, and temperament.

Conformation show an exhibition to determine how well a dog conforms to the standard for its breed. Dogs are exhibited in conformation to become champions.

Dismissal from the Canine Good Citizen test for growling, snapping, biting, attacking or attempting to attack a person or another dog.

Disqualification a condition making a dog ineligible for exhibition at a dog show.

Dog show catch-all for conformation shows and obedience trials.

Dog World Award of Canine Distinction a performance award by *Dog World Magazine* for either conformation or obedience accomplishments.

Draft Dog (DD) a drafting title awarded by the Newfoundland Club of America.

Drives traits our dogs have inherited from their ancestors.

FCh. Field Champion.

Field Trial a competition for hunting dogs, which are judged on their ability to retrieve game and follow direction.

"Gazette" *American Kennel Club Gazette.*

Handler the person handling the dog, usually the owner. The terms handler, owner, or trainer are often used interchangeably.

Heel position with handler and dog facing in the same direction and the dog being as close to the handler as practical, the area from the dog's head to the shoulder is in line with the handler's left hip.

Highest Scoring Dog in Trial (HIT) from either the Novice, Open, or Utility Class, the dog with the highest score.

Latent learning the process of absorbing what is being taught by taking a break.

Leg a qualifying score toward an obedience title.

Match show a practice show at which no championship points or qualifying scores are awarded.

Negative stress manifests itself by the dog becoming lethargic and tired.

Novice Class   see **C.D.**

N.Q.   a non-qualifying performance in an AKC performance event.

Obedience title   C.D., C.D.X., U.D., OTCh., U.D.X.

Obedience trial   dogs compete for obedience titles.

Open Class   see **C.D.X.**

OTCh.   Obedience Trial Champion. An obedience title awarded by the AKC for dogs that have a Utility title and have acquired a specified number of points and first places in obedience competition.

Positive stress   manifests itself by the dog becoming more active, at the verge of being out of control.

Premium list   an announcement for a conformation show and/or obedience trial that contains the form required to enter a dog and the list of judges.

Professional handler   someone who handles a dog for and on behalf of the owner. This person may also be the owner.

Random reward   a reward given in an unpredictable order for the desired response.

Separation anxiety   anxiety experienced by the dog when separated from the owner.

Stifle   the joint between the upper and second thigh; corresponds to the human knee joint.

Stress   see, negative stress or positive stress.

T.D.   Tracking Dog. A title awarded by the AKC to dogs that have passed an AKC tracking test.

T.D.X.   Tracking Dog Excellent. A title awarded by the AKC to dogs that have passed an AKC tracking dog excellent test.

Title   awarded by the AKC for achievements in obedience or conformation exhibiting.

U.D.   Utility Dog. An obedience title awarded by the AKC for dogs that have qualified in three Utility classes. Dogs must have earned a C.D.X. to enter the Utility Class. The exercises are the Signal Exercise, Scent Discrimination, Directed Retrieve, Moving Stand and Examination, and Directed Jumping.

Utility Class   see **U.D.**

U.D.X.   Utility Dog Excellent. An obedience title awarded by the AKC to Utility Dogs that have qualified in the Open and Utility classes at the same trial 10 times.

Water Dog (WD)   a water rescue title awarded by the Newfoundland Club of America.

withers   the highest part of the back at the base of the neck; where the shoulder blades meet.

Index

C

Jumping through arms or hoop trick, 205–6
Juvenile stage, 36–37

K–L

Kirk, Robert, 315

Labrador Retrievers, 16, 17, 18, 278
"Landscaping," 285, 289–90
Latent learning, 110, 338
Leadership training, 55–56
Learning, stress and, 109–10
Learning influences, 73–87
  breed-specific behaviors, 82–85
  emotional needs, 78
  environment of dog, 76
  impact of first impression, 77
  mental sensitivity, 85
  nutritional needs, 82
  physical needs, 78–82
  social needs, 77–78
  sound sensitivity, 86
  touch sensitivity, 86–87
  visual stimuli responses, 85–86
  your attitude, 76
  your expectations, 74–75
Leashes, 134, 140
  for Canine Good Citizen test, 193
  suppliers, 335–36
Leash tests
  Heel on Leash, 215, 216–19, 225
  Walking on a Loose Leash, 187
Leash training, 146
  checking, 156
  heeling and, 148. *See also* Heeling
  leash over shoulder technique, 148–50, 152
  teaching not to pull, 146–47
Left footed, 199
Left turn in place, 262–63
Left turn maneuver, 148, 150, 151
Leg (qualifying score), 215, 338
Lethargy, stress and, 107
"Lie down" command, 64–66
Life expectancy, 4
Linoleic acid, 124
Live ring, 140
Liver treats, 141
Loneliness, 293

Long down exercise, 53–56, 306
Long Down test, 215, 234–35, 239, 306
Long sit exercise, 55, 56
Long Sit test, 215, 234–35, 239
Lure coursing, 279

M–N

Magazines, 333–34
Marking behavior, 51–52
Master Agility, 275
Match show, 338
Meat, 119–20, 129
Mental sensitivity, as influence on learning, 85
Mental stress, 106
Minerals, 127
Most, Konrad, 110
Motivational Retrieve, 245, 247
Mouth, taking something out of, 308
Moving Stand test, 253, 264–65
Muzzles, 306–7

Nail trimming, 80–81
National Association of Dog Obedience Instructors, 334
Natural preservatives, 125
Negative reinforcement, 5, 10
Negative stress, 106–7, 112, 178, 338
Neutering, 39–42
  advantages of, 40
  age for, 40–41
  disadvantages to, 41
Newfoundlands, 86
Newspapers, swatting with, 50
"No," eliminating, 10
No-No training model, 7
Non-reinforced repetitions, 169–70
Non-sporting breeds, 83
Novice Agility, 275
Novice Class, 214–26
  exercises, 215–37
    Figure 8, 215, 223–26, 240
    Heel Free, 215, 225, 240
    Heel on Leash, 215, 216–19, 225
    Long Down, 215, 234–35
    Long Sit, 215, 234–35, 239
    Stand for Examination, 215, 227–31

Nutrition, 119. *See also* Feeding
  carbohydrates and, 123–24
  choosing right food, 118–19
  deficiencies in, 117, 122
  enzymes and, 128
  fats and, 124–25
  as influence on learning, 82
  minerals and, 127
  protein and, 120–22
  vitamins and, 125–26
Nylon collars, 135–36

O

Obedience classes, 322, 323–26
Obedience Regulations, 220, 225, 249
Obedience titles, 214, 339
Obedience Trial Champion, 214, 339
Obedience trials, 213–71, 339. *See also* Novice Class; Open Class; Utility Class
  agility trials compared with, 275
  Canine Good Citizen test compared with, 215
  leg (qualifying score), 215, 338
Object of Attraction, 220
"OK" commands, 58–59, 61
Open Agility, 275
Open Class, 214, 239–51
  exercises, 239
    Broad Jump, 239, 243, 249–50
    Drop on Recall, 239, 241–44
    Figure 8, 215, 223–26, 240
    Heel Free, 215, 225, 240
    Long Down, 239, 306
    Long Sit, 239
    Retrieve on Flat, 239, 243, 244–45
    Retrieve over High Jump, 239, 243, 245–49
Organizations, 334
Other one trick, 201
Out of sight stays, 251
Overfeeding, signs of, 48